Global Technology and Legal Theory

I0891006

The rise and spread of the Internet has accelerated the global flows of money, technology and information that are increasingly perceived as a challenge to the traditional regulatory powers of nation states and the effectiveness of their constitutions. The acceleration of these flows poses new legal and political problems to their regulation and control, as shown by recent conflicts between Google and the European Union (EU).

This book investigates the transnational constitutional dimension of recent conflicts between Google and the EU in the areas of competition, taxation and human rights. More than a simple case study, it explores how the new conflicts originating from the worldwide expansion of the Internet economy are being dealt with by the institutional mechanisms available at the European level. The analysis of these conflicts exposes the tensions and contradictions between, on the one hand, legal and political systems that are limited by territory, and, on the other hand, the inherently global functioning of the Internet. The EU's promising initiatives to extend the protection of privacy in cyberspace set the stage for a broader dialogue on constitutional problems related to the enforcement of fundamental rights and the legitimate exercise of power that are common to different legal orders of world society. Nevertheless, the different ways of dealing with the competition and fiscal aspects of the conflicts with Google also indicate the same limits that are generally attributed to the very project of European integration, showing that the constitutionalization of the economy tends to outpace the constitutionalization of politics.

Providing a detailed account of the unfolding of these conflicts, and their wider consequences to the future of the Internet, this book will appeal to scholars working in EU law, international law and constitutional law, as well as those in the fields of political science and sociology.

Guilherme Cintra Guimarães received his PhD in International Law from the University Roma Tre, Italy. He is a Federal Attorney at the Brazilian Office of the Attorney General of the Union.

Routledge Research in International Commercial Law

Available titles in this series include:

International Commercial and Marine Arbitration
Georgios l. Zekos

International Commercial Arbitration and the Arbitrator's Contract
Emilia Onyema

Jurisdiction and Arbitration Agreements in International Commercial Law
Zheng Sophia Tang

Progressive Commercialization of Airline Governance Culture
Jan Walulik

Economic and Environmental Regulation of International Aviation
From Inter-National to Global Governance
Steven Truxal

Combining Mediation and Arbitration in International Commercial Dispute Resolution
Dilyara Nigmatullina

Global Technology and Legal Theory

Transnational Constitutionalism, Google and the European Union

Guilherme Cintra Guimarães

Routledge
Taylor & Francis Group
LONDON AND NEW YORK

First published 2019
by Routledge
2 Park Square, Milton Park, Abingdon, Oxon OX14 4RN

and by Routledge
605 Third Avenue, New York, NY 10017

First issued in paperback 2021

Routledge is an imprint of the Taylor & Francis Group, an informa business

Publisher's Note
The publisher has gone to great lengths to ensure the quality of this reprint but points out that some imperfections in the original copies may be apparent.

British Library Cataloguing-in-Publication Data
A catalogue record for this book is available from the British Library

Library of Congress Cataloging-in-Publication Data
Names: Cintra Guimarães, Guilherme.
Title: Global technology and legal theory transnational constitutionalism : Google and the European Union / Guilherme Cintra Guimarães.
Description: Abingdon, Oxon ; New York, NY : Routledge, 2019. |
Series: Routledge research in international commercial law | Based on author's thesis (doctoral - Universitáa degli Studi Roma Tre, 2018), issued title: Transnational constitutional conflicts in cyberspace : Google and the European Union. | Includes bibliographical references and index.
Identifiers: LCCN 2019007121 (print) | LCCN 2019007635 (ebook) | ISBN 9780429060021 (ebk) | ISBN 9780367181956 (hbk)
Subjects: LCSH: Internet industry--Law and legislation--European Union countries. | Google (Firm)--Trials, litigation, etc. | Data protection--Law and legislation--European Union countries. | Information services--Law and legislation--European Union countries. | Information technology--Law and legislation--European Union countries. | Information services--Taxation--Law and legislation--European Union countries. | International and municipal law.
Classification: LCC KJE6946 (ebook) | LCC KJE6946 .C56 2019 (print) | DDC 343.2409/9--dc23
LC record available at https://lccn.loc.gov/2019007121

ISBN 13: 978-1-03-224109-8 (pbk)
ISBN 13: 978-0-367-18195-6 (hbk)

DOI: 10.4324/9780429060021

Typeset in Galliard
by Taylor & Francis Books

For Zsuzsanna and Cecília

Contents

Acknowledgments

This book is based on my PhD research at the University Roma Tre, which was carried out between 2014 and 2018. The book itself was last reviewed at the beginning of 2019. Since then, the conflicts between Google and the European Union in the areas of competition, taxation and human rights, which are the main object of the book, have evolved at a fast pace and are still unfolding as I write these words. The whole debate on so-called "fake news", and online disinformation more generally, has also gained especial momentum as the influence of digital media on recent elections and referenda held around the world has shown us some of the possible (un)democratic consequences of digital technologies. The book, therefore, runs the obvious risk of becoming a bit outdated at the very moment I try to update it. This is probably an unavoidable condition of our contemporary society and its fast "acceleration of time". A condition we are still slowly learning how to deal with.

Niklas Luhmann used to say that it is only by accident that a person has a theory. Generalizing this sentence, one might say that it is only by coincidence that someone comes up with a specific thesis or original idea. Well, in my case, this fortunate "coincidence" would be nothing without the help and support of a lot of people and organizations.

I would like to express my deepest gratitude to the University Roma Tre and all its administrative and academic personnel. The PhD course was a wonderful and very stimulating research experience, into which I have put my best efforts in the last four or five years. Special thanks are due to my supervisor, Giuseppe Palmisano, who followed the research with patience and attention, always providing me with great advice and helping me to "keep my feet on the ground". I would also like to thank Professors Leopoldo Nuti, Maria Rosario Stabili, Raffaele Torino, Gaetano Sabatini and Giacomo Marramao for all their help and insightful advice. My PhD colleagues are responsible for turning the whole course into a fun and joyful experience: Valerio Intraligi, Shai Tagner, Chiara Pagano, Sayuri Romei, Gabriele Maestri and Gabriele Marchese. I hope we remain friends for life!

I would also like to express my gratitude to the Corvinus University of Budapest and all its administrative and academic personnel. The research period at the university was also wonderful and very stimulating. Special thanks are due to Professor Erzsébet Kaponyi, who followed my research in Budapest, and Professor

Sándor Gyula Nagy, who helped me with his useful advice. “Nagyon szépen köszönöm!”

Last but not least, my special thanks go to my family and friends for all their love, patience and support. My wife, Zsuzsanna, has helped and inspired me all the time. Our daughter, Cecília, who was born in 2017, has brought me new energy, making me understand a little bit more about the human condition:

> The fact that man is capable of action means that the unexpected can be expected from him, that he is able to perform what is infinitely improbable. And this again is possible only because each man is unique, so that with each birth something uniquely new comes into the world.
>
> (Hannah Arendt)

Acronyms and abbreviations

AEPD	Agencia Española de Protección de Datos
BEPS	Base Erosion and Profit Shifting
CCCTB	Common Consolidated Corporate Tax Base
CIA	Central Intelligence Agency
CJEU	Court of Justice of the European Union
CNIL	Commission Nationale de l'Informatique et des Libertés
CoE	Council of Europe
DNS	Domain Name System
DPD	Data Protection Directive
DRD	Data Retention Directive
DSM	Digital Single Market
ECHR	European Convention on Human Rights
ECtHR	European Court of Human Rights
EDPS	European Data Protection Supervisor
EEA	European Economic Area
EMEA	Europe, Middle East and Africa
EU	European Union
FCC	Federal Communications Commission
FRA	European Union Agency for Fundamental Rights
FTC	Federal Trade Commission
GDP	Gross Domestic Product
GDPR	General Data Protection Regulation
IANA	Internet Assigned Numbers Authority
ICANN	Internet Corporation for Assigned Names and Numbers
ICCPR	International Covenant on Civil and Political Rights
ICT	Information and Communication Technologies
IETF	Internet Engineering Task Force
IGF	Internet Governance Forum
ILO	International Labour Organization
IP	Internet Protocol
ISO	International Organization for Standardization
ISOC	Internet Society
ISP	Internet Service Provider

ITU	International Telecommunication Union
MOSS	Mini One Stop Shop
NSA	National Security Agency
OECD	Organization for Economic Cooperation and Development
PRT	Preferential Tax Regime
SEO	Search Engine Optimization
TEU	Treaty on European Union
TFEU	Treaty on the Functioning of the European Union
TNC	Transnational Corporation
UK	United Kingdom
UN	United Nations
UNCCPR	United Nations Human Rights Committee
UNCTAD	United Nations Conference on Trade and Development
UNGA	United Nations General Assembly
UNHRC	United Nations Human Rights Council
URL	Uniform Resource Locator
US	United States
VAT	Value Added Tax
VoIP	Voice over Internet Protocol
VPN	Virtual Private Network
W3C	World Wide Web Consortium
WP29	Article 29 Data Protection Working Party
WTO	World Trade Organization

Introduction

Our relationship with modern media is rather ambiguous, as Niklas Luhmann once put it a couple of decades ago:

> Whatever we know about our society, or indeed about the world in which we live, we know through the mass media. … On the other hand, we know so much about the mass media that we are not able to trust these sources.[1]

Luhmann's famous statement on the reality of the mass media still resonates with us even with all the changes in social communication, and social organization more generally, caused by the global spread of the Internet since the beginning of the 1990s.

When writing on the mass media, Luhmann was thinking mainly about the dissemination of communication and information by the technologies of printing and broadcasting.[2] The ways in which, with the help of these technologies, the mass media construct social reality through the constant production and reproduction of information, and also the particular and inherent selectivity of their operations, which, in turn, makes the reality created and offered by them so suspicious.[3]

We may draw an analogy, even if a rather rough one, between Luhmann's statement in the middle of the 1990s and our current situation a couple of decades later. In the context of what is commonly referred to as the "society of information" or "network society",[4] a growing part of the knowledge that we get about our society, the world in which we live and even our day-to-day lives, we get through the Internet, particularly with the help of search engines.

1 Luhmann (2000 [1996]) *The Reality of the Mass Media*, p. 1.

2 According to Luhmann (2000 [1996]) *The Reality of the Mass Media*, p. 2, the mass media include "all those institutions of society which make use of copying technologies to disseminate communication".

3 On the "suspicion of manipulation" as a sort of unavoidable paradox of the system of the mass media: Luhmann (2000 [1996]) *The Reality of the Mass Media*, pp. 14, 40–41 and 78.

4 Castells (2010) *The Rise of the Network Society.*

The rise and spread of the Internet as a global and convergent medium of production and diffusion of communication and information has provoked an enormous change in the way society communicates and disseminates information, which seems to have blurred, at least to a certain extent, the very distinction between mass media communication and other forms of communication.[5] Most people continue to read newspapers and watch television,[6] but our daily access to information is now mediated by the new institutions of cyberspace, among which Google is certainly one of the most important, powerful and omnipresent.

I.1 Google and its global reach

Google's ambitious mission is "to organize the world's information and make it universally accessible and useful".[7] That includes not only the indexing of all the information published on the World Wide Web, but also the digitalization of content until now available only in printed form, as in the case of the Google Books Project.[8] Based on the global success of the company and its large market share all over the world,[9] it is fair to say that this mission has been well accomplished. Perhaps it would not be an exaggeration to say that what is not indexed and shown by Google is hard (or almost impossible) to find in cyberspace.

And yet we cannot say that we know enough about Google, and search engines in general, to be able to trust them. We certainly know a lot about how the company was set up by two young American PhD candidates at Stanford University back in 1998, and its rapid growth from a small Silicon Valley start-up established in a little garage to one of the most successful transnational

5 Castells (2010) *The Rise of the Network Society*, p. 355ff. The Council of Europe (2011) *Recommendation CM/Rec(2011)7 of the Committee of Ministers to Member States on a new notion of media*, in its turn, has officially referred to the new forms of communication made available by the "new media" as "interactive mass communication" and "mass communication in aggregate".

6 It seems, however, that the very idea of having to adapt to a pre-programmed TV schedule is hard to understand for the younger generations, given the current possibilities of having access to content on demand. See: Castells (2010) *The Rise of the Network Society*, p. xxvii.

7 Information available on Google's own website: https://www.google.com/intl/en/about. Google undertook a major corporate restructuring in 2015, with the creation of the holding Alphabet and the concentration, under the brand name Google, which is now formally a subsidiary of Alphabet, of the main Internet businesses of the company, especially online search and advertising. More information is available on Alphabet's own website: https://abc.xyz.

8 On the Google Books Project: Darnton (2009) 'Google & the future of books'.

9 According to the website StatCounter (http://gs.statcounter.com), Google has approximately a 90 percent share of the market for online search in the whole world, including Europe and the US. According to the website Statista (http://www.statista.com), Google's share of digital advertising revenues worldwide was 32.4 percent in 2018.

corporations of the Internet economy.[10] We are also aware of the fear it has inspired among its competitors due to its allegedly monopolistic practices,[11] the problems it has caused to governments' tax bases with its aggressive tax avoiding strategies[12] and the risks to people's privacy posed by its data collection techniques.[13] But what do we really know about the "reality" of Google and other search engines?

Search engines strive to get users' attention and collect their data in order to make money by providing targeted advertising. Usually, their main business is not the direct production of content, but the intermediation of information. They "crawl" the whole Web, collect and index its content and then make it available to everyone based on a particular way of ranking and organizing the information searched by the user. The "secret sauce" is the "secret code": the algorithm that ranks the information retrieved according to a specific order of priorities, which is supposed to maximize the relevance of the list of results shown to the user.

As a new kind of media company engaged in the intermediation of information and advertising on the Internet, Google too must make its own "editorial choices". These choices are embedded in the algorithm the company uses to rank its search results, which is a set of mathematical equations and logical commands that determine the relevance of the information made available to the users.

In contrast to traditional media corporations, which provide content based on some explicit or implicit criteria that guide the editorial decisions taken by (or attributed to) concrete persons or a group of persons,[14] the selectivity of Google is technologically automated by a piece of software code that does not depend on direct human intervention for its functioning once it has been designed and implemented. The selectivity is not only less transparent to the users, who generally have no means of getting access to the incomprehensible "deepness of the invisible machine" beyond the "surface of the screen".[15] It is also secret, a business secret considered to be essential to the very competitive advantage of the company.

The "reality" of search engines is, thus, determined, to a great extent, by the "secrecy" of their code. We know that they intermediate and provide information and that they do that in order to make money from targeted advertising,[16] but we do not know exactly how. Paradoxically, we know so much about them and so little about their code that we may not be able to "trust these sources" either.

10 On the history of Google and its worldwide success: Levy (2011) *In the Plex*; Vise and Malseed (2008) *The Google Story*.

11 Döpfner (2014) 'Why we fear Google'.

12 EurActiv (2014) 'Google, Apple and Amazon under fire in OECD war on tax evasion'.

13 Zuboff (2014) 'Dark Google'.

14 On the "the unavoidable yet intended and regulated selectivity" of the mass media and the self-generated criteria for the search for, and production of, information: Luhmann (2000 [1996]) *The Reality of the Mass Media*, p. 27ff.

15 On the effects of the use of computers for communication in general, and the contrast between the "surface of the screen", which does not require too much from the human senses, and the "deepness of the invisible machine", whose commands are unknown to the user: Luhmann (2012 [1997]) *Theory of Society*, p. 180ff.

16 On the open manipulation of information that constitutes the normal business of advertising: Luhmann (2000 [1996]) *The Reality of the Mass Media*, p. 44ff.

Given the normal selectivity of search engines and the important role they play in the circulation of information throughout the Internet and in society at large – to a certain extent, in the very construction of social reality – it is no surprise that they have become a source of growing academic interest and public scrutiny.[17]

The case of Google is particularly interesting. Besides operating the most popular and widespread search engine in the world, the company has progressively expanded its business into other fields and areas of the Internet economy and beyond, from email, social network, city maps, browsers, video streaming and cloud computing to the mobile market for operating software and applications, among many other disparate projects and activities such as space exploration and the design and fabrication of driverless cars. Notwithstanding its wide range of activities, the main business logic of the company is fairly straightforward: to offer free services to the general public in exchange for their attention and personal data, which is generally monetized by means of targeted advertising.[18]

As a big and powerful transnational corporation of the new media sector created by the rise and spread of the Internet, Google takes part in, and is able to influence to a certain extent, the ever more accelerated global flows of money, technology and information that are increasingly challenging the traditional regulatory powers of nation states and the effectiveness of their constitutions. This imbalance or asymmetry may be attributed to certain specific structural conditions of our modern society, especially to the fact that the economy, science and technology and the mass media are able to operate at a worldwide scale with relative independence from national borders, while the functioning of politics and law is still strongly dependent on the territorial segmentation of world society in the form of nation states.[19]

I.2 A new constitutional question?

This brief digression on the "reality" of Google is important to contextualize and provide the background for the presentation of the object and the main theses of the book, which will focus on the analysis of some recent conflicts between Google and the European Union (EU) in the areas of competition, taxation and human rights. Beyond the difficulties and shortcomings of the traditional mechanisms of state regulation, global technology companies like Google seem to represent a challenge to the very descriptive and reflective potential of legal and constitutional theory.

17 König and Rasch (eds) (2014) *Society of the Query Reader*; Becker and Stalder (eds) (2009) *Deep Search*; Introna and Nissenbaum (2000) 'Shaping the Web'.

18 On the details of the "Google economy": Levy (2011) *In the Plex*, p. 69ff.

19 On the description of modern society as a world society, made up of communication, that is internally differentiated into functional subsystems that operate worldwide with variable degrees of independence from territorial borders: Luhmann (1997b) 'Globalization or world society'; Luhmann (2013 [1997]), *Theory of Society*, p. 87ff.

One of the main inspirations of the book comes from the insight or provocation of Gunther Teubner, according to whom companies like Google would be at the center of the "new constitutional question" of our days, prompted by the increasing globalization, privatization and digitalization of the world, which would pose new risks and threats to individual and institutional autonomy. These risks and threats would be analogous to those represented by the liberation of political energies in the historical formation of nation states, and to which traditional constitutions offered a response by means of the regulation of political power and the protection of individual rights.[20]

The aim of the book is to analyze whether and to what extent the recent conflicts between Google and the EU may be described (or framed) as transnational constitutional (or transconstitutional)[21] conflicts related to legal, political and economic disputes that would take place in cyberspace. In other words, do these conflicts have a constitutional dimension that would demonstrate the current expansion of constitutionalism beyond the nation state?

This question has at least two important implications. The conflicts would be transnational because they would transcend the political and legal order of nation states. The conflicts would also be constitutional because they would involve, at least to a certain extent, questions about the constitution/limitation of power and the enforcement of fundamental rights.[22]

The *first set of conflicts* is related to competition. Google was the target of three antitrust proceedings that have recently been carried out by the European Commission. In the first and second proceedings, the company was fined the two biggest antitrust fines ever applied by the Commission: (i) €2.42 billion for abusing its dominant position in the market for general Internet search by giving illegal advantages to its comparison shopping service (Google Shopping) to the

20 In the words of Teubner (2013) 'The project of constitutional sociology', p. 45: "Google is exemplary of the new constitutional question, which is prompted by the tendencies of globalisation, privatisation and digitalisation of the world. In comparison to the old constitutional question of the eighteenth and nineteenth centuries, today different, although no less severe, problems become apparent. While back then the focus was on the release of the nation state's political energies and likewise its effective limitation by the rule of law, today's constitutionalisation concentrates on constraining the destructive repercussions that result from the unleashing of entirely different social energies, which are especially noticeable in the economy, but also in science and technology, in medicine and the new media. Constitutionalisation beyond the nation state occurs as an evolutionary process going in two different directions: constitutions evolve in transnational political processes outside the nation state and, simultaneously, they evolve outside international politics in the global society's 'private' sectors." On the main ideas and theses about this particular form of "societal constitutionalism": Teubner (2012) *Constitutional Fragments.*

21 On the theoretical approach of transconstitutionalism, which will be specifically addressed in section 1.3.1 below: Neves (2013 [2009]) *Transconstitutionalism.*

22 The terms human rights and fundamental rights are used interchangeably throughout the book, since they usually refer to the same set of basic rights recognized by both international law (human rights) and constitutional law (fundamental rights).

detriment of its competitors;[23] and (ii) €4.34 billion for abusing its dominant position in the market for mobile operating systems and applications.[24] In the third proceeding, (iii) the company was also fined a huge fine of €1.49 billion for abusing its dominant position in the market for online search advertising.[25] All three proceedings were initiated following complaints lodged with the Commission by Google's competitors, which include companies that are also transnational corporations, some of them with their headquarters in Europe and some of them with their headquarters in the United States (US).

The main issue behind the investigations and proceedings has been framed as the battle for "search neutrality" or "fair search". Google has been accused of being biased in the presentation of its search results. The bias would be embedded in its algorithm, which would be designed to favor Google's own products and services to the detriment of its competitors. The wider problem of the normal selectivity of search engines, which has significant consequences for the circulation of information in society at large, is reduced here to its narrow economic aspects, as a mere risk to innovation and consumer choice. This is probably a consequence of the very "constitutional design" of the EU, whose major concerns are the establishment of a free market and the protection of competition. The conduct of Google would, then, represent a challenge to the "economic constitution" of the EU and its rules on competition and economic freedom, whose need of greater enforcement has been stressed in the context of the strategy for the establishment (or strengthening) of the "digital single market".[26]

The *second set of conflicts* is related to taxation. Google has been engaging in aggressive tax avoidance strategies in order to minimize its tax liabilities and maximize its worldwide margins of profit. This kind of strategy is common among big transnational corporations and usually involves the use of tax havens and the exploitation of legal loopholes in national and international tax rules. The Internet or digital economy, however, poses new challenges to the fiscal capabilities of nation states due to the intangibility of a large part of the products and services that are transacted through the new means of electronic commerce and also due to the easiness of relocating mobile activities and establishing fake companies around the world as a consequence of the spread of new information and communication technologies.

This is a problem connected with one of the most traditional and important powers of the nation state, the power to collect taxes, the limitation of which is at the very origin of the evolution of constitutional law in Europe and abroad. Recent initiatives on the taxation of the digital economy are being negotiated at

23 European Commission (2017) *Antitrust: Commission fines Google €2.42 billion for abusing dominance as search engine by giving illegal advantage to own comparison shopping service.*

24 European Commission (2018) *Antitrust: Commission fines Google €4.34 billion for illegal practices regarding Android mobile devices to strengthen dominance of Google's search engine.*

25 European Commission (2019) *Antitrust: Commission fines Google €1.49 billion for abusive practices in online advertising.*

26 European Commission (2015) *A Digital Single Market Strategy for Europe.*

the level of the Organization for Economic Cooperation and Development (OECD),[27] and also at EU level,[28] which seems to indicate that the real issue nowadays would not be the limitation, but rather the constitution (or re-constitution) of the public power to collect taxes given the acceleration of the global flows of wealth that are difficult for nation states to regulate.

However, when it comes to taxation, the EU is much more fragmented and less "constitutionalized" in comparison to the enforcement of competition rules. Google has been taking advantage of that, making use of a sort of "arbitrage of laws" in order to avoid taxes, which consequently has a negative impact on public finances and the capacity of Member States and the EU to implement public policies that promote the fundamental rights of their citizens.

The *third set of conflicts* is related to human rights. As the world leading search engine, Google plays an important role in the global flows of information that take place in cyberspace. These flows of information include general data that are important for the very construction of the reality of the society and the world in which we live, and also personal data that potentially affect the social identity and intimate life of individuals. Google's activities have, thus, a relevant impact, on the one hand, on the fundamental rights to freedom of expression and access to information, and, on the other hand, on the fundamental rights to privacy and the protection of personal data. They affect both the memory of society and the private sphere of individuals.

In a recent case involving Google and a Spanish citizen, the Court of Justice of the European Union (CJEU) decided that individuals have a right to request search engines to remove links from their search results pages to certain types of information published by third parties about them – the so-called "right to be forgotten", or more simply, "right to delist".[29] The right applies not only to information that is intimate, defamatory or fake in nature, but to any kind of personal data that is, in the language of the court, "inadequate, irrelevant or no longer relevant, or excessive in relation to the purposes of its original processing", even if the information is true and has been legally published.

In another recent case – this time involving an Austrian citizen and Facebook, not Google – the CJEU has invalidated a decision of the European Commission[30] that approved the rules regulating the transfer of personal data from the European Economic Area (EEA) to the US – the so-called "Safe Harbour Agreement".[31] The main argument of the court was that the Commission's positive assessment

27 OECD (2015) *Addressing the Tax Challenges of the Digital Economy.*

28 European Commission (2014) *Report of the Commission Expert Group on Taxation of the Digital Economy.*

29 CJEU (2014) *Case C-131/12: Google Spain SL, Google Inc. v Agencia Española de Protección de Datos, Mario Costeja González.*

30 EU (2000) *Commission Decision 2000/520/EC of 26 July 2000 pursuant to Directive 95/46/EC of the European Parliament and of the Council on the adequacy of the protection provided by the safe harbour privacy principles and related frequently asked questions issued by the US Department of Commerce.*

31 CJEU (2015) *Case C-362/14: Maximillian Schrems v Data Protection Commissioner.*

on the level of data protection in the US was wrong and could not, then, bind the assessment of national data protection authorities when deciding upon specific complaints lodged with them by individuals who are challenging the lawfulness of the transfer of their personal data to the US.

Both rulings are connected, to a certain extent, with the global flows of information and personal data through the Internet and both of them represent a firm stance on the protection of privacy. The first one directly affects Google and its global activities of intermediation and provision of information. The second one affects the company indirectly by forcing, in practice, a change in the rules for cross-border transfer of personal data between the EU and the US.[32]

Taking into consideration the three sets of conflicts, the economic, technological and media power of Google may be described as threefold: (i) the market power that affects competition and the basic "economic constitution" of the EU; (ii) the financial power that affects the public finances and tax collection capabilities of European nation states; and (iii) the power over global flows of information and personal data that affects the fundamental rights to privacy and freedom of expression of European citizens. Corporations, governments and individuals all seem to be concerned about the power of Google to a greater or lesser extent.

One additional aspect that should also be taken into consideration in the analysis of these conflicts is that the economic, technological and media power of Google, even if autonomous from the US, is also significantly influenced by US political power. Google has its headquarters in the US and is, thus, submitted to the US wide, intrusive and rather convoluted legislation on national security and online surveillance. A legislation that, given the Snowden revelations, seems to work as a means to project the US power and influence into cyberspace, due to the fact that the major companies of the Internet economy have their headquarters in the US and use it to cooperate closely with their intelligence services.

The conflicts between Google and the EU cannot, thus, be disconnected from traditional conflicts that may arise between the US and their European allies. Conflicts which are also manifest in the issues of Internet governance and may imply different constitutional traditions and national (or supranational) positions on questions of competition, taxation and the rights to privacy and freedom of expression.

Notwithstanding the relevant role played by the political, legal and economic interests of different nation states, the conflicts between Google and the EU may also have a prominent transnational constitutional (or transconstitutional) dimension that would deserve deeper investigation in order to shed some light on their wider context, structural conditions and future developments.

32 These new rules have been recently approved and baptized as the "Privacy Shield": EU (2016) *Commission Implementing Decision (EU) 2016/1250 of 12 July 2016 pursuant to Directive 95/46/EC of the European Parliament and of the Council on the adequacy of the protection provided by the EU-U.S. Privacy Shield.*

I.3 Structure of the book

Constitutions, in the traditional sense, may still be the privilege of nation states, or even of advanced forms of supranational organizations such as the EU. But the basic ideas and principles of constitutionalism, related to the democratic organization of power and the protection of fundamental rights, are certainly not. They may transcend the nation state and be invoked in any forum, organization or space of world society. This basic idea will be further developed and qualified in the first two chapters of the book, which, respectively, set the theoretical background of the analysis and show why the Internet or cyberspace may be seen as a special locus of transnational constitutional (or transconstitutional) conflicts.

Chapter 1 deals with the future of constitutionalism in world society. Some ideas and principles of constitutionalism are much older than the modern age. The general organization of society and the definition of some form of public power were already the content of philosophical and political debate in the western tradition long before the rather unexpected invention of constitutions as legal documents that institutionalize the political form of the modern nation state (1.1). The acceleration of the process of globalization, however, tends to increase the perception of nation states and their constitutions as contingent historical phenomena, raising doubts about their future evolution. The full realization of the structural changes brought about by modern society gives rise to semantic uncertainties in the field of constitutional theory (1.2). The result is an inflation of new concepts and descriptions that try to grasp the uncertain future of constitutionalism beyond the state (1.3).

One promising approach is that of transconstitutionalism,[33] which takes a more realistic or skeptical view about the emergence of constitutions beyond the state, focusing instead on actual conflicts between different legal orders of world society that may have a constitutional dimension (1.3.1). Two potentially new constitutional subjects are particularly interesting here: the EU and transnational corporations. The long debate about a constitution for Europe does not seem to have come to an end even after the failure of the constitutional treaty.[34] The European constitution is a persistent idea, notwithstanding the constant dilemma it faces between its economic and political configurations (1.3.2). The worldwide spread of transnational corporations, in turn, raises the question of the new conglomerations of economic power that tend to reduce the range of action of nation states.[35] Even if the claims about their constitutional dimension[36] seem to be overestimated, transnational corporations

33 Neves (2013 [2009]) *Transconstitutionalism*.

34 Habermas (2012) *The Crisis of the European Union*, p. 2ff. Casting some doubt about the very constitutional nature of the failed constitutional treaty: Palmisano (2004) 'Spunti internazionalistici di riflessione sul trattato "costituzionale" e sulla natura dell'Unione Europea'.

35 Marramao (2011) *Contro il Potere*, p. 107ff; Arrighi and Silver (eds) (1999) *Chaos and Governance in the Modern World System*, pp. 97ff and 278.

36 Teubner (2011) 'Self-constitutionalizing TNCs?'; Teubner (2009) 'The corporate codes of multinationals'; Backer (2012) 'Transnational corporate constitutionalism'.

certainly pose new challenges to democracy and human rights at the level of world society (1.3.3).

Chapter 2 deals with the architecture of cyberspace, its basic code, the set of algorithms, logical protocols and legal and practical constrains that determine the possibilities of interaction and communication on the Internet, which is sometimes metaphorically construed, in a material sense, as its "constitution".[37] As a completely artificial invention – an artefact of this world, constructed by "the work of our hands", to quote Hannah Arendt[38] – the Internet or cyberspace may be described as a medium of production and diffusion of communication and information that has paradoxically created, at the same time, unprecedented freedom and unprecedented control (2.1). Its extraterritorial or transnational dimension is the source of constant dispute, which means that the issues of Internet governance cannot be reduced to their more restricted technical aspects, because the legal and political conflicts of the physical space are obviously also present in cyberspace (2.2). An example of that was recently given by the Snowden leaks, which revealed to the whole world the widespread and intrusive practices of mass surveillance online carried out by the intelligence services of the US, as well as the somewhat subservient role played by their transnational corporations in the projection of US political power and influence onto the Internet, with a worldwide negative impact on human rights (2.3).

Transnational corporations, however, cannot be generally depicted as mere agents of their nation states of origin. Google, one of the most successful companies of the Internet economy, has interests of its own. The company seems to be one of the most omnipresent figures in the architecture of cyberspace. Its innovative culture has been universally praised, but its economic, technological and media power has also been increasingly perceived as a source of disruption for governments, individuals and other corporations around the world (2.4).

The last two chapters are dedicated to the analysis of the conflicts described above between Google and the EU in the areas of competition, taxation and human rights. The aim is not to analyze in depth all the aspects of the conflicts, which, besides being complex and multifaceted, are still ongoing. Priority is given

37 Lessig (2006) *Code*. The terms Internet and cyberspace are used interchangeably throughout the book to refer to the global and public "network of networks" that make possible the worldwide communication between non-presents with the help of a computer or mobile device. The Brazilian Internet Civil Act provides a simple, concise and clear definition of the Internet that is worth mentioning: "the system of logical protocols, structured at worldwide scale for public and unrestricted use, which makes possible the communication and exchange of data between terminals through different networks" (Brasil (2014) *Lei Federal n. 12.965, de 16 de Abril de 2014*, Article 5(I)). The World Wide Web (or simply Web), in its turn, is the specific part (or application layer) of the Internet in which webpages made up of a combination of texts, images and sounds are published and linked to each other in the form of hypertexts, which may be located by means of a unique Web address (or Uniform Resource Locator (URL)).

38 Arendt (1998 [1958]) *The Human Condition*.

to the comparative analysis of their transnational dimension and the possible use of the constitutional discourse in the framing of their most important issues.

Chapter 3 deals with the economic and fiscal aspects of the conflicts. The fast and exponential growth of new media companies like Google has been perceived as a threat to both market competition and public finances, particularly in Europe. Given the current structures of the EU, though, the strategies to deal with de-monopolization of cyberspace (3.1) and the avoidance of taxes online (3.2) do not seem to be on an equal footing.

In order to tackle the problems of competition in cyberspace (3.1.1), the EU has activated its well-developed and consolidated corpus of economic law against the allegedly abusive practices of Google (3.1.2). Even if competition law tools may be adequate to deal with the concentration of markets, they seem to stop short of effectively addressing the new constitutional concerns over media pluralism on the Internet. Economic freedom to shop online does not equate to freedom of expression and information. While the current antitrust investigations and proceedings are designed to boost the former, they may end up having no impact at all on the latter (3.1.3).

If EU law may be structurally coupled to the functioning of a supranational "digital single market", the same does not seem to be true for EU politics. Uniform rules for market competition are (mis)matched by fragmented rules on corporate taxation. Besides competition *between* companies, there is also strong competition *for* companies among European nation states. Google's strategy of tax avoidance in Europe is a good example of that. In order to face the challenges to the taxation of the digital economy (3.2.1), the EU seems to be searching in vain for a common tax policy that would allow its Member States to incorporate their legitimate share of the very mobile income of companies like Google (3.2.2).

Chapter 4 deals with the constitutional aspects of the conflicts properly speaking. Beyond competition for data and taxation of data, the traditional and historic meaning of constitutionalism has probably more to do with the very protection from data. That is to say, the protection of people from global data flows and the manipulation of these flows by companies like Google, as well as the intelligence services with which they closely cooperate.

The increasingly automated use of data as a means (or media) to produce ever-new forms of information (4.1) has called for a reconfiguration of the rights to privacy and data protection online (4.2). Besides being a pioneer in the development of a strong legal framework for the protection of privacy, the EU, especially through the case law of its Court of Justice, has recently tried to impose some constitutional limits on the exercise of power over global data flows, as shown by the rulings mentioned above (4.3). Given the impact of digital technologies on the operations of social memory and on the methods of public and private surveillance, these rulings raise important questions about the global or transnational enforcement of fundamental rights such as privacy and data protection in cyberspace (4.4).

The investigation proposed in the book may be classified in the field of sociology of constitutions, since its main theoretical background is the specific sociological version of systems theory developed by Niklas Luhmann.[39] Its main focus, therefore, is on the analysis of the aspects of the conflicts between Google and the EU that are directly related to the protection of fundamental rights, especially the rights to privacy and data protection online. However, the economic and fiscal aspects of the conflicts are also relevant in order to get a glimpse of the "bigger picture" behind them, which may indicate the possibilities of, as well as the actual constrains on, the expansion of constitutionalism in world society.

These conflicts involve a transnational corporation and a supranational organization dealing with legal, political and economic disputes connected with the rather extraterritorial cyberspace. That is why it seems relevant to investigate whether and to what extent questions about the constitution/limitation of power and the protection of fundamental rights may have any relevance at all to their unfolding and better understanding. That is to say, whether and to what extent politics and law may be re-articulated and connected beyond the traditional nation state, at the level of the EU, in order to deal with the economic, technological and media power of a transnational corporation like Google.

One preliminary conclusion may already be drawn, even if it is only a paradoxical or "autological" one. In order to study and research Google, one has almost inevitably to rely on Google itself to get access to data and bibliographical material, and also to investigate how the search engine works. To a certain extent Google is, simultaneously, one of the main objects and one of the main instruments of the investigation presented in the book. An object that directly influences (or frames) the subject who is supposed to observe and describe it.

39 Luhmann (1995 [1984]) *Social Systems*; Luhmann (2008 [1993]) *Law as a Social System*; Luhmann (2012 [1997]) *Theory of Society*. On the sociology of constitutions: Luhmann (1996) 'La costituzione come acquisizione evolutiva'; Corsi (2002) 'Sociologia da constituição'; Neves (2013 [2009]) *Transconstitutionalism*; Thornhill (2010) 'Niklas Luhmann and the sociology of the constitution'; Thornhill (2011) *A Sociology of Constitutions*; Teubner (2013) 'The project of constitutional sociology'; Teubner (2012) *Constitutional Fragments*; Febbrajo and Corsi (eds) (2016) *Sociology of Constitutions*.

1 Constitutionalism and world society

The future of constitutionalism in world society is uncertain. This is certainly no surprise. On the one hand, the future itself is a temporal horizon that cannot be observed in the present. Notwithstanding all rational planning, projects and expectations, "the future cannot begin".[1] On the other hand, constitutions were first invented in a revolutionary context to liberate society from its bonds to the past and provide for its "open future", a future that is now already past.[2]

There is a growing body of literature in the fields of constitutional and international law on the role of constitutionalism in world society. Would constitutionalism, traditionally connected with the historical formation of nation states, still have something to say in the age of accelerated globalization or would we now be facing its twilight?[3]

Although there is no consensus about the answer to this question, the prospect of a unifying global constitution with the same compact, holistic and general features as the national ones does not seem feasible, given the increasing fragmentation of global law.[4] Decentralizing tendencies toward the transnationalization and privatization of global legal regimes pose new and serious challenges to state-centered constitutionalism and call for a re-thinking and renovation of constitutional theory.[5]

This first chapter addresses these more general issues of legal and constitutional theory in order to provide the basic theoretical background for the further development of the book. It initially deals with the modern concept of constitution from a sociological perspective, according to which the novelty of constitutions is not necessarily found in their content, but in the specific way they connect law and politics in the historical formation of nation states (1.1). The idea that nation states and their constitutions are currently being challenged by the process of globalization, which is now a commonplace in the social sciences, is then

1 Luhmann (1982) *The Differentiation of Society*, p. 271ff.
2 Koselleck (2004 [1979]) *Futures Past.*
3 Dobner and Loughlin (eds) (2010) *The Twilight of Constitutionalism?*; Zagrebelsky, Portinaro and Luther (eds) (1996) *Il Futuro della Costituzione.*
4 Fischer-Lescano and Teubner (2004) 'Regime-collisions'; Koskenniemi (2005) *Global Legal Pluralism*; Cassese (2009) *I Tribunali di Babele.*
5 Teubner (2012) *Constitutional Fragments.*

described as a consequence of the gap between the structural changes brought about by modern society and their semantic descriptions. Modern society has always been a world society. The progressive realization of that causes some anxiety in the modern semantics of constitutionalism (1.2). Constitutional theory, thus, reacts with an inflationary use of the concept of constitution, which is itself temporalized with recourse to the category of "constitutionalization" (1.3). Instead of focusing on the potential emergence of global constitutions, it seems more promising for constitutional theory to focus on the transnational constitutional (or transconstitutional) conflicts between different legal orders of world society (1.3.1). Two specific subjects of the current discourse on constitutionalism beyond the state are then briefly analyzed, because of their particular relevance to the main object of the book: the EU (1.3.2) and transnational corporations (1.3.3).

1.1 Constitutions and modern society: content and form

One of the most common distinctions of constitutional law is that between constitutional content and constitutional form. The first refers to the topics that are usually dealt with by a constitution, its content properly speaking, such as the democratic organization of the state and the protection of fundamental rights. The second refers to the formal support provided by law to the institutionalization and self-limitation of power, the fact that the constitution is treated as paramount or higher law, which makes possible the legal control of political decisions, especially the judicial review of legislation.[6]

While some general issues related to the basic organization of society and politics were the object of an ancient philosophical and political debate in the western tradition, including the ideas of separation of powers and inalienable rights initially advanced by early modern theories of the social contract and natural law, the idea of the constitution as a legal norm that institutionalizes the political form of the nation state is definitely a modern invention.[7]

A modern and rather unexpected invention, constitutions were certainly the object of conscious and rational planning by the revolutionaries who tried to overcome the old regime and its stratified form of social organization at the end of the eighteenth century in Europe and North America. However, constitutions are also the result of evolution, in which the intentions and expectations of individual and rational actors play only a limited role.[8]

6 On the role of law as a formal support to the constitutionalization of power and the special case of countries, such as Great Britain, that do not have a written constitution: Sajó (1999 [1995]) *Limiting Government*, p. 9ff.

7 Fioravanti (1999) *Costituzione*; Luhmann (1996) 'La costituzione come acquisizione evolutiva'. On a broad sociological concept of constitution as the institution that provides for the differentiation and abstraction of the medium of political power, a concept that denies a radical distinction between modern and pre-modern constitutions: Thornhill (2011) *A Sociology of Constitutions*, p. 10ff.

8 Luhmann (1996) 'La costituzione come acquisizione evolutiva', p. 83ff.

The full development of the constitutional form, which entails that not only is positive law created by political decisions, but also that politics itself is submitted to the supervision of the courts, is a long process. A process that has been more or less accomplished by a great number of nation states during the nineteenth and twentieth centuries, along with a series of wars, catastrophes, *coups d'état* and authoritarian dictatorships. Despite its close connection with the enlightenment's ideals of progress and emancipation, the history of constitutionalism is also, to a great extent, the history of authoritarianism and the state of exception[9], a history of both inclusion and exclusion. This may indicate that the fears of the past usually overtake the hopes of the future as the main reason for the adoption of a constitution.[10]

In any case, the novelty of the constitution lies more in its form than in its specific content. In the particular way that it connects law and politics and, by doing so, contributes to the stabilization of the new basic structures of modern society. In the language of systems theory, the constitution provides for the structural coupling between law and politics.[11] A process that is itself connected to the functional differentiation of modern society as a whole, and the parallel development, on the one hand, of structural couplings between politics and the economy by means of taxation, the public budget and the regulation of the monetary medium, and, on the other hand, of structural couplings between law and the economy by means of the institutions of property, contract and the modern business enterprise.[12]

The constitution may be sociologically described as an instrument or artefact by means of which the legal and the political systems of modern society can achieve high degrees of autonomy while keeping structural links to each other. A fact that decisively contributed to the dissolution of the hierarchical and stratified order typical of European medieval society. With a common reference to the constitution, both law and politics have progressively disconnected themselves from their bonds to a cosmological semantics that projected its normativity into the present, becoming, thus, able to re-orient their operations toward an open future.[13]

These bonds with the past were represented, mainly, by the rules on dynastic government and the principles of natural law, which provided a normative and hierarchical foundation for the political and legal organization of society. With the

9 Agamben (2003) *Stato di Eccezione.*

10 Sajó (1999 [1995]) *Limiting Government*, p. 1ff.

11 Luhmann (1996) 'La costituzione come acquisizione evolutiva', p. 85ff.

12 Luhmann (1996) 'La costituzione come acquisizione evolutiva', pp. 113–114; Luhmann (2008 [1993]) *Law as a Social System*, p. 381ff. Teubner (2012) *Constitutional Fragments*, p. 108, also mentions the institutions of competition and currency as forms of the structural coupling between the legal and the economic systems. For legal purposes, competition may be understood as a sort of general condition for the lawful use of property and the lawful exercise of the freedom of contract. The modern business enterprise, to the extent that it constitutes a mix of both property and contracts, is also a form of the structural coupling between the legal and the economic systems.

13 Luhmann (1996) 'La costituzione come acquisizione evolutiva', p. 100; Corsi (2002) 'Sociologia da constituição'.

dissolution of the old regime and the secularization of its cosmological semantics, these foundations lost their normativity. As a result, law and politics had to find (or rather invent) their own foundations. The constitution offered, then, an alternative to deal with these new problems (or paradoxes) of self-reference, providing a sort of common mechanism for cross-legitimation and mutual effectiveness.[14]

On the one hand, the new sovereignty of the people, its unlimited power to limit itself, was anchored in a set of organizational, procedural and also substantive norms designed to regulate the self-generation and self-limitation of power by means of power.[15] On the other hand, the complete positivization of law, the fact that law regulates the conditions for its own production, was stabilized with the help of interpretative methods that attributed the creation and modification of law to the political decisions taken by the people and their representatives.[16]

Regular channels of legitimacy and effectiveness were then established between law and politics. The legitimacy of politics became dependent on it being regulated by legal norms, and its effectiveness became dependent on its capacity to translate its decisions into a legal form. The legitimacy of law, in turn, became dependent on its openness to the institutionalized influence of political decisions in the form of legislation, and its effectiveness became dependent on the possibility of the centralized use of force for the implementation of its norms.

The novelty of the constitution lies, therefore, in this structural coupling between democratic politics and positive law, the connection between the constituent power and sovereignty of the people and the institutional constraints and limitations provided by the constitutional form. A form that is inherently paradoxical;[17] that constitutes political power by means of its limitation; that enables decision-making by regulating its procedures and restricting its content; that creates freedom by establishing precommitments;[18] that opens the future at the same time as it tries to bind it.

The traditional content of constitutions is better understood in its specific connection with the constitutional form. Both the protection of rights and the separation of powers are important not exactly because of their concrete meanings, which, besides changing over time, are also dependent on particular cultural and historical contexts. Their importance lies in the fact that they institutionalize a higher level of abstraction in the enforcement of legal norms and the exercise of political power, with the consequent homogenization of the social dimension and the re-orientation of law and politics toward the future.[19]

The fundamental rights of freedom and equality solemnly proclaimed by constitutional texts usually do not specify the conditions for their own enforcement.

14 Luhmann (1996) 'La costituzione come acquisizione evolutiva', p. 87ff; Corsi (2016) 'On paradoxes in constitutions'.
15 Luhmann (1996) 'La costituzione come acquisizione evolutiva', p. 101ff.
16 Luhmann (1996) 'La costituzione come acquisizione evolutiva', p. 91ff.
17 Loughlin and Walker (eds) (2007) *The Paradox of Constitutionalism*; Corsi (2016) 'On paradoxes in constitutions'.
18 Holmes (1988) 'Precommitment and the paradox of democracy'.
19 Corsi (2002) 'Sociologia da constituição'.

They serve, nonetheless, to neutralize the existing social inequalities and concrete restrictions on freedom that may be recognized in the present, while potentially constituting the basis for specific demands for compensation.[20] Politics and law do not have to bind themselves to past privileges and social hierarchies. They are free to orient their operations toward an open future, even if it is a future in which new exclusions will emerge as the consequence of inclusions decided in the past.

The constitution also regulates organizational competences and formal procedures by means of which these rather abstract rights are translated into constitutional principles that may be operationalized in the decision-making practices of specific organizations, such as parliaments, courts and administrative bodies and agencies.[21] Openness to the future is also institutionalized in the democratic organization of the state, so that new parties may come to power, news laws may be approved and old precedents may be changed as part of the regular constitutional process.

The content is, thus, connected with the form. Constitutionalism, as the theory of limited and democratic government, is only fully realized in practice with the establishment of a constitutional form, a structural coupling between law and politics. This structural coupling, however, has only been completely developed in particular national settings, that is to say, in the form of nation states.

The nation state may be described as the historical and contingent form of condensation of the abstract medium of power that has provided both an institutional and a conceptual basis for the functional differentiation of modern politics.[22] A form that has also changed over time, from its initial liberal configuration toward the contemporary paradigm of the welfare and democratic state.[23]

It seems paradoxical that this form comes into question at precisely the time that it has expanded all over the world as the predominant model for the functional differentiation and territorial segmentation of power. This happens because the very process of globalization is commonly perceived as a threat to nation states and their respective constitutions.[24]

20 Corsi (2002) 'Sociologia da constituição', p. 109ff. On the importance of fundamental rights to the functional differentiation of modern society: Luhmann (2002 [1965]) *I Diritti Fondamentali come Istituzione*; Verschraegen (2002) 'Human rights and modern society'.

21 Corsi (2002) 'Sociologia da constituição', p. 102ff.

22 Corsi (2007) 'La finzione dello Stato'. On the distinction medium/form: Luhmann (2012 [1997]) *Theory of Society*, p. 113ff.

23 On the distinct historical formation of the state, as a legal and political organization, and the nation, as a reference for collective identity, and their later fusion in the modern form of the nation state, which is a product of the revolutions of the eighteenth and nineteenth centuries: Habermas (2002 [1996]) *The Inclusion of the Other*, p. 105ff. On the idea of constitutional paradigms and on the internal nexus between constitutionalism and democracy: Habermas (1996 [1992]) *Between Facts and Norms.*

24 Habermas (2002 [1996]) *The Inclusion of the Other*, pp. 105–106; Cassese (2002) *La crisi dello Stato*, p. 3ff. According to Castells (2010) *The Rise of the Network Society*, p. xviii, while being the agents of globalization, nation states lost their capacity to regulate the global and interconnected flows of wealth and information. Marramao (2011)

The contemporary debate on constitutionalism beyond the state clearly makes use of the traditional semantics of constitutionalism. It has an obvious constitutional content, even if the more liberal concerns about the limitation of power usually overtake the republican element of the democratization of decision-making procedures.[25] Nevertheless, this discourse does not seem to be connected with any constitutional form at the global level. It seems to be a sort of "semantics without structural reference".[26]

The next section explores this relationship between social structures and semantics in order to shed some light on the current debate over the legal and political consequences of globalization and its impact on constitutional theory.

1.2 Globalization and world society: structural changes and semantic bifurcations

One of the most important tenets of Niklas Luhmann's systems theory is that modern society is also a world society.[27] Territorial segmentation may still be important to the functioning of law and politics, but modern flows of wealth, knowledge and information have been following a much more borderless logic for a long time. The fashion term globalization, so common in recent decades, only stresses the intensification and acceleration of the functional differentiation that constitutes the basic structure of modern society, as well as its rapid expansion all over the world. The term itself may be seen as a sort of delayed semantic reaction to the way modern society has been functioning since at least the end of the eighteenth century, the age of the great social and technical revolutions that have dissolved the cosmology and the hierarchical order of the old regime.

Functional differentiation also implies that modern society is a society without a top or a center. Social inequalities, social exclusion and social privileges certainly still exist, maybe at a greater level now than ever before, but there is no longer a universal and unifying cosmological vision of the world that is able to justify and legitimate them as a direct imposition of a natural or supernatural order. Inclusion and exclusion are now submitted to the particular functional logic of each social system and none of them is able to guide or control society from above, be it religion or politics.[28]

Contro il Potere, p. 104, refers to the current "crisis of the state" as a paradoxical process by means of which nation states seem to be "declining while still growing".

25 Loughlin (2010) 'What is constitutionalization?', p. 60ff.

26 Neves (2013 [2009]) *Transconstitutionalism*, p. 5ff. According to Luhmann (2008 [1993]) *Law as a Social System*, p. 464ff, there is nothing at the level of world society that corresponds to the structural coupling of the political and legal systems by means of constitutions.

27 Luhmann (1997) 'Globalization or world society'; Luhmann (2013 [1997]), *Theory of Society*, p. 87ff.

28 On the shortcomings of the classic semantics inherited from the enlightenment movement when it comes to doing justice to the hypercomplex, poly-contextual and multi-centered structure of modern society: Luhmann (1995) 'Why does society describe itself as postmodern?'; Luhmann (2013 [1997]), *Theory of Society*, p. 167ff.

There are, however, two social systems that have some kind of primacy in the reproduction of social operations due to their relative independence from territorial segmentation and their predominant orientation toward the cognitive rather than the normative dimension of social communication, two factors that facilitate their generalized functioning worldwide: the economy, associated with the technical knowledge (or simply technology) derived from science, which has some primacy at the basic structural level of world society's organization and reproduction, and the mass media, which are more prominent at the level of the condensation of social semantics, that is to say, when it comes to offering self-observations and self-descriptions of modern society as a whole.[29]

If the term globalization may be described as a somewhat delayed reaction of social semantics to the acceleration and worldwide expansion of functional differentiation, the so-called crisis of the nation state may be understood as a sign that the classical semantics of statehood and nationality, which once offered a hierarchical self-description of society centered on the territorially segmented political system, is finally "making its peace" with the multi-centered and poly-contextual structure of modern society.[30]

The concept of the state as the hierarchical center of society, connected with the idea of sovereignty as absolute or supreme power, is somewhat reminiscent of the old cosmological semantics of medieval Europe, a semantics that reflected the stratified social structures of the time by means of a hierarchical description of the world. This concept is still quite popular in contemporary political and legal theory, even with all the progressive secularization brought about by the advent of modernity and the worldwide expansion of functional differentiation. Some elements of continuity remain, notwithstanding the revolutionary attribution of sovereignty to the people, and the submission of the state, now as a nation state, to the rule of law.[31]

Politics, however, is only one among the many subsystems of the poly-contextual and multi-centered modern society. The nation state, as its conceptual and main institutional basis, the historical form that has provided unity to the differentiation of the medium of power, is not and has never been the center of society. It is only the center of the modern political system at very best, and not exactly in the sense of a hierarchical and privileged space of centralized management and direction, but as the last instance of imputation for collective decision-making.[32]

29 Neves (2013 [2009]) *Transconstitutionalism*, p. 18ff.

30 The very idea of crisis, as well as the constant recurrence of ever-new crises, seems to have been a common feature of modern society since its revolutionary origins. See: Koselleck (1998 [1959]) *Critique and Crisis.*

31 This continuity is at the basis of the famous thesis of Carl Schmitt, for whom: "All significant concepts of the modern theory of the state are secularized theological concepts" (Schmitt (1985 [1922]) *Political Theology*, p. 36). On the metaphor of verticality as a long-term image in medieval and modern political thought: Costa (2004) 'Immagini della sovranità fra medioevo ed età moderna'.

32 Corsi (2007) 'La finzione dello Stato'. On the internal and rather heterarchical differentiation of the modern political system in the subsystems of politics in the strict sense, administration and the public: Luhmann (1990 [1981]) *Political Theory in the Welfare*

The so-called "death of the *Leviathan*" does not necessarily imply, though, that nation states have lost or will lose their institutional importance for the internal organization of the modern political system, at least not in the near future. What is "dying" or "disappearing", like Nietzsche's God, is not the state as an institution or set of formal organizations, but the state as the "mortal God" depicted in Hobbes' *Leviathan,* [33] this long-term self-description of politics, and of state politics, as the hierarchical center of society, a center supposedly able to direct and manage it from above.[34]

As an institution or set of formal organizations, the nation state will probably remain an important actor in the future of world society, even with all the institutional and organizational changes to which it has been submitted in its evolution from the classical liberal model to the contemporary welfare and democratic one, including the more recent wave of de-regulation and privatization of the 1980s and 1990s.

As a consequence of the worldwide spread of functional differentiation, structural trends toward fragmentation have manifested themselves both inside and outside the nation state, showing the growing anachronism of the traditional image of the hierarchical and centralized unity. Domestic centrifugal tendencies, usually coined in terms such as "pluralism", "corporatism" or "polyarchy", were matched by external ones, such as the invasion of the international legal order of "sovereigns" by the new "subjects" of international law and the new "transnational regimes" of global governance[35].

Notwithstanding the autonomy between the various social systems, functional differentiation is not a symmetrical process. As stated above, systems such as the economy, science and technology and the mass media, due to their relative independence from territorial segmentation and their predominant orientation toward the cognitive rather than the normative dimension of social communication, can easily spread worldwide, while the functioning of law and politics is still strongly dependent on the territorial segmentation of world society in the form of nation states, and on the normative structuration of nation states in the form of constitutions.

State. On the idea of nation as a provisory "semantics of reaction" to the functional differentiation of modern society that now works as an "*obstacle épistémologique*" in the social sciences, preventing a more adequate description of world society: Luhmann (2013 [1997]), *Theory of Society*, p. 283. From a different perspective, the nation may also be described as an artefact that once provided cultural substance to the legal form of the state, helping it to promote a highly abstract level of civic solidarity among its citizens. An artefact that, nevertheless, should now be disconnected from the republican ideal of constitutionalism in order to allow constitutionalism itself to address the current challenges of multiculturalism and globalization. See: Habermas (2002 [1996]) *The Inclusion of the Other*, p. 105ff.

33 Hobbes (1651) *Leviathan.*

34 According to Marramao (2000) *Dopo il Leviatano*, p. 23ff, the "death of the Leviathan" was already inscribed in its genetic code with the worldwide expansion of the European system of nation states.

35 Cassese (1986) 'The rise and decline of the notion of state'; Cassese (2002) *La Crisi dello Stato*; Teubner (2012) *Constitutional Fragments*, pp. 15ff and 42ff.

This structural asymmetry is behind the more general diagnosis of the decline of politics, and also law, at least to a certain extent, at the level of world society.[36] While the crisis of the traditional concept of the state as a hierarchical, uniform and centralized instance of command and control may be considered as a mere anachronic and "nostalgic" disillusionment at the level of social semantics,[37] this more general decline of law and politics seems to be the effect of this asymmetric functional differentiation of world society, in which the legal and political systems are usually overtaken by the global functioning of the economy, science and technology and the mass media. Contrary to the former, this latter aspect of the critical self-description of modern politics and law seems to have a clear structural reference, that is to say, a reference to the reality of the concrete operations of world society at the level of its basic structures (or forms of differentiation).

The asymmetric globalization of modern society raises at least two important questions about the future of constitutionalism. One has to do with the possible emergence of new forms of power beyond the nation state, and the other with the consequent risks to democracy and social inclusion.

Formal organizations and informal networks for collective decision-making have existed for a long time alongside the central structure of modern nation states at both the domestic and international levels. However, the obsolescence of the classical concept of the state as a hierarchical and homogeneous unit tends to increase the perception of this fragmentation, while systemic asymmetries at the level of world society tend to put pressure on law and politics to develop new structures in order to cope with the ever more accelerated global flows of money, technology and information.

Beyond the general institutional framework of the United Nations (UN) and its specialized agencies, new organizations and networks for collective decision-making have emerged with varied degrees of autonomy in relation to the nation state, such as the EU, the World Trade Organization (WTO) and the rather decentralized global regime of Internet governance.

The modern business enterprise has also changed its form, with the worldwide expansion of its activities and the progressive transnationalization of its internal organization. Technological innovations in computer science and digital networking, in their turn, have made available new forms for the diffusion of communication and the constant production and reproduction of information at the global level.

36 While the decline of politics seems to be accompanied by a parallel decline of public law, especially constitutional law, private law continues to be important to the organization of transnational economic activities. On the globalization of private law beyond the state: Teubner (1997) 'Global bukowina'; Teubner (2002) 'Breaking frames'; Calliess and Zumbansen (2010) *Rough Consensus and Running Code*. On the incipient globalization of administrative law: Kingsbury, Krisch and Stewart (2005) 'The emergence of global administrative law'; Cassese (2006) 'Administrative law without the state?'; Cassese et al (eds) (2008) *Global Administrative Law*.

37 On the "nostalgic" and "melancholic" elements of the modern theories of the state: Marramao (2000) *Dopo il Leviatano*, p. 25ff.

In the face of all these structural changes, maybe it is still too soon to state if and to what extent the medium of power is being generally displaced or whether it is just changing its form. It is possible to argue that the most recent wave of globalization entails a general shift of the "steering medium", in the sense that money replaces power, with the consequence that the world would then be ruled by the "empire of private law".[38] Another perspective is that globalization implies a trend toward the diffusion of power within and beyond the nation state.[39] We would, thus, be witnessing a new "double movement",[40] in which law and politics are called to fight back the chaotic expansion of the global economic system in the new fora and arenas of the "postnational constellation".[41]

Independently of how it is being depicted, the current scenario of "turbulent evolution"[42] gives rise to semantic uncertainties in constitutional theory about the possibilities of institutionalizing new forms of democratic and inclusive self-government beyond the nation state.[43] This situation may be described as a process of "semantic transition and bifurcation", characterized by an inflationary use of the concept of constitution in the self-descriptions of global law and politics,[44] which is the object of the next section.

1.3 The discourse on constitutionalism beyond the state

The possible ways of re-articulating law and politics at the level of world society are at the basis of the current discourse on constitutionalism beyond the state. No one would doubt that law and politics extend well beyond their more restricted territorial and national configurations. The doubts revolve around the constitutional quality of the global connections between the legal and the political systems and their capacity to institutionalize new mechanisms for the democratic organization of power and the protection of fundamental rights that are able to counterbalance the ever more accelerated and disruptive global flows of wealth, technology and information.

38 Koskenniemi (2011) 'Empire and international law', p. 36. According to Habermas (2001 [1998]) *The Postnational Constellation*, p. 78, the problem lies in the fact that, contrary to power, money cannot be democratized. For another perspective on the possibility, if not of democratizing, at least of constitutionalizing the medium of money: Teubner (2011) 'A constitutional moment?'.

39 Kjaer (2011) 'Law and order within and beyond national configurations', p. 421ff; Thornhill (2011) 'The future of the state', p. 391ff; Marramao (2011) *Contro il Potere*, p. 97ff; Arrighi and Silver (eds) (1999) *Chaos and Governance in the Modern World System*, p. 37ff.

40 Polanyi (1944) *The Great Transformation.*

41 Habermas (2001 [1998]) *The Postnational Constellation*, p. 81.

42 Luhmann (1997) 'Globalization or world society', p. 76.

43 According to Habermas (2001 [1998]) *The Postnational Constellation*, p. 61: "The idea that societies are capable of democratic self-control and self-realization has until now been credibly realized only in the context of the nation-state. Thus the image of a postnational constellation gives rise to alarmist feelings of enlightened helplessness widely observed in the political arena today."

44 Holmes (2011) 'The rhetoric of "legal fragmentation" and its discontents'.

Even if strongly connected with the territorial segmentation of world society in the form of nation states, the political system has multiple ways of operating at the global level. Beyond the traditional forms of diplomacy and power politics backed by military force, world politics has been progressively institutionalized since the late nineteenth century around a set of formal organizations with diverse functional competencies, most significantly the UN and its specialized agencies.

The basic UN institutional framework has been complemented by a variety of regional organizations, informal networks and spontaneous civil society movements that coordinate political processes at the multilevel global system.[45] The procedures for collective decision-making, however, are still very unequal, asymmetric and centered on the north Atlantic, with the United States and its closets allies still being able to exercise what is commonly depicted as a "hegemonic" or "imperial" power, projecting its interests and influence into the main fora and arenas of regional and global governance.[46]

Law, by its turn, is also present at the level of world society, notwithstanding its close ties to the principles of territoriality and nationality and the absence of central legislation and jurisdiction.[47] International law, both public and private, has traditionally provided the means for coordinating the global functioning of the legal system. It has done so by defining the rules and principles for the interaction and cooperation between nation states, and also by regulating the conditions for the applicability of national laws in cases of conflict.

Since the middle of the last century, though, we have witnessed a proliferation of international tribunals and the emergence of global legal regimes with functionally specialized competences, some of them relatively independent from nation states and traditional international organizations.[48] Comparative constitutional law and the growing dialogue between courts have provided, moreover, the means for the global circulation of legal norms and judicial precedents beyond national and territorial borders.[49] The very discourse on human rights may be seen as a trend toward a partial de-territorialization and de-nationalization of the legal system, even if the claim to their universal recognition still lacks a significant degree of effective institutional enforcement.[50]

Alongside this process of evolution of politics and law, traditional distinctions of constitutionalism, such as state/society, public/private and domestic/international,

45 Slaughter (2004) 'Disaggregated sovereignty'; Búrca and Walker (2003) 'Law and transnational civil society'.

46 Koskenniemi (2004) 'International law and hegemony'; Krisch (2005) 'International law in times of hegemony'.

47 Luhmann (2008 [1993]) *Law as a Social System*, p. 464ff.

48 Fischer-Lescano and Teubner (2004) 'Regime-collisions'; Koskenniemi (2005) *Global Legal Pluralism*; Cassese (2009) *I Tribunali di Babele.*

49 Benvenisti (2008) 'Reclaiming democracy'; Tushnet (2009) 'The inevitable globalization of constitutional law'.

50 Neves (2007) 'The symbolic force of human rights', p. 416ff; Marramao (2008) *La Passione del Presente*, p. 173ff.

have lost their original descriptive potential and their associated capacity to serve as clear references for concrete decision-making and political negotiation.[51] On the one hand, successive waves of interventionism and liberalization have blurred both the conceptual and the institutional borders between the state, the market and the organized civil society.[52] On the other hand, the acceleration of the global flows of wealth, technology and information and the parallel multiplication and fragmentation of global legal regimes have weakened the very distinction between an internal or domestic space and an external or international space, with the consequent "re-entry"[53] of the distinction domestic/international and the emergence of new terms such as transnational, multinational, supranational, post-national and so on.

Between the public and the private, the domestic and the international, the organizational and the spontaneous, world society now has a wide variety of regimes and arrangements for regional and global governance that do not match the traditional concepts and categories of constitutional and international law. A brief list would include: the UN general regime of peace and security; international and regional courts (or "quasi-courts") for the protection of human rights; the Bretton Woods institutions of economic governance; the international trade regime centered around the WTO; various arrangements and treaty-bodies to deal with numerous environmental issues; regional organizations for political coordination, military defense and economic integration; private or "hybrid" regimes to deal with disputes between transnational corporations, the regulation of sports and Internet governance; among many others.[54]

World society, therefore, clearly has a global politics, as well as a global law, but it does not seem to have any global constitution, at least not one comparable to the traditional constitutions of modern nation states. Suggestions have been made that the UN Charter would work as a sort of "constitution of the international community,"[55], but, in any case, it would be a very incomplete and asymmetric one, given the limited mandate of the UN, the "absolutist powers" of the five

51 Grimm (2010) 'The achievement of constitutionalism and its prospects in a changed world'.

52 On the process of interpenetration between state and civil society and the corresponding tension between the public and private spheres: Habermas (1991 [1962]) *The Structural Transformation of the Public Sphere.*

53 On the paradoxical concept of the "re-entry" of a distinction into what it has distinguished: Luhmann (2002) *Theories of Distinction*, p. 79ff; Brown (1972) *Laws of Form*, p. 69ff.

54 In order to avoid the constitutional semantics and its consequent paradoxes, these regimes and arrangements of regional and global governance are also usually framed in the language of administrative law. See: Kingsbury, Krisch and Stewart (2005) 'The emergence of global administrative law'; Cassese (2006) 'Administrative law without the state?'; Cassese et al (eds) (2008) *Global Administrative Law.*

55 Fassbender (2009) *The United Nations Charter as the Constitution of the International Community*; Fassbender (2007) 'We the peoples of the United Nations'.

permanent members of the Security Council and the absence of any significant mechanism of judicial review.[56]

In the absence of a clear and unifying global constitution and given the challenges posed by the accelerated globalization of world society, that is to say, by the worldwide expansion of functional differentiation, with all its asymmetries and turbulent effects, constitutional theory has reacted with an inflation of competing concepts and theoretical approaches that try to preserve some of the basic ideals of constitutionalism in the self-descriptions of global law and politics:[57] global or post-national constitutionalism, constitutional pluralism, multilevel constitutionalism, societal constitutionalism, transconstitutionalism and so on.[58]

What seems to be common to most of these approaches is the use of the traditional semantics of constitutionalism in an explicit or implicit prospective way. The main issue is not the actual existence of a global constitution (or constitutions), but rather the possibility of extending the basic ideas and concepts of constitutionalism to political and legal phenomena beyond the territorially segmented nation state. The stress is generally put neither on the constitution as a political act with concrete historical reference nor on the constitution as a legal norm that may be enforced by the courts, but in the current processes of "constitutionalization".[59]

To a certain extent, every constitution has elements of a dynamic process that is constantly pushing for its further realization in practice. The term constitutionalization, however, when applied to the new regimes and decision-making procedures of regional and global governance, seems to raise the very temporalization of the concept of constitution to a new level. While the constitution itself is already a mechanism for opening the future, constitutionalization is a process

56 Habermas (2008) 'The constitutionalization of international law and the legitimation problems of a constitution for world society'; Habermas (2006 [2004]) *The Divided West*, p. 115ff; Cohen (2008) 'A global state of emergency or the further constitutionalization of international law'; Cohen (2010) 'Constitutionalism beyond the state'.

57 Holmes (2011) 'The rhetoric of "legal fragmentation" and its discontents'.

58 Preuss (2010) 'Disconnecting constitutions from statehood'; Kumm (2010) 'The best of times and the worst of times'; Brunkhorst (2010) 'Constitutionalism and democracy in the world society'; Walker (2002) 'The idea of constitutional pluralism'; Walker (2008) 'Taking constitutionalism beyond the state'; Walker (2009) 'Multilevel constitutionalism'; Pernice (2001) 'Multilevel constitutionalism in the European Union'; Teubner (2012) *Constitutional Fragments*; Neves (2013 [2009]) *Transconstitutionalism*. On the skepticism about the possibilities of expanding constitutionalism beyond the nation state: Grimm (2010) 'The achievement of constitutionalism and its prospects in a changed world'; Loughlin (2010) 'What is constitutionalization?'; Palmisano (2010) "Dal diritto internazionale al diritto cosmopolitico?'.

59 On the distinction between constitutionalism, constitution and constitutionalization: Loughlin (2010) 'What is constitutionalization?'. On the meta-political function of constitutionalism, which would consist in the organization and regulation of forms of collective decision-making in the name of some common interest: Walker (2010) 'Beyond the holistic constitution', 295ff.

oriented toward the progressive institutionalization of a form whose main features are currently difficult to guess.

One of the main problems is that the constitutionalization of the actual regimes of regional and global governance tends to highlight the liberal and legal elements of constitutionalism while disregarding its more republican and democratic ones.[60] The overwhelming concern is the limitation and legal control of the exercise of public powers, usually in the name of free trade, competition, fiscal responsibility and the protection of contracts and property rights. The democratization of decision-making procedures and the public debate over their distributional and exclusionary effects do not seem to have the same weight. That is why the discourse on constitutionalism beyond the state is also commonly framed as a counter-project to the so-called "neoliberal constitutionalization" of world society that would have been under way for a couple of decades now.[61]

This discourse, however, has to live up to the fact that constitutions, as artefacts of evolution, cannot be simply imposed on the new regimes of regional and global governance in an automatic and voluntarist way. The very concept of constitutionalization implies a process that cannot be entirely controlled by its eventual agents and planners. One additional setback is that, contrary to the revolutionary context of the late eighteenth century, our present situation, with its recent totalitarian past and the looming risks of an ecological catastrophe, no longer allows an "infinite trust in the future", a trust that was at the basis of classical constitutionalism.[62]

In the current debates over constitutionalism beyond the state, two very popular and common approaches are those of "constitutional pluralism" and "multilevel constitutionalism", which are rather similar and usually tend to overlap. Both were born out of the discussions about the constitutionalization of the EU and are now usually applied to other manifestations of global or post-national constitutionalization. Their focus is on the similarities, differences and conflicts between distinct levels of constitutional ordering that tend to interact, overlap and often clash in the resolution of the regional, sectoral and global problems of world society: nation states, supranational organizations such as the EU and traditional international organizations such as the UN and the WTO.[63]

Another and more heterodox approach is that of "societal constitutionalism", which expands the use of the concepts of constitution and constitutionalization to the analysis of transnational legal regimes that work at the global level with relative (or total) independence from nation states and their intergovernmental

60 Loughlin (2010) 'What is constitutionalization?', p. 60ff.
61 Habermas (2001 [1998]) *The Postnational Constellation*, p. 88ff; Holmes (2011) 'The rhetoric of "legal fragmentation" and its discontents', p. 136ff.; Kennedy (2008) 'The mystery of global governance'; Koskenniemi (2007) 'Constitutionalism as mindset'.
62 Luhmann (1996) 'La costituzione come acquisizione evolutiva', p. 123.
63 Walker (2002) 'The idea of constitutional pluralism'; Pernice (2001) 'Multilevel constitutionalism in the European Union'; Cohen (2010) 'Constitutionalism beyond the state'; Rosenfeld (2008) 'Rethinking constitutional ordering in an era of legal and ideological pluralism'.

organizations, like the ones in charge of the resolution of disputes between transnational corporations (*lex mercatoria*), the regulation of sports (*lex exportiva*) and Internet governance (*lex digitalis*).[64] It is also possible to speak of "corporate constitutionalism" when the focus is on the internal processes of constitutionalization of big transnational corporations whose activities are spread around the world.[65]

Certain aspects of these approaches are briefly analyzed in the following subsections, which deal with some specific issues of the broader debate on constitutionalism beyond the state that are particularly relevant to the further development of the main arguments of the book.

1.3.1 Transconstitutionalism and its realistic approach

This book is less concerned with the best way to describe the allegedly constitutionalization of world society and its various regimes of regional or global governance than with analyzing real and concrete conflicts that may actually present a constitutional and transnational dimension. The main focus is not on emerging constitutional semantics, but on existing legal and institutional structures that may provide mechanisms and solutions for dealing with the new transnational conflicts of world society. That is why the theoretical approach developed by Marcelo Neves, called "transconstitutionalism", is so promising and serves as a reference for the analyses of the following chapters.[66]

With a background on systems theory, this approach recognizes that modern constitutions have developed as a structural coupling between politics and law in numerous national settings, following the territorial segmentation of the legal and political systems. As already referred to in section 1.1 above, constitutions as social structures, and constitutionalism as their semantic reflection, as the theory of constitutions, deal basically with two sets of interrelated problems: the protection of fundamental rights and the legitimate organization of power.[67]

Law and politics, however, have progressively developed beyond their traditional national configurations to such an extent that the usual mechanisms of intergovernmental diplomacy and international law are no longer able to coordinate the legal and political communication of world society. As functional differentiation has spread all over the world and modern society has become ever more "globalized", problems regarding the protection of fundamental rights and the democratic organization of power arise that transcend the limits of any national legal order.[68]

64 Teubner (2012) *Constitutional Fragments*; Teubner (2010) 'Fragmented foundations'.

65 Teubner (2011) 'Self-constitutionalizing TNCs?'; Teubner (2009) 'The corporate codes of multinationals'; Backer (2012) 'Transnational corporate constitutionalism'.

66 Neves (2013 [2009]) *Transconstitutionalism*; Neves (2015) 'Comparing transconstitutionalism in an asymmetric world society; Neves (2016) 'Paradoxes of transconstitutionalism in Latin America'.

67 Neves (2013 [2009]) *Transconstitutionalism*, p. 2ff.

68 According to Neves (2016) 'Paradoxes of transconstitutionalism in Latin America', e-book 82%: "while it is not possible to relinquish classical constitutional state law,

These problems are not only legal, they are also constitutional, because they are closely connected with the very structural coupling between law and politics, with the legal constraints imposed on politics by means of the regulation of power and the protection of rights. Nowadays, political power can easily spread beyond borders with the help of information and communication technologies, raising concerns about the protection of fundamental rights that national courts alone cannot address in a proper way. Mass surveillance online is probably one of the best examples.

In contrast to the structural coupling between law and politics at the national level, world politics does not allow itself to be regulated and constrained by the legal system, at least not to the same degree as provided for in national constitutions. Power politics and strategic national interests have many ways of deflecting and bypassing the ever more fragmented norms and procedures of the international legal order. The rule of force is still much more prominent than any symbolic appeal to some sort of international (or global) rule of law. At the global level, there is a clear asymmetry between the political and legal systems, which prevents the emergence of any incipient form of a global constitution.[69]

Even without a global constitution, world society must somehow face its transnational constitutional problems, which demand dialogue and mutual collaboration among national courts, international and supranational tribunals, as well as other "quasi-judicial" procedures and organizations of the multiple regimes of regional and global governance.[70]

Transconstitutionalism, then, is described as a method to approach and solve conflicts about the legitimate organization of power and the enforcement of fundamental rights that are common to more than one legal order in the multilevel legal system of world society, which encompasses national legal systems, supranational legal orders such as the EU, general international law and various sectoral legal regimes more or less independent from nation states and their intergovernmental organizations (human rights law, WTO law, the law of the sea, *lex mercatoria, lex sportiva, lex digitalis*, etc.). The focus, then, is not on the possible emergence of constitutions beyond the state, but on the concrete ways of addressing transnational constitutional (or transconstitutional) problems and conflicts that no legal order alone can solve, be it national, international, supranational, local or transnational.[71]

generally linked to a constitutional text, constitutionalism is opening up to spheres beyond the state, not exactly owing to the emergence of other (non-sate) constitutions, but rather because eminently constitutional problems, especially those relating to human rights, intersect simultaneously with several legal orders that entangle with each other in their search for solutions".

69 Neves (2013 [2009]) *Transconstitutionalism*, p. 56ff.

70 Neves (2013 [2009]) *Transconstitutionalism*, p. 25ff.

71 Neves (2013 [2009]) *Transconstitutionalism*, p. 74ff. For this specific approach, "transnational legal orders" are those that arise and develop with relative independence from nation sates and traditional intergovernmental organizations, such as the so-called *lex mercatoria, lex sportiva* and *lex digitalis*. See: Neves (2013 [2009]) *Transconstitutionalism*, p. 118ff.

To a certain extent, this approach may be called realistic, or rather skeptical, because it avoids the inflationary use of the concept of constitution to describe global phenomena that do not clearly fit in the traditional meanings of the concept. With the possible exception of the EU, no legal order beyond the state has yet achieved as good a degree of structural coupling to the political system as the national legal orders of existing nation states. As problems related to the legitimate organization of power and the enforcement of fundamental rights arise that no legal order alone can solve, the need to solve them does not necessarily entail the emergence of global constitutions. In fact, what these problems require is a broader and continuous dialogue between the different legal orders involved.

That does not mean that national parliaments and courts are the only ones to enact and enforce constitutional rules. Similar to the theoretical approaches of constitutional pluralism and multilevel constitutionalism, transconstitutionalism also takes the pluralist and multilevel structure of the legal system of world society for granted. This system as a whole encompasses a plurality of legal orders (or subsystems) organized in multiple levels: the national (and holistic) legal orders of nation states, the supranational legal orders of complex entities such as the EU, the many functional areas and subareas of the ever more fragmented international legal order, global (or transnational) legal regimes that are more or less autonomous in relation to nation states and their intergovernmental organizations, and so on. While law and politics are structurally coupled mainly at the national level, constitutional rules circulate among these different legal orders and levels of world society whenever a constitutional problem or conflict arises that transcends the particular national, territorial or functional limits of any of them.

That is why the role of judges, courts and other "quasi-judicial" organizations and procedures is ever more prominent in the multilevel legal system of world society. Even in the absence of uniform rules of competence and attribution, they are the ones with formal mandates to deal in a routinized way with problems and conflicts involving constitutional issues. They may act as a sort of "transition bridge" between different legal orders when transconstitutional problems and conflicts arise.[72] Observing themselves and each other, they also have the privileged opportunity to develop common constitutional rules, in a mutual dialogue that may be more or less contentious and arbitrary.[73]

The Internet is an interesting laboratory to observe and reflect upon these problems and conflicts, as will be shown in the next chapter. Before that, the following subsections briefly deal with the so-called emergence of two potentially new constitutional subjects beyond the traditional nation state: the EU and transnational corporations, and the main theoretical approaches that try to conceptualize them in

72 Neves (2013 [2009]) *Transconstitutionalism*, p. 74ff.

73 On some examples of contemporary legal cases that had to be solved by means of a transconstitutional dialogue between judges, courts and "quasi-judicial" institutions of different legal orders (national, supranational, international, transnational and local): Neves (2013 [2009]) *Transconstitutionalism*, p. 84ff.

a constitutional framework. Some constitutional issues related to the rise and spread of the Internet are then addressed in Chapter 2.

Taking into consideration some of the main ideas and insights of the transconstitutional approach developed by Neves, the analysis of the conflicts between Google and the EU, which are the object of Chapters 3 and 4, is slightly skeptical, or "self-restrained". The aim is to avoid an inflationary use of the concept of constitution. These conflicts are not necessarily described as transnational constitutional because there are actual constitutions at the level of the EU, transnational corporations such as Google or cyberspace itself, but because they involve traditional constitutional issues related to the organization of power and the enforcement of fundamental rights that clearly transcend the national, territorial and functional limits of any specific legal order.

1.3.2 The European Union: between free market and democratic politics

The EU is almost a natural candidate when it comes to identifying the new constitutional subjects of world society. Born out of a project of pacification of rival nation states by means of increasing economic cooperation and integration,[74] the EU has absorbed a significant number of traditional state competences, has achieved a level of institutional density and has been progressively enlarged to such an extent that it can hardly be conceptualized in the classical categories of constitutional and international law.

The EU is neither a federal state, nor a traditional international organization, but a supranational *sui generis* institution.[75] Having given rise to a new form of governance beyond, but at the same time with the state,[76] it is usually described as a multilevel system of governance in which nation states, subnational units and the European institutions share powers and cooperate for the achievement of common goals in a composed constitutional system.[77]

This constitutional system is both plural and multilevel. It is characterized by the dynamic interaction between the multiple constitutions of the Member States and the two basic treaties that establish the EU and regulate its functioning.[78]

74 Habermas (2006 [2001]) *Time of Transitions*, p. 89ff.

75 Pernice (2001) 'Multilevel constitutionalism in the European Union', p. 6. Castells (2010) *End of Millenium*, p. 365ff, has suggested that the EU may be described as a new form of "network state". On the conceptualization of the EU in terms of network theory: Ladeur (1997) 'Towards a theory of supranationality'.

76 Börzel (2010) 'European governance'.

77 Pernice (2009) 'The Treaty of Lisbon', pp. 352–353.

78 The two basic treaties are: (i) the "Treaty on the Functioning of the European Union – TFEU", originally signed in Rome on 25 March 1957 as the "Treaty Establishing the European Economic Community – TEEC" and which came into force on 1 January 1958; and (ii) the "Treaty on European Union - TEU", originally signed in Maastricht on 7 February 1992 and which came into force on 1 November 1993. The main institutions and rules of the European internal market also extend to the European Economic Area (EEA), which, besides the EU Member States, also comprise Norway, Iceland and Lichtenstein. The "Agreement on the European Economic Area" was

Competences are then distributed between the national and the supranational levels in a form of shared sovereignty. Heterarchical and horizontal arrangements for coordinated action prevail over more traditional hierarchical ones. EU law is considered to have "primacy" over national law, even if the continuing dialogue between national and European courts is often very cautious and deferential, so that the potentially unsettling question of final authority remains rather open and undecided.[79]

From the perspective of transconstitutionalism, the EU represents a supranational legal and political order that has somehow been able to coordinate the resolution of transconstitutional conflicts on at least two different levels. On the one hand, inside the EU itself, EU courts and the courts of Member States have already developed their own mechanisms for judicial cooperation and dialogue – like the doctrines of primacy and direct effect of EU law, as well as the practice of referring cases to EU courts for a preliminary ruling – which allow them to provide for more or less uniform solutions to common constitutional problems, especially the ones related to the protection of fundamental rights in the application of EU law.[80] On the other hand, the European institutions themselves have developed their own rules and procedures to deal with the supranational division of powers and the promotion of "European values", which sometimes enter into collision with other legal orders around the world, requiring EU courts to engage in a transconstitutional dialogue with other courts outside the EU.[81]

Notwithstanding the advanced stage of the supranational constitutionalization of the EU polity, the discourse on European constitutionalism has always been under the (in)famous suspicion of a basic democratic deficit, which would be inscribed at the very origins of the post-war project of European integration.[82] Notwithstanding all the optimism and grandiose ambitions of the EU "founding fathers", which would contrast with the more self-restrained and skeptical mood of its current leaders,[83] the project of integration is usually blamed for having been historically pushed by political elites with the passive consent of EU citizens, to the

originally signed in Porto on 2 May 1992 and came into force on 1 January 1994. These institutions and rules extend to Switzerland too on the basis of a number of bilateral treaties signed between Switzerland and the EU.

79 Maduro (2005) 'The importance of being called a constitution', p. 347. According to Walker (2002) 'The idea of constitutional pluralism', p. 337: "Constitutional pluralism … recognizes that the European order inaugurated by the Treaty of Rome has developed beyond the traditional confines of inter-*national* law and now makes its own independent constitutional claims, and that these claims exist alongside the continuing claims of states. The relationship between the orders, that is to say, is now horizontal rather than vertical – heterarchical rather than hierarchical." (Emphasis in original.)

80 On transconstitutionalism between the EU supranational legal order and the legal order of its Member States: Neves (2013 [2009]) *Transconstitutionalism*, p. 96ff.

81 On transconstitutionalism between the EU supranational legal order and some specific functional areas of the international legal order: Neves (2013 [2009]) *Transconstitutionalism*, p. 144ff.

82 Maduro (2005) 'The importance of being called a constitution', p. 334ff.

83 Habermas (2006 [2001]) *Time of Transitions*, p. 89ff.

extent that the technocratic elements associated with the establishment of a free market zone would have once again trumped the ideal of creating a democratic political union.[84]

At the beginning of the 1990s, the conclusion of the Maastricht Treaty and the following discussions over the common currency and the enlargement of the EU to the east drew the attention of public opinion to the advanced level of economic and administrative integration that had already been achieved, and to the existing deficit of democratic legitimation, which, in its turn, prompted the debate about the need for a European constitution properly speaking.[85]

Some of the main issues of this debate were articulated in the famous controversy between Dieter Grimm and Jürgen Habermas back in the mid-1990s. According to Grimm, Europe would still lack the structural conditions for the effective functioning of a supranational democracy: basically, a European-wide public sphere and European-wide institutions for the intermediation and articulation of social interests and conflicts (political parties, trade unions, interest groups, etc.), so that the adoption of a formal constitution would only reinforce the structural deficit of democracy by further curbing the autonomy of the Member States.[86] In Habermas' opinion, however, the adoption of a constitution, especially by strengthening the European Parliament, could institutionalize the necessary conditions for the development of a European-wide process of opinion and will formation that would be required to provide democratic legitimacy to the EU, while also potentially stimulating, in a circular process, the formation of a European identity and a more abstract form of civic solidarity beyond the traditional nation state.[87]

This debate remains relevant even after the failure of the Constitutional Treaty and the later adoption of the Treaty of Lisbon.[88] The deficit of democracy is like

84 Habermas (2015) *The Lure of Technocracy*, p. 3ff.

85 Grimm (1995) 'Does Europe need a constitution?', p. 282ff, who also refers to a conflict between European law and European politics in the divergence between, on the one hand, the constitutional interpretation of the treaties by the then European Court of Justice (ECJ) and, on the other hand, the call of the European Parliament for a democratically legitimated constitution.

86 Grimm (1995) 'Does Europe need a constitution?'.

87 Habermas (1995) 'Remarks on Dieter Grimm's 'Does Europe need a constitution?''. On the Grimm–Habermas controversy and on the process of European constitutionalization in the broader context of the contradictory dynamics of "glocalization": Marramao (2009) *Passaggio a Occidente*, p. 227ff.

88 The ratification of the "Treaty Establishing a Constitution for Europe", which was signed in Rome on 29 October 2004, came to a halt after its rejection by popular referenda in France and the Netherlands in May and June 2005 respectively. Some of the reforms contained in the Constitutional Treaty were later implemented by means of amendments to the TFEU and the TEU by the Treaty of Lisbon, which was signed on 13 December 2007 and came into force on 1 December 2009. On the main changes brought about by the Treaty of Lisbon: Riekmann (2010) 'Constitutionalism and representation'; Pernice (2009) 'The Treaty of Lisbon'. On the main legitimacy problems left unresolved by the Treaty of Lisbon: Habermas (2009) *Europe: The Faltering Project*, e-book 41%ff.

the "original sin" (or paradox) of European integration. Notwithstanding the creative and sophisticated theoretical strategies to conceal it behind the "plural" and "multilevel" forms offered by the self-descriptions of European constitutionalism, it always reappears in one way or another: as the "beheading of the legislator",[89] as a new form of technocratic or post-democratic "executive federalism",[90] as the suspicion and lack of enthusiasm in the east,[91] as the restrictive adjectives that usually precede the very use of the noun constitutionalism in Europe, such as "liberal-legal",[92] "low-intensity",[93] "post-constituent"[94] and so on.

The latest economic crisis, as well as the lack of an effective response thereto, seems to have confirmed all these critical diagnoses of a structural democratic deficit in the EU, a deficit that undermines the very constitutional nature of the process of European integration.[95] The financial crisis of 2008 has developed into a currency and debt crisis and subsequently into a major economic and political crisis that has "entrapped" Europe and put the whole project of further integration and constitutionalization at risk: neither the Member States alone nor the EU as a whole seems able to get out of the crisis and be capable of promoting the joint action needed to provide some degree of political control over the chaotic functioning of the global financial system.[96] The technocratic and rather ineffective crisis policy of the EU has even reinforced the level of euroskepticism and the internal divisions in the continent, fomenting old populist and nationalistic sentiments.[97] The process of withdrawal of the United Kingdom (UK), known as "Brexit", is the most recent example.

The deficit of democracy of European constitutionalism may be contextualized in terms of the more general structural asymmetry in the functioning of the economic, legal and political systems of world society. At the level of the EU, the process of economic integration is at a very advanced stage. It is supported by a strong process of autonomous and supranational law-making that seeks to guarantee broad freedoms for economic transactions, even at the expense of a lack of political legitimacy and the weakening of the ideal of democratic and inclusive self-government. The democratic deficit is, thus, a deficit of politics, which is manifest even at the supranational level of the European institutions: technocratic rule, policy implementation and economic law-making by the European Commission, the European Central Bank and the European Courts usually prevail over the

89 Brunkhorst (2014) 'The beheading of the legislator'.
90 Habermas (2012) *The Crisis of the European Union*, p. 12ff.
91 Sajó (2005) 'Constitution without the constitutional moment', p. 246
92 Loughlin (2010) 'What is constitutionalization?', p. 65.
93 Maduro (2005) 'The importance of being called a constitution', p. 340ff.
94 Walker (2007) 'Post-constituent constitutionalism?', p. 261ff.
95 The deficit of democracy in the EU and its negative effects on the unfolding of the crisis is recognized even by sectors of the media with a strong liberal and market-oriented ideology. See: *The Economist* (2012) 'An ever-deeper democratic deficit'.
96 Offe (2015) *Europe Entrapped*; Habermas (2012) *The Crisis of the European Union*; Habermas (2015) *The Lure of Technocracy*.
97 Habermas (2015) *The Lure of Technocracy*, p. 4ff and 100ff.

political concerns of the democratic legislator, be it the European Parliament, be it the parliaments of the Member States.[98]

In the language of systems theory, we may speak of an imbalance or asymmetry in the structural couplings between law, politics and the economy at the European level. An imbalance that may also be described as the supremacy of the European "economic constitution" over its political one.[99]

First, between the economic and legal systems, there is a strong structural coupling, reflected in the high level of legal protection provided to the four basic economic freedoms, which are meant to promote free trade among the Member States by means of the wide circulation of goods, services, capital and labor in the territory of the EU. Property rights and contracts may count on a stable degree of institutional enforcement, as well as the rules on competition and the restrictions on state aid, which seek to guarantee that the free market is neither "corrupted" by its own failures, nor by potentially disruptive political interventions.[100]

Second, between the economic and political systems, there is a very weak and asymmetric structural coupling. On the one hand, the monetary medium is centralized and strictly regulated by the technocratic and independent European System of Central Banks, which allows most nation states no room for an autonomous monetary policy. On the other hand, the progressive imposition of uniform constraints on national budgets, together with the absence of a common fiscal policy, gives rise to a negative process of inter-state competition for private capital that significantly restricts the redistributive potential of taxation and collective decision-making more generally.[101] The medium of money has, thus, a strong leverage with regard to the medium of power.[102]

Third, between the legal and political systems, that is to say, the constitution in its traditional historical form, the structural coupling is also rather asymmetric.[103]

98 Scharpf (2010) 'Legitimacy in the multi-level European polity'.

99 Brunkhorst (2014) 'The beheading of the legislator', p. 94ff, who also refers to the influence of German ordoliberalism in the inception of the European process of integration, with its focus on competition law and the interconnections between "law and economics", instead of "law and democracy". On the ordoliberal ideals of economic integration and technocratic rule as a sort of "non-constituent constitutionalism": Walker (2007) 'Post-constituent constitutionalism?', p. 252ff. For a critical description of "ordoliberal constitutionalism" as a new kind of natural law derived from the expansionary and "totalitarian" tendencies of the economic rationality: Teubner (2012) *Constitutional Fragments*, p. 30ff.

100 On the role of the then European Court of Justice in the development of the European "economic constitution": Maduro (1998) *We the Court*.

101 On the risks and contradictory economic effects of the establishment of a monetary union without a common fiscal and economic policy by countries with different levels of economic performance, such as in the case of the Eurozone: Offe (2015) *Europe Entrapped*, p. 18ff; Varoufakis (2013) *The Global Minotaur*, p. 194ff; Krugman, Obstfeld and Melitz (2012) *International Economics*, p. 559ff.

102 Offe (2015) *Europe Entrapped*, p. 6ff.

103 On the asymmetry between juridification and democratization, European law and European politics, in the constitutionalization of the EU: Neves (2013 [2009]) *Transconstitutionalism*, p. 65ff.

Even if the Member States retain the monopoly over the legitimate use of force, a wide range of decision-making competencies has been transferred to the supranational level, where democratic legitimation is still weak. The initiative for legislation is a prerogative of the Commission, besides the fact that, in many areas, the Parliament is not on an equal footing with the Council in the legislative process. Though the democratic deficit in the organization of public powers is a limitation of the European "political constitution", the protection of fundamental rights has progressively acquired a stronger level of judicial enforcement, culminating in the proclamation of the Charter of Fundamental Rights and its formal recognition by the Treaty of Lisbon.[104]

Summing up these structural imbalances, while the economy may count on the strong legal institutionalization of a system of supranational free trade and market competition, which gives its organizations significant leverage in European policy-making, democratic politics has very limited room to shape law, and almost no room at all to influence the economy by means of fiscal and monetary policy.[105]

Especially positioned to take advantage of the "fundamental freedoms" provided by the European "economic constitution" are those companies that are able to operate in various national settings and that can rapidly move their assets and capital across borders, that is to say, transnational corporations. Their great leverage allows them to exert massive influence on political decision-making and law enforcement at both the national and supranational levels of the EU polity. They make use of the uniform rules of European law in the defense of their rights and interests, as well as benefit from the political fragmentation of the EU for the purposes of tax avoidance and "law shopping".[106]

The next subsection addresses some contemporary issues and trends in the organization of transnational corporations and the regulation of their activities worldwide.

1.3.3 Transnational corporations: autonomous organizational trends

If the "globalization" of the modern economic system on the side of its markets is a centuries-old trend,[107] the effective transnationalization of its formal organizations is a rather contemporary one.[108] It dates back to the end of the nineteenth

104 Rosas and Armati (2012) *EU Constitutional Law*, p. 160ff.

105 Offe (2015) *Europe Entrapped*, p. 6ff and 32ff.

106 Cassese (2002) *La crisi dello Stato*, p. 109ff; Böröcz and Sarkar (2005) 'What is the EU?', p. 159ff.

107 Arrighi (1994) *The Long Twentieth Century*.

108 The very distinction between market and organization, or horizontal contractual relations and hierarchical decision-making, is an intrinsic part of the modern economy, whose structural features are only partially caught by the term "market economy", since it is also (and increasingly) an "organizational economy". See: Simon (1991) 'Organizations and markets'. On the sociological description of organizations as self-referential systems whose main function is the constant production and reproduction of decisions: Luhmann (2018 [2000]) *Organization and Decision*; Luhmann (2013 [1997]) *Theory of Society*, p. 141ff; Teubner (1993) *Law as an Autopoietic*

century with the overseas expansion of manufacturing activities by European and US industrialists and it gained momentum after the end of the Second World War.[109] It is also a result of the autonomous evolution of the modern business enterprises in relation to their nation states of origin and the progressive differentiation of their economic activities from other administrative and military functions of government, that is to say, the very differentiation between the economic and the political systems.[110]

Transnational corporations, also referred to as multinational enterprises, are usually defined as companies that own assets and engage in direct business activities of a productive nature in more than one country.[111] Mainstream economics tends to explain their existence primarily on the basis of considerations of efficiency and economies of scale.[112] A more far-sighted approach, however, would have to include the strategic advantages that these companies gain by the simple fact of operating in more than one country in terms of the leverage they are able to exert in relation to other actors or organizations that are less capable of coordinating their activities transnationally, such as governments, labor unions, consumers and suppliers.[113]

Foreign direct investment, international (or transnational) production and world trade are currently largely concentrated by big transnational corporations.[114] The increasing degree of transnationalization of the activities of these

System, p. 134ff. On the new hybrid forms of network production between contract and organization: Teubner (2006) '*Coincidentia oppositorum*'.

109 Wilkins (2001) 'The history of multinational enterprise', p. 4ff; Ietto-Gillies (2012) *Transnational Corporations and International Production*, p. 7ff; Calliess (2011) 'Transnational corporations revisited', p. 601ff.

110 On the evolution of the modern business enterprise from the Dutch model of joint-stock chartered companies, which still concentrated significant administrative and military functions of government, to the English model of family manufacturers and later the US model of the vertically integrated multinational corporation, including the more recent trends toward the flexibilization and decentralization of production: Arrighi and Silver (eds) (1999) *Chaos and Governance in the Modern World System*, p. 97ff.

111 OECD (2011) *OECD Guidelines for Multinational Enterprises*, p. 17; Ietto-Gillies (2012) *Transnational Corporations and International Production*, p. 11ff.

112 Krugman, Obstfeld and Melitz (2012) *International Economics*, p. 155ff. For an account of the main literature and theories about the emergence and evolution of transnational corporations: Dunning (2001) 'The key literature on IB activities'; Ietto-Gillies (2012) *Transnational Corporations and International Production*, p. 29ff.

113 Ietto-Gillies (2012) *Transnational Corporations and International Production*, p. 156ff. On this problem of unequal bargaining power: Hymer (1970) 'The efficiency (contradictions) of multinational corporations', p. 446ff.

114 Detailed data on foreign direct investment, which is the kind of investment that usually leads to or increases the activities of international production carried out by transnational corporations, are published annually by the United Nations Conference on Trade and Development (UNCTAD) in its "World Investment Report". See: UNCTAD (2017) *World Investment Report 2017*. It is estimated that two thirds of world trade is the responsibility of transnational corporations and that one third of it takes place on an intra-firm basis. See: Ietto-Gillies (2012) *Transnational Corporations*

companies is also reflected in their internal organization, which spreads across countries in a complex and multifaceted network of corporate structures and contractual arrangements.[115] Their degree of "footlooseness" may be measured by numerous indicators, most of them pointing to the companies' growing autonomy in relation to any specific nation state, including their home countries.[116] Even the conflicts that arise among them are increasingly settled with recourse to a body of law (*lex mercatoria*) that is rather autonomous from state jurisdictions and official law-making.[117]

The proliferation in the number and variety of transnational corporations is usually associated with the corresponding disempowerment of nation states.[118] This disempowerment reveals the organizational side of the worldwide asymmetry between the political and the economic systems. While political organizations are either too limited in their territorial basis, as in the case of state administrations, or too weak in regard to their decision-making powers, as in the case of traditional intergovernmental organizations, transnational corporations, in their turn, are increasingly big, wealthy and ubiquitous enough to exercise significant leverage in political negotiations and policy-making around the world. They are often able to bypass a large number of legal rules enacted to regulate their activities in specific countries, especially regarding tax, labor and environmental issues.[119] It is no surprise, therefore, that society reacts to this imbalance by moralizing the debate and protesting against the perceived unchecked "empire of the corporation".[120]

and International Production, p. 215. On the seminal description of transnational corporations as substitutes for markets in the organization of international exchange: Hymer (1970) 'The efficiency (contradictions) of multinational corporations', p. 441ff.

115 On the evolutionary trend toward the transnationalization of the internal organization of the modern corporation: Westney and Zaheer (2001) 'The multinational enterprise as an organization'. On the interesting paradox of the self-regulating global corporation that is, in theory, able to own itself: Backer (2006) "The autonomous global corporation", p. 552ff.

116 These indicators may be related to the location of assets, sales and employment, which compose UNCTAD's transnationality index, among many other factors, like the nationality of top managers, the board of directors and shareholders, the focus on global markets, and the eventual incorporation under a supranational charter. See: Calliess (2011) 'Transnational corporations revisited', p. 607ff, who also refers, as a sign of transnationality, to the recent fashion trend among European companies, especially German ones, to seek incorporation under EU law as a "*Societas Europaea*". This kind of supranational incorporation is regulated by EU (2001) *Council Regulation (EC) No 2157/2001 of 8 October 2001 on the Statute for a European company (SE).*

117 Teubner (1997) 'Global bukowina'; Teubner (2002) 'Breaking frames'.

118 Arrighi and Silver (eds) (1999) *Chaos and Governance in the Modern World System*, p. 278; Kobrin (2001) 'Sovereignty@Bay'.

119 From the perspective of the economic system, it seems that laws and regulations are increasingly treated as a "commodity" in the "transnational law market", where nation states would compete as suppliers of law-making for the investments of transnational corporations. For an unapologetic defense of the value and efficiency of the emerging "transnational law market": Eidenmüller (2011) 'The transnational law market, regulatory competition, and transnational corporations'.

120 Klein (2000) *No Logo*; Bakan (2004) *The Corporation*. On the "mythology of the multinational", rather common in many protest movements, as an inadequate way to

Beyond protest movements and their activation of the "code of moral",[121] the challenges posed by transnational corporations to democracy and human rights at the level of world society have triggered a wide range of hybrid regulatory initiatives, as well as a renewed debate in constitutional and international law over the possibilities of regulating their activities worldwide.

The initial discussions on the broad theme of Corporate Social Responsibility (CSR) – which, at the beginning, seemed to be restricted to a set of hollow and, thus, non-binding public relations campaigns[122] – have evolved into the emerging debate over the specific relationship between business and human rights. Transnational corporations and other business enterprises, even if not included in the traditional list of "subjects of international law", have begun to be described as addressees of the international norms for the protection of human rights, which has raised the question of their international responsibility, alongside other non-state actors, for the violation of these norms.[123] A parallel debate has resurfaced in constitutional law over the so-called horizontal effect of fundamental rights between private parties and the related legal doctrines developed by different constitutional courts to deal with the issue, such as the US "state action" doctrine and the German doctrine of "third party effect".[124]

A huge set of public, private and "hybrid" codes of conduct has also emerged in order to deal with the regulatory challenges of global business.[125] "Soft law" norms and policy guidelines have been enacted at various levels and with different degrees of "enforceability". Numerous organizations have been involved in this paradoxical form of "non-binding law-making", such as the UN,[126] the

address the complexity of the problems of organized decision-making and risk attribution in modern society: Corsi (2000) 'Protest and decision-making in a society of blame'. Marramao (2011) *Contro il Potere*, pp. 109–110, refers to the thesis of the "imperialism of the multinationals" as a tranquillizing ideological elaboration, a simplistic way of providing a "familiar image of the enemy".

121 Luhmann (1993) 'The code of moral'.

122 Doane (2005) 'The myth of CSR'.

123 Ratner (2001) 'Corporations and human rights'; Muchlinski (2001) 'Human rights and multinationals'; Clapham (2006) *Human Rights Obligations of Non-State Actors*, p. 195ff; Alston (ed) (2005) *Non-State Actors and Human Rights*, p. 141ff. On the debate over the application of human rights norms in the international trade regime: Wai (2003) 'Countering, branding, dealing'; Petersmann (2000) 'The WTO Constitution and human rights'; Petersmann (2006) 'Human rights, constitutionalism and the World Trade Organization'. Detailed and updated information on news, trends and developments around the world are provided by the website of the Business & Human Rights Resource Centre: http://business-humanrights.org

124 Sajó and Uitz (eds) (2005) *The Constitution in Private Relations.*

125 Teubner (2009) 'The corporate codes of multinationals'; Calliess and Zumbansen (2010) *Rough Consensus and Running Code*, p. 181ff; Zumbansen (2010) 'Neither "public" nor "private", "national" nor "international".

126 UN (2014) *Guide to Corporate Sustainability*; UN (2011) *Guiding Principles on Business and Human Rights.* On the evolution of the debate on business and human rights, especially at the level of the UN: Ruggie (2007) 'Business and human rights'. On the main innovations brought about by the UN Guiding Principles on Business and Human Rights, which were endorsed by the UN Human Rights Council on 6 June

International Labour Organization (ILO),[127], the Organization for Economic Cooperation and Development (OECD),[128] the EU,[129] the International Organization for Standardization (ISO),[130] among many other industry- or company-specific initiatives.[131]

Moreover, moving from the "periphery" to the "center" of the legal system,[132] non-governmental organizations and human rights activists around the world have increasingly begun to resort to transnational private litigation as a means to provide the judicial accountability of transnational corporations for violations of human rights. The legal strategies are usually framed in the form of civil liability actions for tort damages, with proceedings often being initiated in countries other than the ones where the supposed violations have occurred.[133]

These new trends and initiatives have resonated with constitutional theory, especially in the latest writings of Gunther Teubner. Against the background of the alleged "neoliberal constitutionalization" of recent decades, which would have provided transnational corporations with unprecedented freedom from the effective regulation of nation states, Teubner proposes a form of "societal constitutionalism" as a sort of "double movement", in which society might fight back the unchecked worldwide expansion of business and the "totalitarian tendencies" of the economic rationality.[134]

2011, and on the thin prospects of the emergence of a formal treaty to deal with the issue: Ruggie (2014) 'Regulating multinationals'.

127 ILO (2017) *Tripartite Declaration of Principles Concerning Multinational Enterprises and Social Policy.*

128 OECD (2015) *G20/OECD Principles of Corporate Governance*; OECD (2011) *OECD Guidelines for Multinational Enterprises*; OECD (2015) *OECD Guidelines on Corporate Governance of State-Owned Enterprises.*

129 On recent trends and innovations in the EU: Schutter (2005) 'The accountability of multinationals for human rights violation in European law'.

130 ISO (2010) *ISO 26000 – Guidance on Social Responsibility.*

131 On the specific sector of information and communication technologies, see the initiatives: "Ranking Digital Rights" (https://rankingdigitalrights.org) and "Global Network Initiative" (https://globalnetworkinitiative.org). For a brief summary of the main issues in the sector: Business & Human Rights Resource Center (2014) *Information Technology.*

132 On the distinction between center and periphery and the position of the courts in the center of the legal system: Luhmann (2008 [1993]) *Law as a Social System*, p. 274ff.

133 Scott and Wai (2004) 'Transnational governance of corporate conduct through the migration of human rights norms'; Wai (2005) 'Transnational private law and private ordering in a contested global society'. On the recent trends in litigation in the US on the basis of the old and controversial "Alien Tort Claims Act": Borden and Rajan (2013) 'Transnational human rights litigation after *Kiobel*'; Grimwood (2013) 'Human rights in a post-*Kiobel* landscape'.

134 Teubner (2011) 'Self-constitutionalizing TNCs?', p. 21ff. For a rather similar perspective on "corporate constitutionalism" beyond the nation state: Backer (2012) 'Transnational corporate constitutionalism'. For a pioneering socio-legal analysis of the risks of corporate power to the "institutional design of a democratic society": Sciulli (2001) *Corporate Power in Civil Society.*

Teubner's main argument is that it is necessary to: (i) generalize the traditional constitutional problem of self-restraining the political system of nation states; and (ii) re-specify it in the global context, in which the expansive and destructive tendencies of other social systems, mainly the economy, pose significant risks to individual and institutional autonomy. As a consequence, human rights should not be reduced to the individual/state dualism and its equivalents in traditional legal doctrine, such as the state's "primary duty to protect" and the "horizontal effect" in private relations. Instead, the actual threats to the integrity of human beings, as well as to the functionally differentiated structure of modern society as a whole, would stem not only from the state or from individual private parties, but from the expansionist and destructive tendencies of the "anonymous matrices" of societal communicative processes.[135]

As formal organizations of the global economic system, transnational corporations are, thus, described as new constitutional subjects, giving rise to an incipient form of "corporate constitutionalism" that challenges the traditional guiding distinctions public/private and national/international of constitutional and international law theory.[136] Furthermore, the problem of their human rights obligations would be better understood as a constitutional one, which requires new legal and political measures to induce the self-restraining of the global economy's "anonymous matrix".

Notwithstanding the innovative and sophisticated framework of this analysis, the claims about the constitutional dimension of corporations seem to be overestimated, at least considering the basic theoretical background advanced above on the role of constitutions in modern society. "Societal" or "corporate constitutionalism" seems to downplay the importance of politics, or "institutionalized politics", as one fundamental side of the constitutional form. The constitutive/limitative function that constitutions have historically performed in relation to modern politics bear little similarity with the actual proposals of regulating and "self-restraining" the activities and the internal organization of transnational corporations. Thus, the broad "generalization" of the form has the risk of preventing its further "re-specification" in a significant and effective manner.[137]

The trend toward the increasingly autonomous organization and worldwide functioning of transnational corporations is, nevertheless, a structural reality that one should count on when analyzing the role of corporations in the actual operations of the modern economic system, as well as the conflicts and disputes

135 Teubner (2012) *Constitutional Fragments*, p. 124 ff; Teubner (2010) 'Fragmented foundations'; Teubner (2006) 'The anonymous matrix'.

136 Teubner (2011) 'Self-constitutionalizing TNCs?'; Teubner (2009) 'The corporate codes of multinationals'.

137 For an explicit argument in favor of the role of civil constitutions beyond traditional politics: Teubner (2012) *Constitutional Fragments*, p. 114ff. For a critical appraisal of Teubner's proposal of "societal constitutionalism" and the related spread of civil constitutions that would represent the structural coupling of law with autonomous subsystems of world society other than politics: Neves (2013 [2009]) *Transconstitutionalism*, p. 70ff.

that constantly arise among them, as well as between them and other organizations and actors, such as governments, international or supranational organizations and individual citizens.

Some contemporary conflicts between Google and the EU are addressed in Chapters 3 and 4. In order to provide a better picture of the context in which these conflicts unfold, the next chapter deals with certain specific and important issues relating to the architecture of cyberspace, a "space" that may prove to be a privileged laboratory for the analysis of the transnational constitutional (or trans-constitutional) aspects of these conflicts.

2 The architecture of cyberspace

Even before the worldwide spread of the Internet, Italo Calvino had already "prophesied" the significance of computer science for the new millennium:

> Today every branch of science seems intent on demonstrating that the world is supported by the most minute entities, such as the messages of DNA, the impulses of neurons, and quarks, and neutrinos wandering through space since the beginning of time … Then we have computer science. It is true that software cannot exercise its powers of lightness except through the weight of hardware. But it is software that gives the orders, acting on the outside world and on machines that exist only as functions of software and evolve so that they can work out ever more complex programs.[1]

Calvino's beautiful evocation of lightness as a literary virtue does not come into direct opposition to heaviness, to the concrete materiality of the things of the world. The evocation suggests more of a relationship of tension and oscillation than one of simple opposition. The lightness of the word does not deny the weight of the world. To a certain extent, it conveys it. Transcending the immediate heaviness of the world within the world would be the task of literature, just as language is supposed to convey meaning beyond the material presence of things, and the software is supposed to put the hardware to work by means of "ever more complex programs".

Even if, according to Calvino, it is the software that "commands", the power of its "lightness" is inseparable from the "weight" of the hardware. A sign, maybe, that neither literature nor language are possible without the worldliness dimension of things. Or, to put it another way, that the production of meaning is dependent upon the "materialities of communication", the specific media and technical apparatuses that store, process and transmit information.[2] The importance of media is also stressed (or overstressed) by the provocative and rather extreme claim that "there is no software" and it is, indeed, the deep hardware which, "protected from the user", really "commands".[3]

1 Calvino (1988) *Six Memos for the Next Millennium*, p. 8.
2 Gumbrecht and Pffeifer (eds) (1994) *Materialities of Communication.*
3 Kittler (2013) *The Truth of the Technological World*, p. 219ff.

The Internet too is made up of "lightness" and "heaviness". Its architecture, or code, is a mix of both software and hardware.[4] Beyond the logical protocols, addresses and standards that provide for the unique interconnection of a multitude of different networks, digital data packets must travel through a "physical layer", as if only to warn us against the simplistic use of common dualities such as virtual and real, cyberspace and physical space, even software and hardware. The "materialities of cyberspace" are present everywhere, even if they are often invisible or hidden in the form of submarine cables lying deep under the sea, wires that usually extend below the earth, electromagnetic waves moving through the air, satellites gravitating in the outer space and last, but not least, the end-point "black boxes" (personal computers, tablets, mobiles and all the various gadgets, devices and appliances of the emerging "Internet of things"), with their bland surfaces and "friendly interfaces".[5]

The rise and spread of the Internet has accelerated the global flows of money, technology and information that are generally controlled (or influenced) by big and powerful transnational corporations of the new media sector such as Google. It has also created new problems for the coordination of the legal and political systems of world society. The governance of this global network of communication has bypassed, to a large extent, the traditional mechanisms of intergovernmental diplomacy and international law. Violations of rights and abuses of power in cyberspace seem to transcend, to a certain extent, the very distinctions national/international and public/private, creating problems that no legal order alone can solve, be it national, international or supranational.

This second chapter addresses some constitutionally relevant issues related to the architecture of cyberspace. The very word constitution is often used, in a metaphorical and material sense, to refer to this architecture. Leaving aside this metaphor, which may be misleading, the chapter focuses on the ways in which the rights and principles enshrined in real constitutional texts and practices interact with the architecture and technical infrastructure of the Internet. It initially describes the innovations brought about by this new medium of production and diffusion of communication and information beyond the traditional and overestimated opposition between freedom and control (2.1). The transnational or extraterritorial character of this new medium, together with the fast and general spread of its multiple uses, poses new legal and political questions regarding its governance and regulation, most of them with a strong constitutional dimension (2.2). The constitutional relevance of these questions has been underscored recently by revelations about the pervasive practices of mass surveillance on the Internet carried out by the US and its closest allies with the help of some big transnational corporations of the Internet or digital economy (2.3). Google is one of them. Besides its collaboration in these practices of mass surveillance online, the activities of the company have become the object of growing public scrutiny

4 Lessig (2006) *Code*, p. 5.
5 Kittler (2013) *The Truth of the Technological World*, p. 209. On the material or spatial dimension of the Internet: Sassen (2004) 'Sited materialities with global span'.

mainly because of its own successes and its innovative business model. Search engines are important "gatekeepers" in cyberspace. The reality of their operations deserves an analysis of its own (2.4).

2.1 The Internet beyond freedom and control

The history of the Internet, like the history of modern media of communication more generally, is closely related to the evolution of warfare and military technology.[6] Just as the precursors of the first digital computers were produced by the Allies for the purpose of breaking German encryption during the Second World War, the Internet was first developed as a research project financed by the US military during the Cold War. State warfare and the industrial-military (or cyber-industrial-military) complex, not some idealized "free market", are at the origins of digital technologies.[7]

The evolution of digital devices and networks, however, has followed a path that cannot be simply reduced to the strict logic of military escalation. The engagement of the academic and scientific community in the development of the Internet and the general spread, first, of the personal computer, and later, of the Net itself, have embedded elements of openness and innovation into the very architecture of cyberspace, something that is also referred to as "generativity".[8]

The military origins of digital technologies have not prevented, however, the emergence of a utopian and libertarian narrative of "Internet freedom" and "cyber-exceptionalism".[9] Nevertheless, the commercial expansion of the Internet and the inevitable legal and political disputes over its governance and regulation have quickly confronted the initial euphoria with the cruder realities of cyber-security, mass surveillance, online censorship, digital borders, "tethered appliances" and the whole range of new "architectures of control".[10]

Following the common narrative, it is possible to say that the Internet has brought, in a paradoxical way, both unprecedented freedom and unprecedented

6 Kittler (1996) 'The history of communication media'.

7 Kittler (2013) *The Truth of the Technological World*, p. 178ff. Contrary to the tenets of the so-called "Californian ideology", private enterprise was only one element of a mixed structure involving state subsidies, defense contracts and amateur engagement in the development of the computer and the Internet. See: Barbrook and Cameron (1996) 'The Californian ideology'.

8 Zittrain (2008) *The Future of the Internet*, p. 67ff. On the origins and evolution of the Internet: Abbate (1999) *Inventing the Internet*; Leiner *et al* (2009) 'A brief history of the Internet'; Hafner and Lyon (1998) *Where Wizards Stay Up Late*; Castells (2010) *The Rise of the Network Society*, p. 45ff.

9 Barlow (1996) *A Declaration of the Independence of Cyberspace*; Johnson and Post (1996) 'Law and borders'.

10 On the move in the self-descriptions of cyberspace, especially among US legal scholars, from the focus on the new freedoms of interaction and communication to the emphasis on the new risks of pervasive control of online behavior: Lessig (2006) *Code*; Goldsmith and Wu (2006) *Who Controls the Internet?*; Boyle (1997) 'Foucault in cyberspace'; Morozov (2011) *The Net Delusion.* On the rise and stall of the generative Net: Zittrain (2008) *The Future of the Internet*, p. 7ff.

control. The new possibilities in terms of free communication, interaction and innovation are only matched by the parallel risks of excessive control of online behavior, a control that may be exercised either directly, by the very design of the code or architecture of cyberspace, or indirectly, by the regulation of intermediaries such as Internet Service Providers (ISPs), search engines, social networks, online platforms, etc.[11]

Beyond the distinction between freedom and control, the Internet may also be described more generally as a new medium of production and diffusion of communication and information. A new medium that also carries a new "message";[12] the message of "multimediality" or "hypermediality". The computer itself already represents a convergence of previous media, in the sense that it is able to reproduce sounds, images and texts, and later "hypertexts", with the only recourse to discrete digital sequences.[13] The Internet goes one step further and links the computer to the telecommunications infrastructure, creating a unique global network of interconnected computers.

As a new medium of communication, the Internet has an impact on almost every sector or system of our modern society: politics, law, economics, science, the arts, education, health, religion, etc.[14] Two specific sectors deserve particular attention here: technology and the mass media.

The "question concerning technology"[15] is an old and complex one. Beyond all forms of technological determinism, infused with either utopian or catastrophic inspiration, the important message of Heidegger seems to consist in stressing the need to overcome pure instrumentalist approaches to technology, especially the ones that tend to oscillate between the poles of freedom and control. The real problem of technology would not lie, thus, in technology itself, but in the illusion that technology is neutral and that society may control it, because this illusion disguises the fact that society is also increasingly dependent upon it – or, in Heidegger's terms: "enframed by its concealed essence".[16]

This is true for the traditional mechanical technologies that deal with the production of energy, as well as for the new information and communication technologies that deal with the management of signs, either through analog or digital

11 Lessig (2006) *Code*, p. 31ff; Goldsmith and Wu (2006) *Who Controls the Internet?*, p. 65ff.
12 McLuhan (1964) *Understanding Media*, p. 7ff.
13 According to Kittler (1999 [1986]) *Gramophone, Film, Typewriter*, p. 1: "The general digitization of channels and information erases the differences among individual media. Sound and image, voice and text are reduced to surface effects, known to consumers as interface. … Inside the computers themselves everything becomes a number: quantity without image, sound, or voice."
14 For a wide range of multidisciplinary contributions on the overall impact of the Internet and its future developments: Szoka and Marcus (eds) (2010) *The Next Digital Decade*. On the impact of digital technologies on the humanities in general: Fiormonte, Numerico and Tomasi (2015) *The Digital Humanist*.
15 Heidegger (1977) *The Question Concerning Technology and Other Essays*.
16 Heidegger (1977) *The Question Concerning Technology and Other Essays*, p. 3ff.

means.[17] Both the "technology of body and things" and the "technology of signs" tend to create a reality of their own, a kind of "second nature" (or "artificial nature") that society increasingly relies upon for the supply of energy and for the automated storage, processing and transmission of information. Instead of control – be it society controlling technology, or technology pre-determining society – the relationship between society and technology is one of mutual dependence and co-evolution.[18]

Technology cannot be reduced, therefore, to a mere instrument for the manipulation of nature and semantic signs. It is, instead, constitutive of social reality, serving as a form of connection between society and its external environment.[19] The growing dependence of modern society on technology means that the very act of thinking and communicating about technology presupposes the use of the technology that is being thought about and communicated. In order to write about the Internet and the computer, for instance, one has inevitably to use the Internet and the computer.[20]

If society is conceived of as communication, it is possible that the Internet and the computer, forming a new medium for the production and diffusion of communication and information, will have (or are already having) an impact on society similar to the invention of writing and the printing press. There is no technological determinism in this diagnosis, however, because there is no teleology or predetermined causality involved. Ubiquitous networking and automated storage, processing and transmission of information generate a drastic increase in the complexity of social communication, with unpredictable effects on the general organization of society and its forms of differentiation.[21]

The "question concerning digital technologies", then, goes beyond the mere use of data and information as the new basic "raw materials" for the production processes of the "information society".[22] It touches upon the most elementary ways in which society observes and describes itself. Communication now flows, ever more rapidly, with the automated support of digital machines, which may dispense of, to a great extent, the intervention or mediation of humans and their traditional scriptographic and typographic media.

The code of cyberspace, its software and hardware, is the channel through which a great part of social communication runs, which means that social reality is

17 According to Kittler (1999 [1986]) *Gramophone, Film, Typewriter*, p. 16ff, the "technologizing of information" did not come about with the invention of the computer. It dates back, instead, to the end of the nineteenth century with the invention of technical media for the storage of data, the famous triad: gramophone, film and typewriter.

18 Luhmann (2012 [1997]) *Theory of Society*, p. 312ff.

19 Luhmann (2012 [1997]) *Theory of Society*, p. 312ff, speaks of technology as a sort of "functional simplification that works" and that provides for the structural coupling between society and its external environment, with all the inevitable risks that come about as a consequence of this coupling. On the relationship between the intensive use of technologies and the concept of risk: Luhmann (2005 [1991]) *Risk*.

20 In the words of Kallinikos (2009) 'On the computational rendition of reality', p. 188: "Informatization models and, at the same time, moulds reality".

21 Luhmann (2012 [1997]) *Theory of Society*, p. 180ff.

22 Castells (2010) *The Rise of the Network Society*, p. 77ff.

increasingly framed by logical protocols and mathematical algorithms that determine the storage, processing and transmission of information with minimal recourse to direct human mediation. Beyond their traditional function of tools for the production of knowledge, mathematical axioms and logical rules have become a constitutive element of the very functioning of society, the artificial medium through which communication and interaction take place.[23] A medium that is also self-referent, given that information is constantly applied to the production of new information, computers are necessary to build new computers, code is needed in order to program new code, etc.

Again, the scenario is best depicted not by reference to humanistic notions of freedom and control, but by reference to structural trends of mutual dependence and co-evolution between society and digital technologies. Communication now depends on the computer, but it may not be causally pre-determined by it. Casualties and surprises are not eliminated, even if they start to become mediated by the combinatory possibilities of the machine.[24]

Here too the real problem lies in the illusion of neutrality, as if the computer were nothing more than an obedient machine that may be controlled or "mastered" by the user.[25] Notwithstanding its "friendly interface", the machine itself is "invisible", in the sense that its inner workings are generally not accessible to the user. While channeling communication and interaction, its functioning remains rather unnoticed and, to a certain extent, beyond meaningful comprehension.[26]

The "invisibility" of the machine is not only a problem for the "ignorant user", who stops at the "surface" and is not able to dig deeper into the "silicon bureaucracy". The "expert user" is also inherently limited in its cognition, given not only the significantly greater computational ability of the machine, especially when globally interconnected with a multitude of other machines, but also the fact that large parts of the code of cyberspace are usually protected or secret.[27]

On the one hand, the almost infinite computational capacity of the network as a whole is beyond the reach of traditional structures of meaning that are particular to both social communication and individual consciousness. To a certain extent, information detaches itself from concrete and identifiable processes of communication.[28] Large amounts of data about the world, society and people in general

23 Kallinikos (2009) 'On the computational rendition of reality'; Esposito (2004) 'The arts of contingency'.

24 Esposito (2017) 'Artificial communication?'.

25 Kittler (2013) *The Truth of the Technological World*, p. 209ff.

26 Luhmann (2012 [1997]) *Theory of Society*, p. 180ff.

27 On the rather pedantic idea of an "ignorant observer": Winthrop-Young (2000) 'Silicon sociology, or, two kings on Hegel's throne?', p. 414ff. According to Burrell (2016) 'How the machine "thinks"', pp. 1–2, computer illiteracy would constitute only one of the "three distinct forms of opacity" that are characteristic of digital technologies, the other two being corporate secrecy and the very "mismatch between mathematical optimization in high-dimensionality characteristic of machine learning and the demands of human-scale reasoning and styles of semantic interpretation".

28 Kallinikos (2009) 'On the computational rendition of reality', p. 189ff; Kittler (1996) 'The history of communication media'.

are stored, processed and transmitted automatically without direct human mediation, so that, when they stimulate communication, it is hard to attribute to someone (and then communicate about) any original intention, because they usually have none. Any meaning thus generated is produced *a posteriori*, because the machine and the network themselves have no need of meaning at all.[29]

On the other hand, the "secret code", generally enforced by various forms of intellectual property, defines the lack of transparency of large components of cyberspace. In the case of search engines like Google, for instance, the secrecy of the code is allegedly the secret of its own success. After all, if everybody knew all the details of the algorithm, the efficiency of the search results would no longer be so trustworthy, because people would be able to cheat the machine.

Even if the major standards and logical protocols that determine the basic functionalities of the Internet are open and non-proprietary, this is generally not the case for a large part of the applications that people browse through, as well as the terminals used to access the Net. That is why the demands for publicity and transparency traditionally addressed to governments are translated in the online environment into demands for the greater use of open standards, free software and more "transparent" algorithms.[30] At issue here is the transparency and publicity of the ways in which communication and interaction take place in society at large. If digital technologies inherently constrain behavior, the counterfactual requirement that they should be transparent is plainly legitimate, which is not the same as saying that this requirement will (or even may) be always implemented in practice.

Nowhere else are the effects and disruptions caused by the pervasive use of digital technologies more visible than in the concrete operations of the mass media. The fact that the Internet has allegedly become the "communicative fabric of our lives", stimulating the emergence of new forms of "mass self-communication", is usually caught by the common slogan: from "one-to-many" to "many-to-many", which means that the diffused audience of traditional mass media have become actively involved in the emission and not just the reception of messages.[31]

29 Esposito (2004) 'The arts of contingency', pp. 23–24; Esposito (2013) 'Digital prophecies and Web intelligence', p. 123ff; Esposito (2017) 'Organizing without understanding'. Regarding the problem of "algorithmic autonomy", Grimmelmann (2014) 'Speech engines', p. 910, raises concern over: "the growing importance of distributed, interactive, algorithmic processes in the sociotechnical co-construction of meaning and authority. Choices made by programmers, publishers, and users feed back into each other recursively with emergent, systemic consequences. At present, we barely have the vocabulary to describe these processes, let alone the theoretical frameworks to explicate them. They are characterized by structures of information aggregation and distribution that are not necessarily intended or even comprehended by any of the contributors to those structures."

30 Lessig (2006) *Code*, p. 138ff; Hildebrandt (2013) 'Profile transparency by design?'.

31 Castells (2010) *The Rise of the Network Society*, p. 355ff. On the emergence of the "networked public sphere": Benkler (2006) *The Wealth of Networks*, p. 212ff. The very idea of the "generativity" of the Net is based on the fact that the user is not simply a passive consumer of information and news, but an active contributor to the circulation of communication and even to the design of code, a target as well as a source of communication flows. See: Zittrain (2008) *The Future of the Internet*, p. 67ff. For a

Creating an institutionalized space for the self-observation of society within society by means of the massive diffusion of communication is the main function of the mass media. With the functional differentiation of modern society and the consequent development by each social system of its own specific memory, the mass media take up the role of providing a sort of immediate memory for everyday communication in society at large. Society, thus, observes and describes itself in its general day-to-day operations with the help of the mass media, which construct a reality and a simultaneous present that may be taken for granted in the specific operations and semantic condensations of other social systems and in the most varied contexts of organizational and interactive communication.[32]

One basic characteristic of the mass media is that, by the use of printing, broadcasting and now digital networking technologies, they enable the massive diffusion of communication and the constant production and reproduction of information throughout society at the same time as they disable, as a general rule, the possibility of direct and meaningful interaction between sender and receiver, which is also a condition for the differentiation of their particular form of communication from the various forms of communication of everyday life.[33] This differentiation, however, does not prevent "the recursive interweaving of mass media communication with everyday communication in the interactions and organizations of society".[34]

Rather than simply transforming the whole audience into a bunch of potential publishers, what the Internet seems to be doing is increasing and intensifying this recursive interweaving.[35] Ubiquitous computing and networking serve as a medium of production and diffusion for any form of communication. On the one hand, what the mass media produce as information rapidly enters the circuits of organizational and interactive communication. On the other hand, the communication going on in the context of formal organizations and informal interactions has a greater chance of being captured and reflected by the mass media, thus reaching a larger audience.

As a global and convergent medium of communication, the Internet is far from being a uniform and universal platform for a more transparent and inclusive public sphere. Communication that takes place online is intrinsically fragmented and opaque. The digital medium itself intermediates the most diverse forms of communication: interactive communication, both public and private, licit and illicit, "true" or "fake"; organizational communication, with its closed intranets and its public relations campaigns; and, of course, mass media communication, whose

rather different perspective, stressing the similarities between new digital media, which like to present themselves as open and neutral "platforms", and the traditional mass media in terms of the centralized control, organization and monetization of content: Gillespie (2010) 'The politics of "platforms"'.

32 Luhmann (2000 [1996]) *The Reality of the Mass Media*, p. 95ff.

33 Luhmann (2000 [1996]) *The Reality of the Mass Media*, pp. 2ff and 71ff.

34 Luhmann (2000 [1996]) *The Reality of the Mass Media*, p. 99.

35 On the "ubiquity" and "social embeddedness" of digital media: Featherstone (2009) 'Ubiquitous media'; Howard (2004) 'Embedded media'.

more traditional institutions (the so-called "quality press") increasingly strive to distinguish themselves as the only sources of "reliable information".[36]

Encompassing all these forms of communication is the ubiquitous code. Beyond all individual decisions related to emission and reception, the whole storage, processing and transmission of information is relatively automated. To a great extent, algorithms, and not real people in real time, define what gets stored, processed and transmitted. This has a significant impact on social memory, largely due to the functioning of search engines like Google.

Prior to analysis of the reality of search engines, the next two sections briefly deal with some specific aspects of the law and politics of cyberspace.

2.2 Internet governance: law and politics in cyberspace

When it comes to the regulation and governance of the Internet, a techno-libertarian common sense would like cyberspace to be free from the legal and political conflicts of physical space, as if they were somehow two different worlds.[37] Even without directly appealing to this naïve and unrealistic duality of worlds, the debate on Internet governance is still influenced by the assumption that some (or even most) issues that require regulation are essentially technical and politically neutral.

Technology, however, is never neutral. By providing for the global interconnection of computers and the worldwide diffusion of communication, the Internet does not create a new world. It is the one and only world society, with its divisive politics and its labyrinthine myriad of conflicting laws, which becomes interconnected. New issues of extraterritoriality and new forms of transnational conflict certainly arise, some of them of a complex technical nature, but they are far from being only technical or politically neutral.

The politics of Internet governance cover a wide range of issues related to the global regulation of information and communication technologies: from the narrower fields of the management of critical Internet resources, as well as the telecommunications "backbone" infrastructure, to the broad areas of content regulation, network security and stability and the protection of intellectual property.[38] Questions about the democratic organization of decision-making powers, as well as the enforcement of human rights, especially the rights to privacy and

36 Marramao (2011) *Contro il Potere*, p. 112ff, speaks of the Net as a "meta-medium" in which a plurality of "diasporic semi-spheres" (*semiosfere diasporiche*) emerge. The fragmentation of the public sphere as an effect of the spread of the Internet is also stressed by Habermas (2009) *Europe: the Faltering Project*, e-book 75%.

37 Barlow (1996) *A Declaration of the Independence of Cyberspace*; Johnson and Post (1996) 'Law and borders'.

38 On the main issues and debates in the global regime of Internet governance: Mueller (2002) *Ruling the Root*; Mueller (2010) *Networks and States*; DeNardis (2010) 'The emerging field of Internet governance'; DeNardis (2014) *The Global War for Internet Governance*; Kurbalija (2014) *An Introduction to Internet Governance.*

freedom of expression, are a fundamental part of the regime, which means that the medium cannot escape the constitutional disputes of the "real world".

Given the role of the US government in the original development of the Internet, the regulation of critical Internet resources was first institutionalized under its auspices at the end of the 1990s. The Internet Corporation for Assigned Names and Numbers (ICANN) was created in 1998 as a non-profit organization, incorporated according to the laws of the state of California, for the regulation and coordination of the domain name system (DNS) and the system of Internet Protocol (IP) numbers, the names and numbers that constitute the basic addresses and identifiers that allow digital communications to flow uniformly around the world.[39]

In theory, ICANN is an independent and "multistakeholder" organization. Even if nation states are formally represented in its Governmental Advisory Committee (GAC), ICANN itself does not follow the intergovernmental rules and procedures typical of traditional international organizations, which are usually established by means of an international treaty. Its main regulatory activities, however, were until recently under the supervision of the US government through the Department of Commerce, which held ultimate authority over the root servers that are at the center of the global system of uniform addresses and identifiers – the so-called Internet Assigned Numbers Authority (IANA) functions. Notwithstanding some elements of formal autonomy of the ICAAN regime, this more than symbolic "authority over the root" was the digital monopoly of the US government.[40]

The international community, on the initiative of the EU and some so-called "developing countries", has reacted to this situation of "unilateral globalism" by arguing for the need to internationalize the activities of ICANN, if possible under the umbrella of an intergovernmental organization of the UN system such as the International Telecommunication Union (ITU). Global issues of Internet governance were addressed at the World Summit on the Information Society in 2005 and have since then been regularly discussed by a multiplicity of actors and stakeholders at the Internet Governance Forum (IGF), organized annually by the United Nations (UN).[41].

39 On the institutionalization of the ICANN regime, which marked the initial "taming of cyberspace": Mueller (2002) *Ruling the Root.*

40 Mueller (2002) *Ruling the Root*, p. 197ff; Mueller (2010) *Networks and States*, p. 215ff. As the global regime of Internet governance is somewhat decentralized, the concrete functioning of the Internet, which, in a technical sense, is nothing more than a network of networks, depends on the collaboration and coordination of a multitude of different networks that need a uniform set of addresses and identifiers (domain names and IP numbers) in order to exchange data with each other. The "root servers" are the central servers that consolidate the authoritative list of these addresses and identifiers, as a kind of big and official "phone book" of cyberspace. By having formal authority over the root, the US government had, until recently, the final say on the changes and updates made on this consolidated list.

41 On the reaction of the International community to the US "unilateral globalism" and the specific form of "multistakeholderism" that characterize the global regime of Internet governance: Mueller (2010) *Networks and States*, p. 55ff.

Despite all the intergovernmental and multistakeholder debates, the final authority over "names and numbers" in cyberspace remained with the US government, which tended to respond to international criticism by rhetorically appealing to the risks of the fragmentation or "balkanization" of the Internet that would allegedly follow from any change to the then current regime.[42] The real risk of fragmentation, however, seemed to be posed by this particular form of unilateral global power that could not count on any check or balance able to provide it with legitimacy before world society as a whole. A very fragile situation that incited other governments to look for alternatives to the US monopoly over the root, threatening the stability of the very system of uniform addresses and identifiers that makes the global interconnection of networks possible in the first place.

After the Snowden revelations and because of mounting international pressure and mistrust, the US government finally agreed on a plan to reform the governance structures of ICANN and to definitely transfer to the organization and its "multistakeholder" constituency the ultimate authority over the root servers, which formally took place on 1 October 2016.[43] Therefore, ICAAN itself now has the final say on the changes and updates made on these servers, which are needed in order to keep the global coordination and resolution of addresses and identifiers running smoothly.[44]

Beyond the regulation of critical Internet resources in the context of the ICANN regime, various issues of Internet governance are currently addressed by means of the direct engagement of the technical community and the business sector. The main network protocols and standards are formulated by the Internet Society (ISOC) and its Internet Engineering Task Force (IETF). The protocols for the applications of the Web are defined by the World Wide Web Consortium (W3C).[45] Big telecommunication carriers and other ISPs negotiate the private arrangements that govern important aspects of the flow of data through the Internet's "physical layer". The terms of service imposed by online platforms and content providers determine the default rules for the general provision of services to the users and the collection of their personal data.[46]

42 On the reality and myths around the whole rhetoric of fragmentation or "balkanization" of the Internet: Mueller (2017) *Will the Internet Fragment?;* Alves Jr (2014) 'The Internet Balkanization fragmentation'.

43 Wired (2016) *The Internet Finally Belongs to Everyone*; *Guardian* (2016) Quietly, symbolically, US control of the Internet was just ended.

44 More information is available on ICANN's website: https://www.icann.org/stewardship-accountability.

45 On the innovations in terms of standard setting brought about by the technical community, especially the IETF, and their democratic potential: Russell (2006) "Rough consensus and running code and the Internet-OSI Standards War'; Froomkin (2003) 'HABERMAS@DISCOURSE.NET'.

46 On the role of the private sector in the provision of services that have a strong impact on the exercise of fundamental rights online: MacKinnon (2012) *Consent of the Networked*, p. 114ff; Rosen (2012) 'The deciders'; Belli and Venturini (2016) 'Private ordering and the rise of terms of service as cyber-regulation'.

Notwithstanding the absence of traditional intergovernmental regimes directly dealing with the central issues of Internet governance, the nation state is also an important actor. The global reach of the Internet and its ubiquitous presence, however, tend to pose a wide range of new problems of jurisdiction and territoriality for the exercise of traditional public powers over activities that take place online, such as the regulation of offensive and defamatory speech, the enforcement of antitrust rules, the taxation of digital transactions and the protection of intellectual property and fundamental rights. The traditional field of conflict of laws is rapidly evolving in order to deal with new matters of extraterritoriality and transnationality of conduct, while ever more efficient technologies for geolocation and geoblocking increasingly make it possible to frame online conflicts with the help of traditional rules on territorial jurisdiction.[47]

Law is particularly challenged by the ubiquitous presence of digital technologies. The very design of these technologies tends to embody rules and commands that directly constrain behavior. In cyberspace, as Lawrence Lessig famously stated, "code is law".[48] The combination of software and hardware put immediate constraints on what may be said and done with the help of computers. Contrary to legal texts that must be interpreted and enforced in the context of specific institutional procedures, "digital rules" are self-enforced by the machine itself without any need for mediation. Perfect enforcement substitutes for the guarantees of due process.[49]

This specific form of regulation by technology, or regulation by code, creates some "latent ambiguities" for the legal regulation of code, especially for the translation of fundamental rights into the online environment.[50] Technology must be taken into consideration if constitutional principles and rules are to be adequately applied to the new conflicts related to the Internet. These rules and principles must be applied not only to the resolution of conflicts that involve the use of computers and networks, but also to the very design of digital technologies in the first place.[51]

If the equality of access that is so important for the generativity of the Internet is to be preserved, then specific rules on net neutrality must be implemented in order to guarantee that ISPs will give equal treatment to all packets of data and will not discriminate Internet traffic to the benefit of particular content providers. If freedom of expression and access to information is to be adequately enforced,

47 On the continuing importance of territorial borders for the regulation of the Internet: Goldsmith and Wu (2006) *Who Controls the Internet?*. On the assertion of state jurisdiction with the help of technological means: Reidenberg (2005) 'Technology and Internet jurisdiction'.

48 Lessig (2006) *Code*, p. 5. The digital embodiment of rules and commands by information and communication technologies was also early stressed by Reidenberg (1997) 'Lex informatica'.

49 Lessig (2006) *Code*, p. 83ff; Zittrain (2008) *The Future of the Internet*, p. 107ff; Karavas (2009) 'The force of code', p. 471ff.

50 Lessig (2006) *Code*, p. 157ff; Tribe (1991) 'The constitution in cyberspace'.

51 On the role of law and politics in the regulation of code: Lessig (2006) *Code*, p. 61ff.

technical restrictions on the management and sharing of digital content must be properly assessed and carefully regulated. If privacy is to be meaningfully protected online, pervasive technologies for the collection and processing of personal data may have to be ruled out or significantly restrained.[52]

These new challenges require a continuous dialogue between law practitioners and technology experts. Just as legal research "has to face the task of taking the machine, the computer into account",[53] engineers and programmers have to count on the counsel of constitutional lawyers in order to translate fundamental rights and constitutional principles such as fairness and due process into the digital architecture of cyberspace.[54]

From the perspective of transconstitutionalism, the whole debate on Internet governance is exemplary of the need to articulate and promote a sort of dialogue among the multiple legal and political orders of world society in the resolution of the new digital conflicts that transcend the limits of any of these orders. To deal with these conflicts, national, supranational and international orders all have to take into consideration the so-called *lex digitalis*, which is a mix of hybrid organizations, technical communities, technological standards and the internal rules and practices of big transnational corporations that dominate the digital economy.[55]

The evolving governance and regulation of the Internet creates all sorts of conflicts and dilemmas regarding the legitimacy of decision-making powers, such as those relating to ICANN and other technical communities, as well as the enforcement of fundamental rights such as privacy and freedom of expression, conflicts and dilemmas that are common to the multiple legal and political orders of world society. The decision-making powers of hybrid organizations like ICANN are a source of dispute not only among nation states, but also between nation states and international organizations that would like to extend their mandate into cyberspace – not to mention the "Internet community" itself, with its self-asserted claims to the transnational democratization of the net beyond restricted national configurations. Moreover, the very global or transnational functioning of the Internet potentializes the effects of the mass violation of rights online, which spread around the world with little concern for specific national laws or international human rights standards.

52 On the application of the theoretical approach of societal constitutionalism to the Internet: Teubner (2004) 'Societal constitutionalism'. On the horizontal effect of fundamental rights in the online environment: Karavas and Teubner (2005) 'www.CompanyNameSucks.com'. On the formulation of specific legal principles for the regulation of the Internet: Solum and Chung (2004) 'The Layers Principle'. On the changes in the self-descriptions of cyberlaw and the move from the initial ideas of borderless networks, bordered laws, regulation by code and self-regulation to the ideas of bordered networks, borderless laws, regulated code and government regulation: Geist (2003) 'Cyberlaw 2.0.'.

53 Karavas (2009) 'The force of code', p. 481.

54 Zittrain (2008) *The Future of the Internet*, pp. 173–174.

55 On the interaction between *lex digitalis* and national legal orders as a source of transconstitutional problems: Neves (2013 [2009]) *Transconstitutionalism*, p. 118ff.

These specific problems and issues of Internet governance reflect, therefore, the more general problems and issues of a world society whose global flows of wealth, technology and information increasingly outpace the regulatory capacities of the legal and political systems. The greater dependence of law and politics on territorial segmentation is a clear limitation when it comes to the governance and regulation of a technological medium that operates globally and that significantly accelerates the worldwide circulation of money and information.

Law seems to react to this situation by reflecting upon its own media dependence.[56] The main advice of cyberlaw scholars is that code should be taken seriously. In an interconnected world society, technology becomes an asset as well as a target for legal regulation. Just as the new techniques of geolocation and geoblocking may help to define some form of territorial jurisdiction in the regulation of online conduct, the application of constitutional rules and principles to the very design of code may mitigate some of the concerns over the power of digital technologies to impose direct constraints on behavior.

Regarding politics, its first task seems to be to reaffirm itself against the illusions of technological neutrality and the elitism of entrenched technical communities. Real asymmetries of power and wealth create ever-new digital divides. As shown by the recent transfer of ultimate authority over addresses and identifiers to ICANN, collective decision-making in the governance of critical Internet resources is too important an activity to be left to the exclusive discretion of technical experts and the business sector, under the auspices of a single self-empowered nation state. Especially when this nation state seems to act in an arbitrary and rather authoritarian fashion.

2.3 Mass surveillance online: the US and its transnational corporations

Mass surveillance and bulk data collection online were already widely suspected (or even acknowledged) much earlier than specific revelations were made about the details of these intrusive practices. The collection of personal data for the purposes of targeted advertising, price discrimination and risk management by the business sector is as old as the commercialization of the Internet itself. Government surveillance, in its turn, is much older. The traditional secrecy surrounding the US National Security Agency (NSA), together with its institutional mandate to collect and process signals intelligence, has always served as a reminder of the military origins of digital technologies and the role of the "crypto-industrial complex" in the development of (and also intrusion into) global networks of communication.[57]

56 Karavas (2009) 'The force of code', p. 474ff.

57 Kittler (2014 [1986]) 'No such agency'; Barlow (1992) 'Decrypting the Puzzle Palace'. On the history and evolution of the NSA, its "extra-legal status" and its intrusive and long-established methods of mass surveillance: Bamford (1982) *The Puzzle Palace*; Bamford (2002) *Body of Secrets*; Bamford (2008) *The Shadow Factory*. The European Parliament had already demonstrated at the beginning of the

This suspicion has been recently confirmed. In July 2013, the ex-contractor of the NSA Edward Snowden leaked to the international press a series of secret documents that contained detailed information about the policy of mass surveillance carried out by the US and its closest allies, especially after the terrorist attacks of 11 September 2001[58].

The main objective of the policy may be summarized as "collect it all".[59] It means literally to collect all information possible about every bit of data that flows daily though the Internet (emails, chats, Voice over Internet Protocol (VoIP) calls, access to websites, use of search engines like Google and Bing, etc.), and also information about telephone calls and other telecommunication services provided through the same infrastructure of wires, cables and satellites that are used for the transmission of data through the Internet.

Given the worldwide scope of the US mass surveillance policy and its abusive and unrestricted collection of all kinds of data, which has a huge negative impact on the human rights of hundreds of millions of citizens around the world, the leaks spawned an avalanche of criticism in the media and in the international community.[60]

The official discourse of US authorities in response to these critiques reveals a lot about the structure of rights violation in cyberspace. About the widespread collection of telephone calls and personal emails even in the absence of specific judicial warrants, the then US President Barack Obama declared: "[T]his does not apply to US citizens, and it does not apply to people living in the United States",[61] who are protected, at least in theory, by the rights and guarantees of the

millennium the existence of a global network of surveillance among the secret services of the US, the UK, Canada, Australia and New Zealand, the so-called ECHELON program. See: European Parliament (2001) *Report on the existence of a global system for the interception of private and commercial communications (ECHELON interception system)*.

58 On the details of the leaks and the policy of mass surveillance carried out by the US and its closest allies (according to the (in)famous NSA parlance, the "Five Eyes": US, UK, Canada, Australia and New Zealand): Greenwald (2014) *No Place to Hide*.

59 Greenwald (2014) *No Place to Hide*, p. 90ff. According to the NSA document "New Collection Posture", the policy consists indeed in: "sniff it all", "know it all", "collect it all", "process it all", "exploit it all", "partner it all". All the leaked documents are available at: https://snowdenarchive.cjfe.org.

60 Alves Jr (2013) 'Internet governance in the age of surveillance'; Human Rights Watch (2014) *With Liberty to Monitor All*; The Privacy Surgeon (2014) *A Crisis of Accountability*; Blau (2014) 'NSA surveillance sparks talk of national Internets'. Specifically at the level of the UN: UNGA (2013) *Resolution on the right to privacy in the digital age*; UNGA (2014) *Report of the Special Rapporteur on the promotion and protection of human rights and fundamental freedoms while countering terrorism*; UNHRC (2014) *Report on the right to privacy in the digital age*; UNCCPR (2014) *Concluding observations on the fourth periodic report of the United States of America*, pp. 9–10.

61 *Wall Street Journal* (2013) 'Transcript: Obama's remarks on NSA controversy'. On the suspicion that the NSA had been spying on the content of telephone calls and emails of US citizens even in the absence of specific judicial warrants: *Guardian* (2014) 'NSA performed warrantless searches on American's calls and emails'.

US Constitution.[62] Later on, when announcing the measures adopted to overhaul the methods and strategies of the NSA, President Obama also stated that: "We will not apologize simply because our services may be more effective",[63] given that spying on the Internet would be a common practice among governments. On the one hand, a global power that recognizes no territorial limits, on the other hand, a limited constitution that is only effective inside the borders of a restricted territory.[64]

Independently of whether or not all governments are actually engaged in the same practices of mass surveillance, the US President was surely right: the spying services of the US are certainly the most effective. Two of the main instruments used for the universal collection of data by the NSA take advantage of the privileged position of the US regarding the economic power of its companies and the very infrastructure of the Net: (i) the PRISM program, which provides direct access for the NSA to the servers and databases of the biggest companies that operate on the Internet, which are subjected to the US national security laws because their headquarters and main servers are located in US territory (Microsoft, Apple, Google, Yahoo!, Facebook, Amazon, etc.); and (ii) the UPSTREAM program, which allows the direct interception of data that flow through the global infrastructure of wires, cables and satellites, because a great part of this infrastructure is controlled by the US, their closest allies, such as the UK, and their major telecom companies.[65]

Besides their multiple strategies and instruments for tapping the "materialities of cyberspace", which guarantees a sort of "perfect enforcement" for their policies of mass surveillance,[66] the intelligent services have also directly engaged in industrial espionage, as well as the targeted surveillance of the personal communications of political leaders and government officials around the world, even of nation states usually considered to be allies or friends.[67] The personal communications of members of international organizations would also have been targeted, including the specific EU Commissioner responsible for antitrust investigations and proceedings against US companies such as Microsoft and Google.[68]

The leaks also demonstrate the strategic importance of exerting some form of control over the business sector. The biggest companies of the Internet economy

62 According to the Fourth Amendment of the US Constitution: "The right of the people to be secure in their persons, houses, papers, and effects, against unreasonable searches and seizures, shall not be violated, and no Warrants shall issue, but upon probable cause, supported by Oath or affirmation, and particularly describing the place to be searched, and the persons or things to be seized".

63 *New York Times* (2014) 'Obama's speech on N.S.A. phone surveillance'.

64 Human rights treaties like the International Covenant on Civil and Political Rights, whose Article 17 expressly guarantees the right to privacy for all, do not seem to have any weight here.

65 For more details: Greenwald (2014) *No Place to Hide*, p. 90ff.

66 On the specific risks of designing code for the purpose of mass surveillance, especially in regard to the so-called "tethered appliances": Zittrain (2008) *The Future of the Internet*, p. 109ff.

67 *New York Times* (2013) 'N.S.A. spied on allies, aid groups and businesses'.

68 *Financial Times* (2013) 'Brussels furious over claims UK and US spied on Almunia'.

are transnational corporations. Even if they have subsidiaries and affiliates spread around the world, their headquarters and main servers are usually located in US territory, which automatically submit them to the US wide, intrusive and rather convoluted legislation on national security and online surveillance. By providing the most diverse range of services and content for people all over the world, they are the perfect intermediaries to be targeted by governments. Controlling local intermediaries is a necessary requirement for the exercise of extraterritorial control over the Internet as a whole.[69]

Having the headquarters and the main servers of the major Internet companies under their direct jurisdiction is an exclusive privilege of the US. It is also a growing source of animosity between the US and their European allies, especially in matters of antitrust, taxation and the protection of personal data.[70]

Notwithstanding the collaboration of the intelligence services of several of its Member States with the NSA,[71] the reaction to the US practices of mass surveillance online revealed by the Snowden leaks has been particularly strong in the EU. The EU Parliament has immediately condemned the intrusive methods and practices of pervasive online surveillance, speaking of a "crisis of confidence" between the EU and the US and within the EU itself.[72] Reforms to the EU data protection legislation proposed earlier by the EU Commission gained special momentum.[73] Even the CJEU has given signs of reaction by invalidating the polemic Data Retention Directive (Directive 2006/24/EC),[74] as well the rules regulating the transfer of personal data from the European Economic Area (EEA) to the US (the so-called "Safe HarbourAgreement").[75]

69 Goldsmith and Wu (2006) *Who Controls the Internet?*, p. 65ff. On the US framing of Internet security as a national security issue and the risks of the militarization of the Internet in the context of the globalization of surveillance: Mueller (2010) *Networks and States*, p. 159ff. On the increasingly significant role of large technology firms as providers of national security: Kello (2017) *The Virtual Weapon and International Order*, p. 229ff.

70 The French media has even come up with specific acronyms to account for the dominance of US businesses on the Internet economy. After GAFAM (Google, Apple, Facebook, Amazon and Microsoft), the new fashion acronym seems to be NATU (Netflix, Airbnb, Tesla and Uber). See: Rue89 (2015) 'Après les Gafa, les nouveaux maîtres du monde sont les NATU'.

71 Besides the "Five Eyes" (US, UK, Canada, Australia and New Zealand), NSA documents also contained reference to the "Nine Eyes" ("Five Eyes" + Denmark, France, Norway and the Netherlands) and the "Fourteen Eyes" ("Nine Eyes" + Germany, Belgium, Italy, Spain and Sweden). See: European Parliament (2014) *Inquiry on electronic mass surveillance of EU citizens*, pp. 28–29.

72 European Parliament (2014) *Inquiry on electronic mass surveillance of EU citizens*, p. 43ff.

73 European Commission (2012) *Commission proposes a comprehensive reform of data protection rules to increase users' control of their data and to cut costs for businesses*; European Commission (2015) *A Digital Single Market Strategy for Europe.*

74 CJEU (2014) *Joined Cases C-293/12 and C-594/12: Digital Rights Ireland and Seitlinger and Others.*

75 CJEU (2015) *Case C-362/14: Maximillian Schrems v Data Protection Commissioner.*

The question of whether and to what extent the leaks have influenced the unfolding of recent conflicts between Google and the EU is further addressed in Chapters 3 and 4. However, the next section deals with the role of Google and search engines in general in the architecture of cyberspace.

2.4 Google and the reality of search engines

Search engines are media institutions enhanced by a powerful technology. Like traditional mass media, they too operate on the basis of the constant production and reproduction of information and they also make use of copying technologies – more specifically, digital networking technologies – as a medium of diffusion. Their particular form of producing information out of information – or more specifically, information out of data[76] –however, is rather different from traditional mass media. Their "dual reality" seems to be of a special kind.[77]

If the role of the mass media is to diffuse communication between senders and receivers beyond direct interaction, search engines intermediate this process of diffusion at a different level. Given the exponential multiplication of publishers and publicly available content provided by the spread of the Internet and the World Wide Web, their main function is to allow publishers and content to be identified and found by interested users. Content already published in a decentralized and rather chaotic manner is then collected, indexed and finally ranked in answer to a particular query and according to specific criteria.

Search engines turn the huge set of disordered data present on the Web into an ordered list of potentially useful information. The passive receiver becomes the active searcher and the active sender becomes the hidden publisher that must be constantly found. Instead of editors, journalists, advertisers and entertainers, the operations of search engines are carried out, first and foremost, by engineers, programmers, computers and algorithms.

The production and diffusion of information by search engines is automated to such a degree that the traditional operations of selection of a message, emission and reception – in system theory's terms: information, utterance and understanding[78] – are unbundled and relatively disconnected. Information is automatically stored, processed and transmitted without any reference to particular and meaningful forms of emission (or utterance) and reception (or understanding). The machine itself has no original intention, but only combinatory possibilities. It does not have to understand the information either.[79] It only has to store, process

76 The distinction between data and information is further elaborated below at section 4.1.

77 On the "dual reality" of the mass media, that is to say, the reality of their concrete operations and the reality of the observations offered by them: Luhmann (2000 [1996]) *The Reality of the Mass Media*, p. 3ff.

78 On the concept of communication as the unity of the three operations (or selections) of information, utterance and understanding: Luhmann (2002) *Theories of Distinction*, p. 155ff.

79 Esposito (2017) 'Organizing without understanding'.

and transmit it according to previous information (or data), which may either be objective information about the answer to the query of the users, or personal information about the users themselves. Information is, therefore, produced and reproduced by search engines without direct reference to specific and previous communication in a constant feedback loop.[80]

This automated and decentralized form of intermediation of information, however, neither means that search engines are "neutral" or "unbiased", nor undermines the important role of users as both producers and searchers of content. Search engines too must make their own "editorial choices", selecting where to "crawl", what to index and how to rank and present their results. These operations, moreover, depend on the way people publish and classify content on the Web, and particularly on the present and past behavior of users in their search for online content. Every search starts with a query, which may trigger a rather unpredictable chain of communications from the automated information produced by the search engine in the form of a list of results.[81]

The unavoidable selectivity of the operations of search engines and their reflexive relationship with users have raised some serious concerns over the way they order and present information about the world, society and people in general, which determines the very "reality" that may be observed through them. The "suspicion of manipulation" that constitutes the "deadly sin" of the mass media[82] also afflicts search engines, notwithstanding their automated and decentralized ways of operation.

The selectivity of the operations of crawling, indexing and particularly ranking necessarily creates biases in the storage and retrieval of information. Either by conscious design, casual "editorial" interferences or by means of its combinatory and random possibilities, the algorithm always produces some order that makes certain sources and content more visible and prominent than others. In this sense, no search is ever neutral.[83]

The suspicion of manipulation may also be attributed to the very business model of most commercial search engines, which monetize their users' attention by means of targeted advertising. Even if ads (or "sponsored links") are usually

80 Esposito (2013) 'Digital prophecies and Web intelligence', p. 123ff. It seems that algorithms are also increasingly able to directly stimulate the production of communication by automatically processing the voluntary contributions, as well as the involuntary digital traces, left by people in cyberspace and, then, offering back to users a sort of "virtual contingency" that feeds back the communicative process. This would be a sort of "artificial communication" not between machines themselves, but between users and algorithms. See: Esposito (2017) 'Artificial communication?'.

81 For an interesting account of the unpredictable uses made of the information provided by search engines in terms of social communication and the formation of individual identities: Ginzburg (2010) *A História na Era Google*. For a user-centric theory of search engines as advisors that help connect searchers with the content they are looking for: Grimmelmann (2014) 'Speech engines'.

82 Luhmann (2000 [1996]) *The Reality of the Mass Media*, p. 44.

83 Goldman (2006) 'Search engine bias and the demise of search engine utopianism'; Goldman (2011) 'Revisiting search engine bias'.

indicated as such and spatially separated from the general list of results ("organic results"), there always remains the possibility of programming the algorithm and designing the results page in order to make the ads the most attractive links to be clicked.

Furthermore, the fact that the ranking algorithm is usually treated as a business secret, which is justified in order to avoid "spamming" by webpublishers and search engine optimizers,[84] only transfers the suspicion of manipulation from the publishers to the search engine itself. This is particularly so when search engines, such as Google, offer a varied set of specialized search services (e.g. for products, places, images, videos, news, academic articles, etc.) that may be privileged in the presentation of general results to the potential detriment of competitors – in other words, when the search engine decides to self-promote its own services.

Beyond this more general suspicion of manipulation that is common to traditional mass media, search engines are also often accused of reinforcing specific biases in the behavior of users, both as a whole and individually considered. On the one hand, by usually ranking the content of webpages according to the number of references (or links) made by other webpages, as well the rate of visit by users, search engines allegedly give rise to a popularity bias that would tend to reinforce majority trends, giving more visibility to already popular websites and creating obstacles to the diffusion of new and less popular ones.[85] On the other hand, by personalizing and customizing the list of results according to the personal data available about specific users, especially their past behavior and their

84 There is a whole industry of Search Engine Optimization (SEO) dedicated to improving the ranking of websites in the results page of search engines, so as to attract more traffic and, consequentially, more revenue. Some practices of SEO are considered legitimate ("white hat SEO") and consist in increasing the visibility of a website by improving its content, layout, metadata, etc. Some practices of SEO, however, are considered to be spam ("black hat SEO") and consist in consciously trying to cheat the algorithm of search engines by creating artificial incoming links, using unrelated keywords, introducing deceptive metadata, etc. Search engines usually develop best practices, procedures and algorithmic methods in order to detect spam (or "black hat SEO") and to punish websites that make use of it, with sanctions like the demotion on the search results page or even the exclusion from the index. See: Google (2010) *Search Engine Optimization Starter Guide*. For a critical overview of Google's attitude toward SEO: Pasquale (2010) 'Trusting (and verifying) online intermediaries' policing', p. 350ff. More recently, the issue of the spreading of "fake news", associated with online campaigns of disinformation, has attained great public attention due to the new possibilities of using digital media in order to openly "manipulate the public opinion", a "suspicion of manipulation" that is not always raised directly against digital platforms such as Google, but against the "malicious" and "misleading" use of these platforms by third parties. See: European Commission (2018) *A multi-dimensional approach to disinformation*.

85 Introna and Nissenbaum (2000) 'Shaping the Web'; Hindman, Tsioutsiouliklis and Johnson (2003) '*"Googlearchy"*'. For a different perspective, stressing the role of topical interests and more specified searches for the diffusion of content published by a variety of less popular websites that typically address "non-mass interests" and the "long-tail of queries": Fortunato *et al* (2006) 'The egalitarian effect of search engines'; Granka (2010) 'The politics of search'.

automatically inferred interests, search engines would tend to create filters that allegedly reinforce personal habits and ingrained beliefs and prejudices, reducing the probability of exposing users to different and divergent opinions and perspectives not already shared by them.[86]

Although it is still hard (and probably too soon) to measure the real impact of these seemingly opposing biases of standardization and customization in the overall circulation of information throughout the Internet, these concerns, together with the unavoidable suspicion of manipulation of the algorithm, reflect the new sorts of problems and paradoxes that modern society has to face when digital technologies increase, to the traditional audience of centralized mass media, the active "query reader" of search engines. Readers who constantly take part, consciously or not, in the automated processes of production of information out of information (or information out of data).

As media institutions, search engines have a significant impact on the general memory of society. Memory should be understood here not as a storehouse for information and content, but as a dynamic and complex mechanism that involves both remembering and forgetting. While remembering allows operations to be reproduced and connected through a common basis of already established meaning and experimented social patterns, forgetting provides the selectivity that is necessary in order to filter details and construct abstractions.[87]

The worldwide spread of digital technologies is usually associated with a "data deluge" or "information overload". Computers and networks have provided the means for an almost infinite capacity for storage of data that may be later retrieved with the help of search engines and data mining techniques.[88] Now that storage and retrieval may be almost perfectly automated, remembering replaces forgetting as the new default value: it becomes increasingly easier to remember and increasingly harder to forget.[89] The ever-growing accumulation of data also implies that the past is constantly flowing into the present, as if society would become unable to leave anything behind and would be constrained to operate in a sort of "broad present".[90]

Whereas the machine or the network as a whole has a potentially "perfect memory", which means that it may be able to remember, but also to forget almost

86 Pariser (2011) *The Filter Bubble*. On the negative effects on democracy and free speech of the excessive personalization and customization of online content in general: Sustein (2007) *Republic.com 2.0*.

87 On the concept of social memory: Luhmann (2012 [1997]) *Theory of Society*, p. 348ff; Esposito (2001) *La Memoria Sociale*; Esposito (2008) 'Social forgetting'. On the close relationship between social memory and the media: Zierold (2008) 'Memory and media cultures'.

88 On the shift from the focus on storage to the focus on retrieval in the functioning of "digital memories": Sluis (2010) 'Algorithmic memory?'.

89 Esposito (2013) 'Digital prophecies and Web intelligence', p. 129; Mayer-Schönberger (2007) 'Useful void'; Vaidhyanathan (2011) *The Googlization of Everything*, p. 178; Rosen (2010) 'The Web means the end of forgetting'.

90 Gumbrecht (2014) *Our Broad Present*.

anything,[91] the memory of society is always imperfect and inherently selective. While the former only involves the automated storage, processing and transmission of information, the latter involves communication: someone must read, listen or watch something in order for the information to be understood (or misunderstood) and for further communication to take place, so that a certain topic is brought out as an object of communication, while others are not.

The intermediation of information carried out by search engines is always selective. Their internal mechanisms of crawling, indexing and ranking the content of the Web, as well as the way people publish and search for this content, are very dynamic, unpredictable and rather evasive.[92] There always remains some degree of self-produced instability that influences which information will gain entry in social communication and which will not, which one will be remembered and which one will be forgotten. As a specific case analyzed in Chapter 4 shows, the European citizen who first got the formal right to be delisted from a Google's results page is already being remembered (and probably will always be) for having asked to be forgotten.

Search engines influence the dynamics of social communication by constraining what society at large is able to construct as reality in its present operations. They increase the selectivity of the general social memory provided by the mass media, which means that more things may be remembered, as well as more may be forgotten. Their primary focus, however, is always on the findability of data currently available on the Web, and not necessarily on their preservation as digital objects or artefacts for future generations, which seems to remain, to a great extent, the function of traditional memory institutions, such as archives, libraries and museums.[93]

The contemporary online media landscape of world society, and thus its general memory function, is significantly shaped by one search engine in particular: Google. Given its leading market share all over the world, the company is usually considered to be one of the main "gatekeepers" of the "information society", being sometimes depicted as a "digital sovereign",[94] as well as a "digital monopolist".[95]

Google's mission is essentially global: "to organize the world's information and make it universally accessible and useful".[96] As a business and media organization that operates on the basis of a powerful technology, Google takes part in, and is able to influence to a certain extent, the ever more accelerated global flows of money, technology and information that are increasingly challenging the

91 Everything that is stored may also be deleted, as well as code may be designed to retrieve, but also to hide (or encrypt) data.

92 Kallinikos, Aaltonen and Marton (2010) 'A theory of digital objects'.

93 On the transformation of memory institutions in the digital age: Marton (2011) 'Social memory and the digital domain'.

94 MacKinnon (2012) *Consent of the Networked*, p. 131ff.

95 Pollock (2010) 'Is Google the next Microsoft'.

96 Information available at the company's own website: https://www.google.com/about.

traditional regulatory powers of nation states and the effectiveness of their constitutions.[97]

Google deals basically with information (or data) and its findability. By organizing the world's information and making it "universally accessible and useful", the company creates order out of disorder. The decentralized and rather chaotic data that circulates through the Web is turned into valuable information for users, publishers and advertisers. A powerful and ever-changing technology allows the company to transform the global flows of data and information into global flows of money.[98]

The successful code of Google is a combination of both software and hardware (the so-called "Googleware"): a complex, sophisticated and constantly updated set of algorithms, as well as a growing network of interconnected servers, datacenters and fiber cables spread all over the world that provide the company with massive, resilient and rather distributed computing power.[99]

The company first developed an original algorithm, called PageRank, in order to rank the relevance of online content based on the number and quality of the references made to a certain webpage, which is reflected in the structure of its incoming links, the existing links on the whole Web that point to it. Similar to the common practices of the scientific community, the more qualified references (or links) there are to a certain webpage, the more relevant and trustworthy its content should be considered to be.[100]

Besides this link-based approach to webpage ranking, Google's current ranking algorithm contains more than two hundred criteria (or signals), which are constantly being changed and improved. More important than the specific criteria its ranking algorithm applies at any given moment is the fact that the company strives to learn the best way to organize online content from the very behavior of its users, whose online habits and personal data are routinely collected, analyzed and tested.[101] Its obsession with data and the "physics of clicks" makes it a sort of "artificially intelligent company".[102] Its intelligence, however, is the intelligence of the distributed network itself, which is made up of the hundreds of millions of

97 The global reach of Google, however, is not necessarily at odds with the territorial segmentation of world society, given that the company increasingly differentiates its own products, services and routines according to the laws, policies and practices of the countries where it conducts its business. The company has different national versions of its main website, and also makes available the possibility of selecting the language to be used on its different versions. See: MacKinnon (2014) 'Playing favorites'.

98 According to Levy (2011) *In the Plex*, p. 6ff, Google's two "black-boxes", which constitute the very basis of its success, are its search engine and its advertising model.

99 Vise and Malseed (2008) *The Google Story*, p. 2 and 45ff; Levy (2011) *In the Plex*, pp. 9ff and 167ff.

100 Brin and Page (1998) 'The anatomy of a large-scale hypertextual Web search engine'.

101 Details about the search process as a whole, and the data-driven approach to algorithm changes, which are usually preceded by experiments conducted with the users themselves, are provided by Google at the webpage: http://www.google.com/insidesearch/howsearchworks/?rd=1.

102 Levy (2011) *In the Plex*, p. 118ff and 385.

users and computers who are constantly exchanging data and information throughout the Internet. An intelligence that Google permanently tries to grasp with the help of algorithms, data mining and machine learning techniques.[103]

Google deals with all sorts of information, including those related to the three traditional "programming areas" of the mass media: news, advertising and entertainment.[104] The company began with the intermediation of content already published online and the selling of advertising space on its own website. Since its foundation in 1998, it has constantly updated and improved its search engine, launching ever-new search tools, such as specialized (or "vertical") search options for different kinds of content (products, places, images, videos, news, academic articles, etc.), which may be simultaneously explored by means of a standard "universal search". It has also evolved to become a direct provider of a variety of online content and services, always with a view to retaining users on its own website instead of quickly sending them off to third-party websites: email, social networks, city maps, video streaming, cloud computing, browsers, operating software and applications for the mobile market and many more.[105]

Notwithstanding its wide range of products and services, the business model of Google is pretty straightforward: to offer free services to the general public in exchange for their attention and personal data, which is generally monetized by means of targeted advertising. The company has become the biggest and richest "ad broker" of the Internet economy. It is able to cater for large corporations and well-known brands, as well as for the "long tail" of business. Big and small companies and entrepreneurs buy advertising space from Google – especially by means of an online auction for specific keywords – and big and small producers of content sell advertising space through it.[106]

103 Esposito (2013) 'Digital prophecies and Web intelligence', p. 124ff.

104 Besides making the most of its money by means of targeted advertising, Google also provides a specific news aggregator (Google News) and an online platform for video streaming (YouTube), which was acquired by the company in 2006. On the internal differentiation of different areas of programming as "the most important internal structure of the system of the mass media": Luhmann (2000 [1996]) *The Reality of the Mass Media*, p. 24ff.

105 On the "portalization" of Google: Goldman (2011) 'Revisiting search engine bias', p. 103ff; Crane (2012) 'Search neutrality as an antitrust principle', p. 1200ff. A list of Google's products and services is available at the webpage: http://www.google.com/about/company/products. Since 2010, Google has started to provide telecommunications and related services, such as broadband access to the Internet, cable TV and telephone, in some US cities through its own network of fiber cables (Google Fiber). On Google Fiber: https://fiber.google.com/about.

106 Google sells advertising space on its own websites and on the websites of its partner publishers through the online auction platform "AdWords". Its partner publishers form a network of content websites that display advertising based on a program known as "AdSense", which selects and targets the best ad to be served on the websites based on their own content, as well as the personal data of the users. In simple terms, "AdWords" is the main platform to deal with advertisers, and "AdSense" is the main platform to deal with webpublishers. On the details of the "Google economy": Levy (2011) *In the Plex*, p. 69ff. Summing up Google's main business processes in the words

Google's omnipresence and leading position in the markets for online search and advertising allow the company to offer a huge set of free services that increase its access to data, as well as stimulate the very sharing of data by its users, which, in turn, increases ad revenues. Flows of information generate flows of money that generate more flows of information, and so on, in a very profitable business cycle.[107]

Given its global dominance and overall influence, the moral slogans officially proclaimed by the company, such as "don't be evil" or "do the right thing",[108] are obviously not enough to protect it against all forms of criticism[109] and a non-stoppable avalanche of legal actions in the most diverse areas, such as antitrust, intellectual property, taxation, privacy, free speech, defamation and content regulation in general.[110]

In the debates over the "politics of search", Google usually serve as a reference (either negative or positive) for the invention of new terms in order to denote the opposing theses of, on the one hand, the alleged standardization of online content and the negative effects on public opinion and mass culture of the concentration of the search market ("Googlearchy"), and on the other hand, the diversification of content and the democratization of access thereto that would be an effect of the operation of search engines ("Googlocracy").[111]

of one of its ex-engineers, Alan Eustace: "When a Google user searched for Nike shoes … there were sets of algorithms that determined search results and another set that figured out which ad should appear alongside the results; then another set of algorithms would run an instant auction. But the system was always learning" (in Levy (2011) *In the Plex*, p. 215). The automation of the whole process based on self-learning algorithms and data mining does not mean the system always works smoothly. It is not uncommon, for example, to see the ads of big brands being shown alongside "extremist" or "offensive" content, especially on YouTube. See: *Guardian* (2017) 'Google ad controversy'; *The Economist* (2017) 'YouTube highlights problems with digital advertising'.

107 In the words of another of Google's ex-engineers, Andy Rubin: "We don't monetize the things we create …. We monetize the people that use it. The more people that use our products, the more opportunity we have to advertise to them" (in Levy (2011) *In the Plex*, p. 229).

108 *Wall Street Journal (2015)* 'Google's "Don't be evil" becomes Alphabet's "Do the right thing"'.

109 The most common critiques usually made against Google range over the "techno-fundamentalism" or "techno-determinism" of its business ideology, its privacy threatening techniques of wholesale collection of personal data and its close ties with the US industrial-military complex. See: Vaidhyanathan (2011) *The Googlization of Everything*; Morozov (2011) *The Net Delusion*, p. 1ff; Miconi (2014) 'Dialectic of Google'; Ippolita (2014) 'The dark side of Google'; Assange (2014) *When Google Met WikiLeaks*.

110 On the main legal challenges currently faced by Google: Lopez-Tarruella (ed) (2012) *Google and the Law*. On the main legal issues posed by search engines in general: Grimmelmann (2007) 'The structure of search engine law'.

111 Introna and Nissenbaum (2000) 'Shaping the Web'; Hindman, Tsioutsiouliklis and Johnson (2003) '*"Googlearchy"*'; Fortunato *et al* (2006) 'The egalitarian effect of search engines'; Granka (2010) 'The politics of search'; Westwood (2010) 'How to measure public opinion in the networked age'.

As a consequence of the inherent selectivity of search engines, Google has a significant power over the global flows of information that circulate through the Internet. A tweak on its algorithm may have huge unintended (as well as suspiciously intended) effects, affecting the overall traffic of large portions of the Web and potentially condemning some websites to a sort of "death penalty".[112]

By treating its algorithm as a business secret – even if justified by the alleged interest on the reliability of search results, a paradoxical form of "security through obscurity"[113] – Google only feeds the general suspicion of manipulation so common to the mass media. A suspicion that tends to be even greater in relation to a company so powerful and omnipresent, which, at the same time as it seems so attached to the principles of transparency and the use of open standards, also cultivates the utmost secrecy about some of its technologies and business practices.[114]

The very distinction between transparency and opacity seems to be at the center of most legal and political controversies over the governance of cyberspace. Either because of the opacity produced by the exercise of intellectual property rights over "code" or because of the opacity produced by the regular operations of the digital medium itself – which is programmed, to a large extent, to automatically manage data without any reference to their meaning – it seems that the "network society" is still trying to cope with its paradoxical need to exercise "control over the lack of control".[115] In other words, to build structures for the heterarchical coordination of social actions and operations while renouncing the possibility (or illusion) of hierarchically controlling them.

The economic and media activities of companies like Google contribute to simultaneously increase both transparency and opacity, freedom of communication and behavior control. Automatic storage and retrieval of data increase the possibilities of access to information, including information about the users themselves. In theory, though, for the algorithm to be efficient, it cannot be widely known. So, we get more and more information on the Net, but we get to know less and less about how the Net really works, including how it gets to know ourselves.

112 Zittrain (2008) *The Future of the Internet*, pp. 147 and 218.
113 Zittrain (2008) *The Future of the Internet*, p. 220.
114 Levy (2011) *In the Plex*, p. 354. Notwithstanding all the suspicion and criticism, Google has taken the lead when it comes to promoting transparency online. See: MacKinnon (2012) *Consent of the Networked*, p. 243ff. The company regularly publishes detailed data on how current laws and policies affect its activities online and its interface with its users in its "Transparency Report": https://www.google.com/transparencyreport/?hl=en-US. Moreover, Google usually has the highest scores among Internet and telecommunication companies in the "Corporate Accountability Index" of the "Ranking Digital Rights" initiative, which assesses the overall performance of companies in the ICT sector with regard to the implementation of global standards of freedom of expression and privacy online: https://rankingdigitalrights.org. It has also received a positive assessment of compliance in the last round of rather similar evaluations carried by the "Global Network Initiative", a multistakeholder forum established to advance the global dialogue on the protection of human rights in the ICT sector. See: Global Network Initiative (2016) *Public Report on the 2015/2016 Independent Company Assessments.*
115 Esposito (2001) *La Memoria Sociale*, p. 216ff.

As the Internet works on a global scale, as do most companies that make a profit out of it, not to mention the intelligence services that are constantly trying to tap it, any solution to the conflicts and controversies related to its regulation has necessarily to take its extraterritorial or transnational dimension into consideration. This includes the attempts to extend the protection of fundamental rights to the online environment, as well as the attempts to curb the power of online intermediaries by the enforcement of antitrust rules and the implementation of effective mechanisms of taxation. That is why the Internet, as a technical medium for the global production and diffusion of communication and information, may be seem as a privileged laboratory or locus to analyze whether and to what extent the expansion of constitutionalism beyond the nation state may effectively take place.

Turning again to Google, it seems that its rapid worldwide expansion has triggered a defensive, though not necessarily concerted reaction to its activities in the EU. As a big and powerful transnational corporation of the new media sector, Google's presence in Europe has been a source of problems to the national legal orders of EU Member States, as well as to the supranational legal order of the EU itself. The transnationality of the company, together with the mobility and opacity of its main digital assets, create new conflicts that Member States alone cannot address properly, having, thus, to rely on the supranational institutions of the EU, which have different degrees of legitimacy and enforcement capacity depending on the issues involved.

The next two chapters address some recent conflicts between the transnational business and media activities of Google and the supranational attempts to counter them legally and politically (to a certain extent, also constitutionally) at EU level.

3 Disrupting markets and tax bases

It may not at first sight be clear how a company can pose constitutional problems to the functioning of a union of states. Especially considering that the constitutional character itself of the EU is still the subject of fierce controversy. The project of integration has always aimed to facilitate economic activities beyond national borders. Law and politics at the supranational level have as their primary goal to sustain the growth and development of the internal market. Would the worldwide expansion of Google represent a threat to the stability and competitiveness of this market? Could this threat be characterized as a constitutional one?

Constitutions are historical artefacts that provide the structural coupling between law and politics. While connecting the legal and political systems, they also sustain the structural links between these systems and the economy. The structural coupling between law and the economy through the institutions of property, contract and competition, together with the structural coupling between politics and the economy by means of taxation, the public budget and the regulation of the monetary medium are usually dealt with by contemporary constitutional texts, including the founding treaties of the EU. The democratic organization of power and the protection of fundamental rights depend, to a large extent, on the legal and political conditions for the exercise of economic activities.

In our world society, however, while the economy and its formal organizations operate more easily at the global level, the functioning of law and politics is still strongly restricted by territorial segmentation. Democracy and human rights, the two sides of constitutionalism, are inevitably affected by this structural asymmetry or imbalance. The openness and inclusiveness of decision-making processes, as well as the integrity and autonomy of individuals, are significantly limited (or substantially violated) by the inability of law and politics to deal with the ever more accelerated global flows of wealth, technology and information.

This is the background against which the conflicts between Google and the EU will be analyzed. On the one hand, Google may be seen here as a sort of "proxy" for the new media sector created by the rise and spread of the Internet, a sector strongly dominated by big transnational corporations that have their origins, headquarters and main business activities in the US. On the other hand, the EU represents the most developed attempt until now to expand law and politics, as well as the very idea of constitution, beyond the traditional configuration of the modern nation state. The conflicts may indicate, then, some trends, limits, possibilities and contradictions regarding the future of constitutionalism in world society and its current expansion in cyberspace.

The fast and exponential growth of Google has generated some apprehension among its competitors, among governments, and also among individuals around the world. While corporations and governments often want, for different reasons, to be "remembered" by Google, in order to compete and to collect more revenues, people increasingly want to be "forgotten" by it for the sake of the protection of their intimate life and social identity. These conflicts may require legal and political solutions, as well as changes in the very code of cyberspace, the technology used by Google and other companies of the Internet economy in the provision of their services.

This chapter addresses some recent conflicts between Google and the EU in the areas of competition and taxation. It deals, basically, with the disruption caused by Google in Europe in terms of the digital economy's connections, on the one hand, with EU law, and on the other hand, with EU politics. The unfolding of these conflicts may help to shed some light on the prospects of the enforcement of fundamental rights by the EU to counter the disruptions on privacy also caused by companies like Google, which is the subject of the fourth and last chapter.

As the world's most popular search engine, Google has been condemned by the European Commission for abusing its dominant market power. The high levels of concentration in the new digital markets seem to be perceived as a threat to the European "economic constitution", with its focus on competition law (3.1). European nation states also seem to be threatened by the digital economy. Their public finances tend to suffer significant losses because of the financial power and the tax avoidance strategies of companies like Google (3.2).

However, while the alleged disruption of markets caused by Google has been addressed by the well-established and usual institutional mechanisms for economic law enforcement at the supranational level, the disruption of tax bases remains mainly a national problem with little prospect of an effective solution at the EU level. This disparity is yet another indication that the internal market – or, in this case, the "digital single market" – may be more easily connected with EU law than with EU politics.

3.1 "We're afraid of Google"

The rhetoric of fear is commonly used by state authorities to justify the imposition of restrictive and repressive measures of all sorts, measures that citizens would otherwise have no reason to accept. A strategy that somehow changes the burden of proof. While fear may be presupposed and more easily manipulated, countering it requires patience, rational arguments and a more balanced way of reasoning. Elements that may not always prevail against the strength and appeal of hysterical emotions.

It is curious, therefore, to observe this kind of rhetoric being used against a company like Google by some of its competitors and overall critics, who denounce its "absolute power" and its "hegemonic project" to monopolize data in order to create a "digital superstate".[1] This rhetorical exaggeration has the clear aim to put pressure on EU institutions to be "harsh" with Google and to defend the "autonomy" of the European digital economy.

Media campaigns and public relations disputes apart, the rhetoric of fear does not suit the rather prosaic competition conflicts currently unfolding between Google and the EU. This is possibly an indication that there are more serious and less paranoid concerns over the business activities of Google that recent antitrust investigations and proceedings cannot deal with.

This section initially introduces the general issues of competition in the Internet or digital economy prompted by the EU's initiative to promote and strengthen its "digital single market" (3.1.1). The recent antitrust investigations and proceedings initiated by the European Commission against Google are then analyzed in the context of this overall policy (3.1.2). The high levels of concentration in the new digital markets, however, pose real problems in terms of media pluralism that go well beyond the more restricted concerns of competition law. Problems that the European "economic constitution" alone may not be able to address adequately (3.1.3).

3.1.1 Competition in cyberspace

The very evolution of the modern economic system has shown that competition cannot be taken for granted as a natural feature of a capitalist economy. Instead, it must be counterfactually protected against the structural trends toward concentration that tend to make whole sectors of the economic system coalesce into their formal organizations. The rights to property and to freedom of contract are conditioned by this overall requirement of maintaining a competitive and open market wherever and whenever possible.

Together with the four fundamental freedoms of movement, competition is usually described as a fundamental value of the EU, an essential pillar of its "economic constitution".[2] Providing a level playing field for the free exercise of economic activities by private parties is seen as the best way to promote welfare, innovation and consumer choice. That is why "the establishing of the competition rules necessary for the functioning of the internal market" is an area of exclusive competence of the EU (Article 3(1)(b) TFEU).

The rise and spread of the Internet has created new and different markets for digital products and services and has transformed the whole landscape of the

1 Döpfner (2014) 'Why we fear Google'; Lima (2014) 'Google ou la route de la servitude'. For a more realistic and balanced assessment in the media of the actual risks posed by Google's business model and the resulting concerns, "both paranoid and justified", that it has induced: *The Economist* (2007) 'Who's afraid of Google?'

2 In the words of the EU Commissioner for Competition, Margerethe Vestager: "Apart from the need for government safeguards to fix market failures, our founding fathers saw that competition policy was needed to build an internal market for the more united Europe they had in mind" (Vestager (2015) 'Competition policy in the EU').

traditional media sector, with a strong impact on the advertising and entertainment industries.[3] These new markets, often characterized by significant "economies of scale" and "first-mover advantages", are usually dominated by big TNCs of US origin. Their high levels of concentration tend to generate a lot of competition conflicts that catch the attention of antitrust and regulatory authorities around the world.[4]

The levels of concentration may be analyzed from two different, but interrelated perspectives. On the one hand, from a narrow economic perspective, concentration means basically market share and the ability of dominant companies to unilaterally influence the whole market independently of the behavior of their competitors. The concentration of online traffic and the power over global data flows are seen as instruments for the generation of revenue, usually by means of subscription and transaction fees, as well as targeted advertising, price discrimination and risk management. Concentration is perceived mainly as a threat to innovation and consumer choice.[5]

On the other hand, from a broad media perspective, the concentration of traffic and data has significant consequences for the circulation of communication and information throughout society at large and for the distinction between the public and private spheres. Users are seen beyond their more passive consumer role, as producers of content and information that flow through the Web. Media pluralism, freedom of expression and privacy add up to the concerns over economic welfare and technological innovation. Competition for traffic and data go beyond the mere expansion of market shares and the consolidation of dominant positions. It has a direct impact on the way people communicate and interact online.[6]

Beyond the legitimate concerns over economic and media policy, the Snowden revelations have shown that state power over companies of the ICT sector is a

3 Beyond the basic service of access to the Internet, usually provided by well-established telecommunications companies, new markets have emerged for the online sale of products and provision of services (e-commerce), online banking, online search, online news, online advertising, video and music streaming, social networking, cloud computing, mobile devices and applications, etc. On the impact of information and communication technologies on the economy and the main features of the so-called digital economy, which is also, increasingly, the whole economy: OECD (2015) *Addressing the Tax Challenges of the Digital Economy*, pp. 35ff and 51ff; European Commission (2014) *Report of the Commission Expert Group on Taxation of the Digital Economy*, p. 11ff; UNCTAD (2017) *World Investment Report*, p. 155ff.

4 Evans (2008) 'Antitrust issues raised by the emerging global internet economy'.

5 This is the approach usually adopted by antitrust authorities and law and economics scholars. See: Evans (2008) 'Antitrust issues raised by the emerging global Internet economy'; Ballon and Van Heesvelde (2011) 'ICT platforms and regulatory concerns in Europe'; Argenton and Prüfer (2012) 'Search engine competition with network externalities'; Pollock (2010) 'Is Google the next Microsoft'.

6 This approach results from the incorporation of broader legal, political and media perspectives that go beyond the narrow focus of neoclassical economics and competition law. See: Benkler (2006) *The Wealth of Networks*; Pasquale (2010) 'Trusting (and verifying) online intermediaries' policing'; MacKinnon (2012) *Consent of the Networked*; Becker (2009) 'The power of classification'.

matter of major geopolitical and geoeconomic relevance. Promoting competition in cyberspace and weakening or even breaking the monopoly of dominant US firms may have greater consequences for Internet governance at large than the more restricted goals of competition law may suggest.

If the global economy is moving online, so is the European "economic constitution". As part of its overall strategy of sustainable economic growth for the second decade of the millennium ("Europe 2020 Strategy"), the EU launched the "Digital Agenda for Europe" in 2010, whose main goal is to strengthen the European "digital single market" (DSM) by removing "digital borders" and regulatory barriers that hamper cross-border e-commerce and digital transactions in the territory of the EU.[7] Exploiting the opportunities of a "connected digital single market" was also listed as a priority by the Commission that came into office in November 2014.[8]

Specific policy actions have been adopted since then in order to boost the European digital economy. In 2012, the EU launched an action plan to increase the volume of e-commerce in the continent.[9] In 2015, it launched its "Digital Single Market Strategy", comprising sixteen different initiatives, among which are: a specific antitrust inquiry into the e-commerce sector, the review of the rules on privacy in electronic communications, the promotion of the "free movement of data" in the EU, a comprehensive analysis of the role of online platforms in digital markets and the modernization of copyright law.[10]

This more recent set of initiatives has been described as an opportunity to close the gap between the EU and the US in terms of the contribution of information and communication technologies to overall Gross Domestic Product (GDP) growth.[11] In other words, as the digital economy is currently dominated by companies of US origin, the EU seems to aspire to a larger share of the cake. This would explain its strong focus on the promotion of competition in cyberspace, especially to counter the power of online platforms such as Google.[12]

The very concept of "platform" is rather broad and multifaceted.[13] It has been strategically used by new media companies in their lobbying activities and public relations campaigns in order to differentiate themselves from traditional mass media and to demand a more favorable regulatory environment. In contrast to the centralized and hierarchical "old media", new online platforms would operate in a more decentralized way that enhances the democratic potential of user-generated

7 European Commission (2012) *Europe 2020*; European Commission (2014) *Digital agenda for Europe.*

8 Juncker (2014) *A New Start for Europe.*

9 European Commission (2012) *Stimulating growth and employment.*

10 European Commission (2015) *A Digital Single Market Strategy for Europe.*

11 European Commission (2015) *A Digital Single Market Strategy for Europe*, p. 5.

12 European Commission (2015) *A Digital Single Market Strategy for Europe*, p. 52ff.

13 According to the European Commission (2015) *A Digital Single Market Strategy for Europe*, p. 52: "Online platforms can be described as software-based facilities offering two-or even multi-sided markets where providers and users of content, goods and services can meet".

content, favoring the emergence of a more dynamic and transparent public sphere.[14]

The economics of online platforms and the complex and dynamic character of their business models seem to be as controversial as their politics. In economic terms, what matters is their "multi-sidedness", the fact that they intermediate economic activities by matching consumers to producers, buyers to sellers, publishers to advertisers, searchers to content generators, thereby reducing "transaction costs". Acting as intermediaries or "online brokers", platforms have the opportunity to benefit from "network externalities" and to gather huge amounts of data about the behavior of a varied set of users (or customers), which may give rise to significant risks of monopolization and abuse of market power.[15]

In order to promote the European digital economy, the EU seems to be inclined to counter the power of online platforms by enforcing (and perhaps overstretching) specific rules of its complex and sophisticated body of competition law.[16] Google would, thus, be the perfect target.

3.1.2 Antitrust investigations and proceedings

Google is by far the most popular search engine in Europe.[17] It operates as a sort of Internet "gatekeeper" in the continent, the media most Europeans use to get access to information and content online, which also includes access to the digital economy. Buying goods and services on the Web often involves, first of all, finding the right seller or provider with the help of Google. As data and money flow through the Internet, the company appropriates a large share of both.

Some changes in the technology and the business strategy used by Google in the provision of its services have raised specific concerns among its competitors, and also among European competition authorities. Two of them seem to be of great relevance.

First, following the increasing "portalization" of its website and the progressive offer of a varied set of online services, in 2007 Google began to move toward a new "paradigm" for the presentation of its search results that was baptized "universal search". Instead of showing only general links to other websites, the results page began to integrate different kinds of content from different sources, including Google itself: products, places, images, videos, news, academic articles, etc. The general or "horizontal" search results were, then, blended with specialized or "vertical" search results.[18] In practical terms, if a user searched for "smart

14 Gillespie (2010) 'The politics of "platforms"'.

15 Ballon and Van Heesvelde (2011) 'ICT platforms and regulatory concerns in Europe'.

16 Graef (2015) 'Stretching EU competition law tools for search engines and social networks'.

17 According to the website StatCounter (http://gs.statcounter.com), Google has approximately a 90 percent of share in the market for online search in Europe and around the world.

18 Search Engine Land (2007) 'Google launches "universal search" & blended results'; Search Engine Land (2007) 'Search 3.0: the blended & vertical search revolution'.

phones", instead of getting the old "ten blue links" to websites that contain information about the product – including commercial websites for online shopping and price comparison – Google itself began to show, in a prominent space on its search results page, a list of smart phones from its own specialized search service for products (Google Shopping), with information about prices and vendors.[19]

Second, with the huge and rapid spread of mobile devices and their increasing use for ubiquitous networking, Google decided to make its move into the mobile market. In 2008 the company launched the Android operating system for smartphones and tablets, together with an alliance of manufacturers of mobile devices, called the "Open Handset Alliance". Android is an open source software, which means it can be freely changed, adapted and used by anyone without the need for a specific license. It is usually offered together with a set of Google's services, platforms and applications, including Google's search engine box. It has become the worldwide leading operating system for mobile devices.[20] Developing and offering an operating system for free was the strategy Google found to expand its presence in the mobile environment, where an increasing part of online traffic and global data flows tend to be concentrated.[21]

Both the moves toward "universal search" and into the mobile market ended up motivating the recent antitrust investigations and proceedings initiated against Google by the European Commission, which decided to take up the cases given the inherently cross-border nature of Google's activities and its wide presence in the continent. The unfolding of events is described below.[22]

According to Google (2007) 'Google begins move to universal search': "Google's vision for universal search is to ultimately search across all its content sources, compare and rank all the information in real time, and deliver a single, integrated set of search results that offers users precisely what they are looking for. Beginning today, the company will incorporate information from a variety of previously separate sources – including videos, images, news, maps, books, and websites – into a single set of results. At first, universal search results may be subtle. Over time users will recognize additional types of content integrated into their search results as the company advances toward delivering a truly comprehensive search experience".

19 Initially, the specialized or "vertical" search service for products (originally called "Froogle", then "Google Products" and now "Google Shopping") was based on the same model of general or "horizontal" search, in which algorithmically generated "organic" results are clearly separated from advertisements. Since 2012, however, Google has begun to charge merchants for the inclusion of its products in Google Shopping based on a pay-per-click method. For more information about Google Shopping: https://www.google.com/shopping.

20 According to the website StatCounter (http://gs.statcounter.com), approximately 75 percent of all mobile devices in the world run on the Android operating system, while only 70 percent do so in Europe.

21 On Google's move into the mobile market: Levy (2011) *In the Plex*, p. 213ff. On the legal aspects and controversies about the use of open source software and open standards by Google: Bain (2012) 'Google Chrome and Android'; Katz (2012) 'Google, APIs, and the law'.

22 Given the confidentiality of the official files, the information available about the investigations and proceedings is published by the European Commission mainly in the form of press releases and factsheets. According to Article 16(1) of Commission

Based on a series of complaints filed by Google's competitors, especially by providers of specialized or "vertical" search services, the European Commission opened an antitrust investigation against Google in November 2010 for alleged abuse of a dominant position in the markets for online search and advertising (Article 102 TFEU).[23] The competition concerns may be summarized as follows: (i) Google had given preferential treatment on its search results page to its specialized search services to the detriment of similar services provided by its competitors, be it by manipulating the algorithm used for the generation of "organic" results, be it by manipulating the ranking of "sponsored" results (advertisements); (ii) Google had imposed exclusivity obligations on its advertising partners, as well as on computer and software vendors, with a view to eliminating competition to its services and platforms; and (iii) Google had also restricted the portability of advertising campaigns from its own advertising platform to competing ones.[24]

Google offered a first set of commitments to address the competition concerns of the Commission in April 2013, and two improved versions of them in October 2013 and February 2014. In the last version, Google committed itself to implementing significant changes on the display of its search results page: every time one of its specialized search services was to be shown with prominence, links to competing search services would also appear side by side.[25] The commitments initially received a positive assessment from the Commission and a final solution to the investigations seemed to be approaching.[26]

However, the commitments were finally rejected by the Commission, which decided to send a Statement of Objections to Google in April 2015, formally

Regulation (EC) No 773/2004/EC of 7 April 2004, which regulates the conduct of antitrust investigations and proceedings: "Information, including documents, shall not be communicated or made accessible by the Commission in so far as it contains business secrets or other confidential information of any person". Official information on all the investigations and proceedings involving Google is available at: http://ec.europa.eu/competition. The three cases described below are: (i) Case Number 39740: Google Search (Shopping); (ii) Case Number 40099: Google Android; and (iii) Case Number 40411: Google Search (AdSense).

23 According to Article 102 of the TFEU (ex Article 82 of the TEC): "Any abuse by one or more undertakings of a dominant position within the internal market or in a substantial part of it shall be prohibited as incompatible with the internal market in so far as it may affect trade between Member States".

24 European Commission (2010) *Antitrust: Commission probes allegations of antitrust violations by Google.* Later on, in May 2012, another concern was announced by the Commission: Google had used, in its own specialized search services, content aggregated from third party websites without prior authorization, a practice known as "scrapping". See: European Commission (2012) *Statement of VP Almunia on the Google antitrust investigation.*

25 European Commission (2014) *Antitrust: Commission obtains from Google comparable display of specialised search rivals.*

26 According to the then EU Commissioner responsible for competition policy, Joaquín Almunia: "the concessions we extracted from Google in this case are far-reaching and have the clear potential to restore a level playing-field in the important markets of online search and advertising. No antitrust authority in the world has obtained such concessions" (European Commission (2014) *Statement on the Google investigation*).

accusing the company of a very specific breach of European competition rules: the company would have abused its dominant position in the market for general online search by systematically favoring its specialized search service for online shopping (Google Shopping) on its search results page to the detriment of similar services provided by its competitors. The Commission announced that its ongoing investigation into other business practices of Google would continue. It also decided to open a separate investigation into the Android mobile operating system.[27]

Regarding this second investigation, the Commission decided to send a Statement of Objections to Google in April 2016, formally accusing the company of additional breaches of European competition rules. According to the Commission, Google's strategy for the mobile market would have been implemented in order to strengthen and consolidate its dominant position in the market for general online search. While developing and offering Android for free, the company would have imposed restrictions that, in practice, tied the use of Android to the parallel use of Google's search engine, its specific browser (Google Chrome) and its platform for software applications (Google Play Store). In other words, Android would be a sort of "Trojan horse", whose overall spread and adoption would have been stimulated by Google in order to lock-in consumers and manufacturers of mobile devices to the use of its other proprietary services, platforms and applications, particularly its search engine.[28]

After reviewing the defense presented by Google regarding the case on Google Shopping, the Commission sent a supplementary Statement of Objections in July 2016 with additional data and evidence to reinforce its initial conclusion on the abuse of a dominant position by the company. Additionally, it decided to open a third case and to send a new Statement of Objections alleging that Google had also abused its dominant position in the specific market for online search advertising.[29]

In this third antitrust case, the Commission accused Google of imposing anticompetitive restrictions on third party websites that make use of its special platform to sell search advertising space ("AdSense for Search"). These third parties are publishers who make use of Google's search and advertising technology on their own websites, sharing with the company the revenues they get from advertisers. According to the Commission, contractual restrictions imposed by Google prevented

27 European Commission (2015) *Antitrust: Commission sends Statement of Objections to Google on comparison shopping service; opens separate formal investigation on Android.* For a summary of some of the arguments used by Google to counter this first Statement of Objections: Google (2015) 'Improving quality isn't anti-competitive'.

28 European Commission (2016) *Antitrust: Commission sends Statement of Objections to Google on Android operating system and applications.* For a summary of some of the arguments used by Google to counter this second Statement of Objections: Google (2016) 'Android's model of open innovation'.

29 European Commission (2016) *Antitrust: Commission takes further steps in investigations alleging Google's comparison shopping and advertising-related practices breach EU rules.*

these third parties from contracting similar ad-brokering services provided by Google's competitors.

In June 2017, the Commission reached a decision on the first case, the one regarding Google Shopping. It concluded that Google had abused its dominant position in the market for general Internet search in order to boost its position in the adjacent market for comparison shopping services. According to the Commission, taking advantage of its dominance in online search, Google had given illegal advantages to its comparison shopping service by: (i) providing it with a prominent place in the display of general search results and (ii) demoting the position of rival services in its search results page. Both the prominence given to Google Shopping and the demotion of competitors had been achieved by means of the manipulation of the ranking algorithm, which had been consciously designed and changed in order to increase online traffic to Google Shopping to the detriment of competing services. As a result, Google and its parent company, Alphabet, received a major fine of €2.42 billion, the highest fine ever imposed until then by the Commission in an antitrust case. The Commission also ordered the company to stop the illegal activities and to provide its competitors with "equal treatment", which may now use the Commission's findings as a basis to sue the company for civil damages in the courts of Member States. The decision itself acknowledges that it could serve as a precedent for the further analysis of other eventual breaches of antitrust law by Google regarding other specialized search services offered by the company (e.g. "vertical search" for places, city maps, images, videos, etc.).[30]

In July 2018, the Commission reached a decision on the second case, the one regarding Android. It concluded that Google had abused its dominant position in the markets for mobile operating systems and app stores as part of an overall strategy to consolidate its dominance in the market for general Internet search. The illegal conduct consisted of imposing contractual restrictions on mobile manufacturers and network operators in order to guarantee that traffic from Android devices would go mainly to Google's search engine. The restrictions were threefold: (i) requiring manufactures to pre-install both Google's search app and browser app (Chrome) as a condition of licensing Google's app store, which is the main platform to buy and download apps on Android devices; (ii) making payments to manufactures and network operators that exclusively pre-install the

30 European Commission (2017) *Commission Decision of 27.6.2017 relating to proceedings under Article 102 of the Treaty on the Functioning of the European Union and Article 54 of the Agreement on the European Economic Area (AT.39740 – Google Search (Shopping))*; European Commission (2017) *Antitrust: Commission fines Google €2.42 billion for abusing dominance as search engine by giving illegal advantage to own comparison shopping service.* Although the Commission found that Google is the dominant search engine in all the thirty-one countries of the EEA, with a market share of more than 90 percent in most of them, the company has launched its comparison shopping service in only thirteen countries, and in all these countries the Commission found that Google has abused its dominant position to illegally favor Google Shopping. These countries are: Germany, the UK, France, Italy, the Netherlands, Spain, Czech Republic, Austria, Belgium, Denmark, Norway, Poland and Sweden.

Google search app on their devices; and (iii) preventing manufactures from pre-installing Google apps on devices running on other versions of Android that were not approved by Google itself ("Android forks"). As a result, Google and its parent company, Alphabet, received a major fine of €4.34 billion, almost double the fine imposed in the previous case, and now the highest fine ever imposed to date by the Commission in an antitrust case. As in the previous case, the Commission also ordered Google to stop the illegal conduct, while acknowledging that the company is liable to face civil actions for damages in the courts of Member States.[31]

Google then appealed against both the decisions to the Court of Justice of the European Union (CJEU), whose General Court may still take several years to give a final ruling on the appeals.[32]

Finally, in March 2019, the Commission reached a decision on the third case, the one regarding AdSense for Search. It concluded that Google had abused its dominant position in the market for intermediation of online search advertising by imposing undue restrictions on its partner webpublishers that prevented them from properly placing advertisements of Google's competitors on their own websites. According to the Commission, Google would have illegally stifled competition, first, by imposing exclusivity clauses that prohibited webpublishers to contract the services of rival ad-brokering services, and then, by imposing restrictive clauses that reserved the most profitable advertising spaces on their search results pages for Google itself, besides giving the company the power to approve changes in the way rival advertisements were displayed. As a result, Google and its parent company, Alphabet, received a fine of €1.49 billion, which is lower than the two previous (and record) ones, but still big enough even by European antitrust standards.[33]

It is not easy to predict how the cases will unfold, especially before the European courts. Notwithstanding its current concerns over the market power of Google, the European Commission did approve previous acts of concentration that increased Google's presence in the market for online advertising, as well as its expansion into the mobile environment.[34] Moreover, in a very similar investigation carried out by

31 European Commission (2018) *Antitrust: Commission fines Google €4.34 billion for illegal practices regarding Android mobile devices to strengthen dominance of Google's search engine.*

32 *Guardian* (2017) 'Google appeals against EU's €2.4bn fine over search engine results'; EurActiv (2018) 'Google appeals record EU fine over Android'.

33 European Commission (2019) *Antitrust: Commission fines Google €1.49 billion for abusive practices in online advertising.* Like the other two cases, Google is also expected to appeal against the decision to the CJEU.

34 On the acquisition by Google of DoubleClick, a US company specializing in the provision of online advertising technology: European Commission (2008) *Mergers: Commission clears proposed acquisition of DoubleClick by Google.* On the acquisition by Google of Motorola Mobility, a US company specializing in the development of smartphones and tablets: European Commission (2012) *Mergers: Commission approves acquisition of Motorola Mobility by Google.* Google later sold Motorola Mobility to the Chinese group Lenovo, while retaining the majority of its significant portfolio of

the Federal Trade Commission (FTC) in the US, Google was cleared of any wrongdoing after agreeing to implement some minor changes in its business practices in January 2013. The FTC considered that although specific changes in Google's ranking algorithm and search results page display, implemented in the context of its move toward "universal search", may have harmed its competitors, they did not violate US antitrust law.[35]

Nevertheless, given the particularities and nuances of EU competition law, usually considered to be more rigorous and to cover a wider range of issues than its US counterpart[36] it is likely that the results will be different in Europe. The European Commission has a recent history of investigating and punishing big US TNCs in the ICT sector for anti-competitive behavior, such as Intel and Microsoft.[37] Google has also been recently investigated by antitrust authorities in Italy and France, which both expressed concerns over the anti-competitive effects of some of its business practices.[38] As shown in the previous chapter, the size of the company, its ubiquity in cyberspace and its power over global flows of data and information tend to raise serious suspicions about abuse and manipulation.

As most details about the investigations and proceedings are kept confidential, allegedly in order to protect the business secrets and strategic information of the companies involved, the public is prevented from getting an adequate picture of

patents, considering it to be strategic in order to provide legal certainty for the development and spread of the Android operating system. See: *Guardian* (2014) 'Google to sell Motorola Mobility to Lenovo in $2.9bn deal'.

35 According to the FTC (2013) *Google agrees to change its business practices to resolve FTC competition concerns in the markets for devices like smart phones, games and tablets, and in online search*: "the FTC concluded that the introduction of Universal Search, as well as additional changes made to Google's search algorithms – even those that may have had the effect of harming individual competitors – could be plausibly justified as innovations that improved Google's product and the experience of its users. It therefore has chosen to close the investigation." On rather similar grounds, Google won a private lawsuit against one of its competitors (the comparison shopping service Buscapé) in Brazil in 2012 over allegations of anti-competitive behavior in the favorable treatment of Google Shopping by Google's general search engine. See: Search Engine Land (2012) 'Google wins major antitrust victory in Brazil'.

36 For a brief and comparative account of competition policy in the EU and the US: European Parliament (2014) *EU and US competition policies.*

37 On the possible impact of the precedents against Intel and Microsoft on the current case against Google: Diez (2012) 'Google, in the aftermath of Microsoft and Intel'.

38 Loon (2012) 'The power of Google', 19ff. The investigations in France made in the context of a broad inquiry into the online advertising sector concluded in 2010 and no official decision was taken by the French antitrust authority (*"Autorité de la Concurrence"*). The Italian antitrust authority (*"Autorità Garante della Concorrenza e del Mercato"*) also terminated its formal investigations and accepted the commitments offered by Google to address its concerns over Google's advertising network and over the news aggregator service Google News. See: Autorité de la Concurrence (2010) 'L'autorité de la concurrence estime que Google est en position dominante sur le marché de la publicité liée aux moteurs de recherche'; Autorità Garante della Concorrenza e del Mercato (2010) 'Antitrust accetta impegni di Google e chiede al parlamento di adeguare le norme sul diritto d'autore'.

the cases and from assessing some of the main arguments of the parties to the conflicts. The remaining source of information, besides the generic press releases and factsheets published by the European Commission and the edited versions of some its main decisions, is a fierce media war waged between Google and its competitors.

Google's competitors have launched a series of coalitions to claim for "search neutrality" or "fair search".[39] Given Google's prominence in the intermediation of information and advertising online, they ask public authorities – in the present case, European antitrust and regulatory bodies – to enforce some sort of neutrality principle in online search, which is supposed to make ranking algorithms more transparent and to prevent companies like Google from manipulating its technology to favor its own services and to harm its competitors.

The front of Google's opponents is rather diverse and multinational in origin, which shows that wholesale criticism of European protectionism in the recent investigations and proceedings against the company should be seen with caution.[40] Beyond eventual national alliances, what TNCs that compete with Google really want is a larger share of the digital economy for themselves, independent of their countries of origin. These include European companies that provide specialized search services (Foundem, Ciao, Ejustice), as well as some of their American counterparts (Expedia, TripAdvisor, Yelp), European media conglomerates (Axel Springer, Lagardère, Mediaset) and American giants of the ICT sector (Microsoft and Oracle), among many others.[41]

Google itself has reacted with a very aggressive lobbying and public relations campaign both in Brussels and worldwide. The strategy of the company and its many lobbyists is to highlight the strong competition between many different online platforms for user attention and advertising revenues, as well as Google's contributions to the growth of the digital economy in Europe and abroad.[42]

Even the European Parliament has directly engaged in the dispute, stressing the need to improve competition and consumer protection in the digital single market and welcoming the further investigations of the Commission into the business practices of search engines. It went even further than these more general exhortations, expressly highlighting the importance of "unbiased search results" for the digital economy and suggesting that "unbundling" search engines from other

39 See the websites: http://fairsearch.org; http://www.searchneutrality.org/about; http://i-comp.org

40 On the arguments of protectionism: Renda (2015) 'Antitrust on the "G string"'; Erixon (2015) 'The Google case and the promotion of the European digital economy'.

41 Greene (2011) 'Why Microsoft is taking on Google in Europe'; Microsoft (2011) 'Adding our voice to concerns about search in Europe'; *New York Times* (2015) 'European publishers play lobbying role against Google'.

42 Schmidt (2014) 'A chance for growth'; Ars Technica (2015) 'Google ramps up EU lobbying as antitrust charges proceed'; *Guardian* (2015) 'Revealed: how Google enlisted members of US Congress it bankrolled to fight $6bn EU antitrust case'.

commercial services might be necessary in order to tackle the concentration in the market for online search.[43]

It is doubtful, however, whether the limited instruments of competition law may live up to the inflated expectations created around the conflicts. Given the secrecy of most official files, the stakes involved and the information actually propagated (and manipulated) by media and public relations campaigns, the recent investigations and proceedings seem to be exclusively concentrated on the narrow and opposing interests of Google and its competitors, notwithstanding all the rhetoric on the promotion of wealth, innovation and consumer choice. Law itself has its limits when it comes to the implementation of broad policy goals. Legal decisions remain valid despite what the future may bring as a direct (or retroactively attributed) consequence of them. Given the fast and rather unpredictable pace of technological evolution, this point is often made regarding the specific limits of antitrust law in the ICT sector.[44]

The European Commission may be able to deal with the narrower economic aspects of the conflicts, sanctioning eventual abuses of dominant position and potentially making market power more evenly distributed between Google and its competitors. The rights of users, however, go beyond the promised increase in choices for online shopping and mobile navigation. They also involve matters of freedom of expression and access to information. Recent claims for "search neutrality" or "platform neutrality" might have an appeal here, but the interrelationships between technological neutrality, media pluralism and market competition are deeper and more complex than current corporate coalitions and economic disputes seem to suggest.

3.1.3 Neutrality, pluralism and competition

The discourse on neutrality in cyberspace has gained prominence in recent years.[45] The discourse itself may be understood as a form of translation of general principles such as equality and fairness into the technological environment of the

43 European Parliament (2014) *Resolution on supporting consumer rights in the Digital Single Market.* Regarding specifically the situation of Google: "The Google case … may provide a window of opportunity for the Commission to clarify some aspects of competition law with regard to digital practices, and to close the difficult gaps between the rights of market dominant companies, free competition and consumer protection" (European Parliament (2015) *Google antitrust proceedings*). On the alleged pressure exercised by national governments: EurActiv (2014) 'France, Germany back MEPs against Google'.

44 The arguments for self-restraint in competition law and policy are usually based on an "error cost analysis" and the risks of "false positives", that is to say, the risks of the actual condemnation of new and innovative business practices that might prove to increase competition and innovation in the future. See: Manne and Wright (2011) 'Google and the limits of antitrust', p. 178ff.

45 Krämer, Wiewiorra and Winhardt (2013) 'Net neutrality'; Odlyzko (2009) 'Network neutrality, search neutrality, and the never-ending conflict between efficiency and fairness in markets'; Renda (2015) 'Antitrust, regulation and the neutrality trap'.

Internet. The equal and fair treatment of global flows of data and information by online intermediaries would be a necessary requirement for the establishment of a level playing field for the exercise of economic activities and for the promotion of innovation and media pluralism online.

As already stressed in the previous chapter, technology itself is never neutral. The complex interrelations between society and its technologies always produce specific dynamics of inclusion and exclusion. It is in order to regulate the wide consequences of this selectivity for the circulation of communication and information online that the whole discourse on neutrality has emerged. It is precisely because technology is not neutral that society may counterfactually demand some degree of neutrality on the part of its technological intermediaries (or simply media, in a broad sense), whose private interests may often conflict with the rights of the public in general.

There is a significant difference, however, between different forms (or "layers") of intermediation.[46] The original discourse in defense of net neutrality was tailored to address specific issues at the infrastructure or physical layer of the Internet. This discourse has resonated all over the world and recent legislation has been adopted at EU level and in other countries in order to legally inscribe net neutrality as a sort of "constitutional principle" of the Internet.[47]

In simple terms, network neutrality requires the companies that own the telecommunications infrastructure and that provide the service of access to the Internet (ISPs) do not discriminate between online traffic based on its origin, destination and content.[48] Strict exceptions are usually allowed in order to tackle network security and stability issues and to guarantee the continuity of basic public services, utilities and infrastructures. But the main idea is that control over access to the network should not extend to control over the content that circulates through it. Websites providing lawful content, applications and services may not be blocked, slowed down or obtain preferential treatment from ISPs.

46 On the concept of layers in Internet law and governance and the basic distinction between the infrastructure or physical layer, the Internet protocol and transportation layers and the application and content layers: Solum and Chung (2004) 'The Layers Principle'; Kurbalija (2014) *An Introduction to Internet Governance*, p. 35ff.

47 The EU has recently adopted Net neutrality rules by the enactment of Regulation (EU) 2015/2120 of the European Parliament and of the Council of 25 November 2015, which lays down measures concerning open Internet access and amends the existing rules on roaming on public mobile communications networks within the EU. In the US, the Federal Communications Commission enacted at the beginning of 2015 a new regulation to enforce Net neutrality rules, the so-called "Open Internet Order" (FCC 15–24). See: FCC (2015) *FCC adopts strong, sustainable rules to protect the open Internet.* However, the FCC itself repealed these rules less than three years after their enactment, at the end of 2017. See: *New York Times* (2017) 'F.C.C. repeals Net neutrality rules'.

48 According to Article 3(3) of Regulation (EU) 2015/2120: "Providers of internet access services shall treat all traffic equally, when providing internet access services, without discrimination, restriction or interference, and irrespective of the sender and receiver, the content accessed or distributed, the applications or services used or provided, or the terminal equipment used".

The neutrality of the infrastructure is a condition for the plurality of the information and communication that circulate through the Internet. Guaranteeing to all users, consumers and producers equal treatment of the traffic generated by them is a way of neutralizing, at least to a certain extent, the direct transposition of actual hierarchies and inequalities in the distribution of power and wealth into the online environment. If all bits are treated equally, more companies have the chance to compete in the market, and more sources of information have the opportunity to gain prominence in public discourse. So equality of access to cyberspace is a counterfactual requirement for the diversity of content, applications and services online.

The discourse on neutrality, however, has been strategically moved to the upper layers of the Internet, to its application and content layers. In both the US and Europe, what was originally a specific demand of Internet users and some media companies for an open and non-discriminatory network infrastructure has become a sort of panacea for all cyberspace problems. Demands for neutrality are now made against search engines and online platforms in general, which would also be expected to be neutral or unbiased.[49] As if some of the priorities on the agenda of Internet governance would have somehow moved from the debate over net neutrality to the debate over search neutrality and platform neutrality.

To a certain extent, this might be seen as a normal development. The discrimination and filtering neutralized at the infrastructure or physical layer would, then, re-enter at the application and content layers. Once the neutrality of the network is established, the next logical move would be the neutrality of applications and content providers.[50] From a narrow economic perspective, this may even make some sense. If the main issue is to guarantee a level playing field for the competition between private companies for the eye-balls and purchasing power of consumers, the market power of search engines and other online platforms would be as worrisome as the market power of common carriers of the telecommunications sector. Furthermore, if all intermediaries can potentially abuse their power, it would be reasonable to submit all of them to similar neutrality or non-discrimination rules.[51]

The argument, however, ignores a basic difference between the two levels of intermediation. Electronic signals and data packets do not flow, and should not be treated, in the same way as information and content. Economically, both may be artificially reduced to quantitative considerations over costs and prices. But they have very different effects on society at large. Electronic signals and data packets are the "materialities" through which information and content are stored, transmitted and processed by networks and machines. While the former are certainly essential to the technological infrastructure of modern society, only the latter have

49 Renda (2015) 'Antitrust, regulation and the neutrality trap'; Krämer, Wiewiorra and Winhardt (2012) 'Net neutrality', p. 809ff.

50 Odlyzko (2009) 'Network neutrality, search neutrality, and the never-ending conflict between efficiency and fairness in markets'.

51 Pasquale (2008) 'Internet non-discrimination principles'; Pasquale (2010) 'Trusting (and verifying) online intermediaries' policing'.

a symbolic dimension for social interaction and communication, for the very constitution of meaning.[52]

Information and content are not neutral and do not have to be so. The fundamental right to freedom of expression is a structural guarantee of the autonomy and integrity of different spheres of communication and meaning in a society that has renounced the possibility of wide and long-standing forms of social homogeneity and normative consensus.[53] The counterfactual requirement of a neutral infrastructure, of the equal and non-discriminatory treatment of electronic signals and data packets, only makes sense as a strategy for promoting the plurality and diversity of information and content. Network neutrality and content diversity are, then, two sides of the same coin.

The transposition of the discourse on neutrality to online platforms in general, and to search engines in particular, besides being inadequate and rather contradictory, risks missing the real issue, or at least framing it in the wrong way.[54] Market and media concentration at the upper layers of the Internet are certainly a real problem. The solution, however, is not to enforce neutrality, but rather to protect and promote diversity. Market competition and media pluralism are two different (even if somehow interrelated) strategies for that. While market competition may increase technological innovation and consumer choice, media pluralism may enhance freedom of expression and access to information online.

Google itself is at the center of the neutrality debate. Once a fierce proponent of net neutrality – since an open and non-discriminatory network infrastructure tends to favor its business model, which is based on the provision of a huge set of free services that consume a lot of online traffic – the company has adopted mixed and contradictory positions with regard to neutrality for mobile access.[55] Nevertheless, from an active sponsor of net neutrality, it has become a target of the campaign for search neutrality in Europe and abroad.[56]

52 On the differences between electrical or mechanical signals, which are relevant for statistic and engineering purposes, and semiotic signs, which are relevant for social communication and the production of meaning: Eco (1975) *Tratatto di Semiotica Generale*, pp. 34ff and 47ff.

53 Luhmann (2002 [1965]) *I Diritti Fondamentali come Istituzione*; Verschraegen (2002) 'Human rights and modern society'.

54 For a critical assessment of the limits and contradictions of the idea of search neutrality or unbiased search and its inadequacy to deal with the real problems posed by the operations of search engines: Goldman (2006) 'Search engine bias and the demise of search engine utopianism'; Goldman (2011) 'Revisiting search engine bias'; Grimmelmann (2010) 'Some skepticism about search neutrality'; Crane (2012) 'Search neutrality as an antitrust principle'; Crane (2014) 'After search neutrality'; Manne and Wright (2012) 'If search neutrality is the answer, what is the question?'; Renda (2015) 'Antitrust, regulation and the neutrality trap'.

55 Ars Technica (2014) 'Google changes stance on Net neutrality four years after Verizon deal'.

56 ISPs have taken part in the campaign as a way of counteracting Google's defense of neutrality at the network layer, a move in which they joined forces with Google's competitors for the provision of content, applications and services online. See:

For methodological and theoretical reasons, the whole case against Google may be better understood and analyzed if we draw a distinction between two basic sets of concerns over the company's overall activities. On the one hand, the market power of the company may be seen as a threat to competition and innovation. On the other hand, its media power has political and cultural consequences that go beyond the narrower economic considerations. Both the economic and the media aspects are clearly connected, however the remedies proposed to deal with them may differ. Neutrality, moreover, is not the solution to deal with either of them.

Competition law and policy are the "specialty" of the EU, the core of its "economic constitution". Although, in its overall policy for the digital single market, the EU still seems rather ambiguous about the best way to deal with the power of online platforms, in its investigations and proceedings against Google, the European Commission did not expressly embrace the argument for search neutrality. It has chosen to frame the case in more traditional antitrust terms, focusing on the anti-competitive effects of the alleged exclusionary conduct adopted by Google as a dominant market player.[57]

As already stated, the EU has, at least in principle, the competence and instruments to deal with the market power of Google. The challenge, however, is to consistently fit the company's complex and innovative business model into the traditional categories, concepts and rules of competition law. Potential difficulties and shortcomings have already been noticed by antitrust experts,[58] and the Commission's recent decisions regarding Google Shopping and Android may provide an opportunity to test these difficulties in the European courts. First, it is not clear what is the relevant market or markets in which Google operates. As a "multi-sided online platform", Google provides a diverse set of services: online search, online advertising intermediation, browsers for Internet navigation, operating systems for mobile devices, platforms for the purchase and sale of software applications, etc. Second, depending on the definition of the relevant market or markets, the range of Google's competitors, and the assessment of its dominant

Anderson (2010) 'Google demands neutrality (just don't apply it to them)'; Anderson (2010) 'Search neutrality?'.

57 Renda (2015) 'Searching for harm or harming search?', p. 19ff. The very limits of competition law to deal with the wide range of concerns of the EU over the activities of Google had already been recognized by the former EU Commissioner responsible for competition policy, Joaquín Almunia: "There is no doubt that the power held by Google poses numerous challenges to our economy and to our society. To name a few, concerns related to the way the Android environment works, to the gathering and use of vast amounts of personal data, to the use of third party content and compliance with intellectual property rights, and to tax planning practices equally deserve the attention of public authorities. Each should be addressed using the right policy instrument. The Commission's ongoing antitrust proceedings against Google are only one piece in that puzzle. But it is a piece that could solve concrete competition problems which require a solution as soon as possible" (Almunia (2014) 'We discipline Google').

58 Manne and Wright (2011) 'Google and the limits of antitrust'; Loon (2012) 'The power of Google'; Renda (2015) 'Searching for harm or harming search?'.

position, may vary substantially.[59] Third, assuming that Google effectively has a dominant position in any given relevant market, it is not clear, and it is even more difficult to prove, that it has abused its market power in order to voluntarily harm and exclude competitors.

Even if competition law may be adequate to deal with the eventual abuse of market power, it cannot address the broader concerns over the media activities of the company. It seems that the real monopoly or dominant position of Google, assuming that there is one, is not necessarily over a specific market, but over the more general global flows of data and information on the Internet as a whole. Antitrust sanctions may have the potential to indirectly limit or disturb this monopoly or dominant position, but their effect will probably be limited, given that the main problem is not one of economic welfare, consumer choice and technological innovation, but one of media pluralism, freedom of expression and access to information.[60]

The real challenge, moreover, is not to promote some form of neutral, fair or unbiased search. As with any other media, search engines are selective and biased by nature. In their specific case, the selectivity is inscribed in the very design of their code. Even if the use of algorithms to index and rank information allow them to operate in a more automatic and decentralized way, the "suspicion of manipulation", nonetheless, remains.

As the most popular and widespread search engine in the world, Google cannot avoid this suspicion, which tends to be as strong as its media power over global flows of data and information. A power that goes beyond its more restricted market aspects, the ones usually dealt with by competition law, such as the alleged bias of the company's general search engine toward its own specialized search services. Google's media power has larger political and cultural consequences. It affects the very way society observes and describes itself, the way it constructs its own reality with the help of its ever more complex and selective memory.[61]

59 On the broad competition faced by Google with other giants of the Internet economy: Singer (2012) 'Who competes with Google Search?'.

60 From the wider, and rather controversial, perspective of societal constitutionalism, such as developed by Teubner (2013) 'The project of constitutional sociology', pp. 44–45: "Google's information monopoly becomes a problem for the constitution of the new media which cannot be reduced to economic issues. Its worldwide digital networking activities, which have enabled massive intrusions into the rights to privacy, informational self-determination and freedom of communication, represent typical problems for the constitution of the global internet. And the lack of transparency in Google's governance structures points to constitutional questions of democracy and of public controls." Teubner (2004) 'Societal constitutionalism', pp. 22–23, also speaks of the need for competition law to develop: "non-economic criteria for the legal structure of information 'markets' in order to allow for a high variety of code-regulations".

61 On the media power of Google and its broad political and cultural aspects: Grimmelmann (2009) 'The Google dilemma'; Röhle (2009) 'Dissecting the gatekeepers'; Rieder (2009) 'Democratizing search?'; Becker (2009) 'The power of classification'; Rogers (2009) 'The Googlization question'; Miconi (2014) 'Dialectic of Google'; Vaidhyanathan (2011) *The Googlization of Everything*.

Beyond the strict limits of economic law, various regulatory and policy proposals have been suggested in order to deal with the media power of Google and search engines in general and to increase competition and pluralism in cyberspace. Three sets of proposals deserve to be briefly mentioned here: (i) official monitoring and supervision over indexing and ranking decisions; (ii) active and more intrusive regulatory measures to promote competition in online search and advertising; and (iii) funding and provision of a public index of the Web.

First, given the important role of search engines as intermediaries of information on the Internet, especially dominant ones like Google, the risk of the voluntary and malicious exclusion or demotion of competing websites and undesired content may constitute a serious reason for concern over anti-competitive behavior and online censorship. The normal selectivity and bias of search engines may not justify the intended and unreasonable exclusion from their indexes or demotion on their search results pages of lawful content, provided either by competitors or by politically controversial publishers.

How law should deal with this selectivity for antitrust and tort purposes is an open question.[62] It may be necessary to strike some balance between the "editorial discretion" of search engines and the rights to freedom of expression and access to information of Internet users.[63] Simply mandating algorithmic transparency, however, would defeat the very purpose of search engines, given that the ranking algorithms work well exactly because their inner workings are secret and cannot, thus, be easily cheated by spammers and search engine optimizers.

Instead of just letting the courts decide eventual private lawsuits on a case-by-case basis, one controversial option would be to assign the competence to deal with complaints of voluntary and malicious exclusion and demotion to a specialized commission or body, which would have restricted access to the confidential business information of search engines, including their algorithms.[64]. A formal and independent procedure for exclusion and demotion appeals would allegedly improve the transparency and accountability of their operations. However, the risks of abuse and overregulation may well speak against this specific proposal.

Second, taking into consideration the alleged trends toward concentration and monopolization in the markets for online search and advertising, which would be characterized by high "fixed costs" and "network effects", more active and intrusive regulatory measures have also been suggested. The basic argument is that the hardware and data infrastructure of a dominant search engine like Google

62 On the case for the implementation of a limited obligation on search engines to avoid the imposition of specific disadvantages to their rivals: Crane (2012) 'Search neutrality as an antitrust principle', p. 1207ff; Crane (2014) 'After search neutrality', p. 402ff.

63 For a description of search engines as online "advisors" in an attempt to overcome the limits of the two extreme options of either fully protecting the free speech rights of search engines as "subjective editors" or considering them to be mere "objective conduits" of information that is supposed to be neutral: Grimmelmann (2014) 'Speech engines'.

64 Pasquale and Bracha (2008) 'Federal search commission'; Pasquale (2010) 'Trusting (and verifying) online intermediaries' policing'.

constitutes a sort of "essential facility", justifying the imposition of a specific "duty-to-deal".[65]

One option would be to compel search engines, and Google in particular, to share their anonymized data on the search behavior of users among themselves. The aggregated data on previous queries and clicking trends would be available for all search engines, including new entrants. All of them would, thus, have the same opportunities to develop and improve their ranking algorithms based on the behavior and preferences of the whole community of Internet users (or searchers).[66]

Another similar, even if much more intrusive option would be to "break" or "unbundle" the activities of the monopolist or dominant firm (Google, of course) for regulatory purposes into the provision of "service" and the provision of "software". On the "service" side, the monopolist would be required to share its computer grid and search index with other players in the market, which would be exempted from the huge fixed costs involved in the development of basic search infrastructure. On the "software" side, all companies would be free to compete on the basis of the quality and accuracy of their ranking algorithms. This would, then, encourage competition, innovation, transparency and software diversity.[67]

Both options rely on some form of regulated market competition to solve most of the concerns over the operation of search engines. The interesting insight is that the critical elements of competition (or the absence thereof) are related to the access to computer power and databases and to the development and improvement of algorithms, the basic infrastructures and assets of the "information economy".

However, what these more limited economic approaches do not seem to get in their fullness are the broader media aspects of search engines. Search engines, as well as their hardware, software and data infrastructures, are more than mere economic and technological "facilities". They are also "cultural and political facilities" for social communication and interaction at large.[68]

The *third* set of proposals takes this broader cultural and political dimension into account. The political culture and the knowledge capital of modern society increasingly depend on the global flows of data and information that are intermediated and framed by search engines. Social memory and human knowledge are "public assets" that deserve a special form of protection. A protection that cannot be provided by market competition alone.

65 Argenton and Prüfer (2012) 'Search engine competition with network externalities'; Pollock (2010) 'Is Google the next Microsoft'.

66 Argenton and Prüfer (2012) 'Search engine competition with network externalities', p. 91ff.

67 Pollock (2010) 'Is Google the next Microsoft', p. 25ff.

68 For a description of dominant search engines as an "essential cultural and political facility": Pasquale (2010) 'Dominant search engines'. For a critical perspective of the idea of search engines as "essential facilities": Manne (2010) 'The problem of search engines as essential facilities'.

Therefore, suggestions have also been made for the development of a public and independent index of the Web.[69] The basic idea is to provide a public infrastructure of computers, networks and databases that would be open and universally accessible. A variety of ranking algorithms and specialized search services might, then, be tested and implemented with minimal cost by a larger number of actors and organizations. This would potentially enhance media pluralism and diversity, with a positive impact on freedom of expression and access to information online.

The project would certainly require a significant amount of initial funding, which could be provided by intergovernmental cooperation, as well as public-private partnerships. A sort of "pan-European" initiative to develop multimedia search engine technology was launched by the governments of France and Germany back in 2005 (the Quaero Project). The initiative, however, ended up being much less ambitious than originally announced, with mixed results in terms of technological innovation and infrastructure development.[70]

All three sets of proposals show that there is a potential range of alternative solutions to address the concerns over Google's activities. From competition law to regulatory and industrial policy, the EU seems to be able, at least in theory, to deal with the economic and media power of Google and search engines in general beyond the restricted focus of the recent antitrust investigations and proceedings. It remains to be seen, though, if it will be able and willing to do so.

Countering Google's power may require more public scrutiny over Google's "code", the mandatory sharing of some of its critical assets and even some form of public (or public-private) direct provision of technological infrastructure with a view to increasing the diversity and variability of "code" itself. In any case, market competition and media pluralism may be promoted and enhanced in cyberspace without any need to divert attention away from the important and "constitutionally" relevant debate over network neutrality to the inadequate extension of neutrality to other layers of the Internet ecosystem.

69 Lewandowski (2014) 'Why we need an independent index of the Web'. On the proposal of a publicly funded search engine: Pasquale (2010) 'Dominant search engines', p. 415ff. On the more ambitious Human Knowledge Project, which aims to create an open and public "knowledge ecosystem" beyond what is currently offered by Google and other search engines: Vaidhyanathan (2011) *The Googlization of Everything*, p. 199ff. On the merits and limits of Google's mission, which is "to organize the world's information and make it universally accessible and useful", in regard to the wide democratization of access to knowledge, and on the continuing importance of public libraries for the diffusion of knowledge and information: Darnton (2009) 'Google & the future of books'; Darton (2009) 'The library in the information age'. The founders of Google themselves had once acknowledged the need for an independent and transparent search engine that is not guided by advertising and other commercial concerns. See: Brin and Page (1998) 'The anatomy of a large-scale hypertextual Web search engine'.

70 *The Economist* (2006) 'Attack of the Eurogoogle'; *New York Times* (2006) 'Europeans weigh plan on Google challenge'; *La Tribune* (2013) 'Pourquoi Quaero n'a pas créé le "Google européen"'; Rude Baguette (2013) 'Quaero: sorry no results found'. More information about the Quaero Project is available on the website: http://www.quaero.org

The most promising long-term alternative would probably be to insist on the development of a public and independent index of the Web. An open and universally accessible infrastructure that might offset the limits of market competition, and the European "economic constitution" more generally, in order to promote media pluralism and content diversity online.

This would involve, of course, the engagement of public finances. Freedom of expression and access to information are certainly noble ends. The means, however, may seem problematic, especially in a period of economic crisis and instability. Fundamental rights also have their costs. And the EU still seems to be divided when it comes to the establishment of a common fiscal policy, notwithstanding recent initiatives and measures promoted to deal with the tax challenges of an ever more digitalized global economy, which are the subject of the next section.

3.2 Fighting digital tax avoidance

The power to collect taxes is one of the most traditional and important powers of the nation state. The very differentiation of the political and economic systems presupposes a structural coupling through the mechanisms of taxation and public spending. It also presupposes a monetary economy in which the monetary medium cannot be entirely controlled either by administrative or business bureaucracies.[71]

Taxes and money are, then, two sides of the same coin. On the one hand, the creation and circulation of economic value may gain autonomy from politics by relying on a standardized and legally enforced currency, whose value may be influenced only by the circumscribed mechanisms of monetary and fiscal policy. On the other hand, political decision-making may influence economic cycles and the very process of value creation and redistribution by the collection of revenues and the direction of public spending, with the regulation of the monetary medium assigned to a more or less autonomous central bank.

Asymmetries in the functional differentiation of world society, however, entail a relative dissociation between taxes and money, or more generally, between public and private finance. While the former is territorially limited and ever more regulated and restricted, especially by the recent trends toward austerity and fiscal consolidation, the latter is increasingly globalized and relatively immune to any form of national regulation. The requirements of fiscal responsibility at the level of public and national finance are completely mismatched by the parallel irresponsibility and lack of transparency and accountability at the level of private and international finance. The current economic crisis and the failed policies to deal with it are probably the best example of this mismatch or asymmetry.[72]

71 On the differentiation and structural coupling between the political and economic systems: Luhmann (1997) 'Capitalisme et utopie'. On the complementarity between the market economy and the tax state: Schumpeter (1918) *The Economics and Sociology of Capitalism*, p. 99ff.

72 On the constitutional dimension of the current economic crisis, interpreted in the framework of systems theory: Kjaer, Teubner and Febbrajo (eds) (2011) *The Financial Crisis in Constitutional Perspective*.

Constitutional law originally evolved from the regulation of territorially localized conflicts over taxation and warfare financing in medieval Europe. The disputes between the monarchy and Parliament in seventeenth century England, as well as the liberal revolutions of the eighteenth and nineteenth centuries, all had their fiscal backgrounds and revolved, to a large extent, around the social distribution of fiscal burdens and the fight against the privileges and immunities related thereto.[73]

If the old constitutional problem was connected with the limitation and regulation of the public power to collect taxes, the real issue nowadays seems to concern the (re)constitution, rather than the limitation, of this power. The fast globalization of financial markets, the autonomous evolution of TNCs and, especially, the acceleration of tax competition between nation states tend to bring taxation to the center of the international political debate.[74]

Interstate competition for mobile capital is itself an essential feature of the modern economic system.[75] Beyond market competition between private companies, nation states also compete with each other for the enlargement of their tax bases and the creation of national wealth in order to sustain public spending through taxation and sovereign debt. The political and economic landscapes of the last decades, however, seem to have changed the dynamics of this competition. The liberalization of finance, the reduction of capital controls and trade barriers, the spread of TNCs, the privatization of public services and the growth of the knowledge component in contemporary systems of production all have contributed to increase the mobility of capital and to accelerate the interstate competition for private investment. Not only has tax competition increased, it has also become easier for wealthy individuals and companies operating in multiple locations to legally avoid or illegally evade taxes.[76]

Global flows of money seem to be ever more immune to national forms of taxation, especially when profits are generated by inherently mobile digital technologies, and fiscal revenues are collected by territorial entities in fierce competition with each other. Google's tax strategy in Europe is a good example of that. While the EU is still trying to come up with a common solution to the taxation of an ever more digitalized global economy, Google and other TNCs have been

73 Gordon (2002) *Controlling the State*, p. 223ff; Paixão and Bigliazzi (2008) *História Constitucional Inglesa e Norte-Americana*.

74 On the recent initiatives of the G20 and the OECD to tackle the contemporary problems of tax avoidance and evasion, especially by TNCs: OECD (2013) *Addressing Base Erosion and Profit Shifting*; OECD (2013) *Action Plan on Base Erosion and Profit Shifting*.

75 Weber (1978 [1922]) *Economy and Society*, pp. 353–354; Arrighi and Silver (eds) (1999) *Chaos and Governance in the Modern World System*, pp. 31–32.

76 Zucman (2013) *La richesse cachée des nations*; Zucman (2014) 'Taxing across borders'. On the recent trends toward regressive and diminishing taxation and the consequent transformation of tax collecting states into debt depending states: Streeck (2013) 'The politics of public debt'; Streeck (2011) 'The crises of democratic capitalism'. On the difficulties of establishing the borders between the legal avoidance and the illegal evasion of taxes: Simser (2008) 'Tax evasion and avoidance typologies'.

taking advantage of the tax fragmentation of the EU in order to avoid taxes in the continent.

After a brief introduction to the current debate on the challenges to the taxation of the digital economy (3.2.1), this section analyzes how Google has been avoiding taxes in Europe and the current initiatives of the EU to tackle the issue of digital tax avoidance in general (3.2.2).

3.2.1 Challenges to the taxation of the digital economy

Given the structural asymmetry between the political and economic systems of world society, global flows of money and wealth tend to be increasingly immune to traditional forms of taxation. The world economy as a whole is able to expand and contract its liquidity and capital flows with relative independence from the control exercised by nation states and central banks. Financial value is created and circulates globally, while public revenues are collected and spent mainly at the national level.

Based on the standards and model conventions developed, initially, by the League of Nations, and later, by the Organization for Economic Cooperation and Development (OECD)[77] and the United Nations (UN),[78] nation states have created a dense network of bilateral tax treaties to regulate the taxation of cross-border economic activities. The original purpose was to avoid the double taxation of these activities by different countries, with a view to stimulating international trade and investment.[79]

From the original concern over double taxation, the main focus of nation states and international organizations nowadays seems to be, instead, on the complex issues of double or multiple non-taxation.[80] The increased mobility of capital, the growth and spread of TNCs and the acceleration of tax competition between nation states have created a whole range of new opportunities for the legal avoidance and the illegal evasion of taxes, especially with the intermediation of tax havens and the use of opaque financial transactions.[81]

TNCs are strategically positioned to take advantage of mismatches and loopholes in national and international tax rules, prompted in many cases by tax competition between nation states. Operating in multiple locations, they are able to engage in the most varied forms of arbitrage of laws in order to artificially shift profits to low-tax jurisdictions, thereby diminishing their worldwide tax liabilities.

77 OECD (2014) *Model Tax Convention on Income and on Capital.*

78 UN (2011) *Model Double Taxation Convention between Developed and Developing Countries.*

79 Eden (2001) 'Taxes, transfer pricing, and the multinational enterprise', p. 598ff; Zucman (2014) 'Taxing across borders', p. 122ff; OECD (2015) *Addressing the Tax Challenges of the Digital Economy*, p. 24ff.

80 OECD (2013) *Addressing Base Erosion and Profit Shifting*, p. 6ff.

81 Zucman (2013) *La richesse cachée des nations*; Zucman (2014) 'Taxing across borders'; Christensen (2011) 'The looting continues'; European Parliament (2013) *Corporate tax avoidance by multinational firms.*

The most aggressive strategies of tax planning usually make use of the manipulation of transfer prices, which are the prices charged in transactions involving two branches or subsidiaries of the same corporate group. In theory, international rules and standards require these prices to be set as if the two parties were unrelated, so that the prices should be the same as those prevalent in the market. However, this artificial requirement, officially known as the "arm's length principle", may be easily bypassed by large corporate groups, especially when the transactions involve the provision of technical and specialized services or the transfer of intangible assets that are very difficult to put a price on, such as intellectual property rights.[82]

Consequently TNCs are able to generate a sort of "stateless income" that is very mobile, an income derived from concrete economic activities that end up not being taxed anywhere.[83] Physical infrastructure and human capital, that is to say, material things and bodies with a specific geographic location are used in a productive process whose profits escape the official tax base of any one nation state: a sign of the asymmetric and very loose coupling between global wealth and national taxes.

The evolution and worldwide spread of information and communication technologies have contributed to the increase in opportunities for the erosion of national tax bases and the artificial shifting of taxable profits on a global scale, as both TNCs and financial markets have become more connected and integrated. They have also given rise to the so-called digital economy, which specializes in the production and provision of information and communication products and services and which is progressively encompassing most sectors of the world economy, the overall knowledge component of which tends to increase.

The digitalization of the world economy puts additional pressure on national tax bases. Traditional rules on jurisdiction and territoriality are even more difficult to apply when transactions are conducted over computer networks, which are relatively detached from physical locations. The material presence of computers, servers and cables may be unrelated to the concrete location of economic activities for tax purposes. Moreover, the very products and services being transacted may also lack a material component, such as software programs, cloud services and digital media content. Like money and financial assets more generally, technology and information, which make up the main assets and outputs of the digital economy, can also flow globally with little regard to territorial borders.[84]

82 On the main issues and problems related to the manipulation of transfer prices by TNCs: Eden (2001) 'Taxes, transfer pricing, and the multinational enterprise'. International standards on transfer pricing are set by the OECD (2017) *Transfer Pricing Guidelines for Multinational Enterprises and Tax Administrations.*

83 On the phenomenon of "stateless income" and the possible ways to deal with it: Kleinbard (2011) 'Stateless income'; Kleinbard (2011) 'The lessons of stateless income'.

84 Corkery *et al* (2015) 'Taxes, the Internet and the digital economy'; OECD (2015) *Addressing the Tax Challenges of the Digital Economy.*

Given the increased mobility of their main assets and outputs, big TNCs of the digital economy tend to adopt very aggressive tax planning strategies.[85] They are usually able to conclude transactions over the Internet without a significant presence for tax purposes in the country of many of their customers, such as selling software and digital media content online, as well as providing information storage, transmission and processing services from remote locations. This gives them additional leverage in the artificial allocation of profits.

Profit shifting may also be easily achieved by the manipulation of transfer prices. Intangible assets such as patents, copyrights and innovative business models, whose market prices are difficult to assess because of their unique character, can be artificially transferred to low-tax jurisdictions and remunerated by overvalued royalties and service fees paid by other branches and subsidiaries of the corporate group located in high-tax jurisdictions.[86]

Taxing the digital economy, therefore, is basically taxing the money that comes from technology and information flows, which are increasingly mobile and immaterial. Intangible assets and digital products and services may be located, paradoxically, nowhere and everywhere, and that is probably why the metaphor of the "cloud" is so catchy. When the world economy meets the globally interconnected medium of cyberspace, opportunities to bypass territorially segmented systems of taxation tend to multiply. The result is an increase in the "stateless income" generated by double or multiple non-taxation.

The debate over the taxation of e-commerce and the digital economy more generally has gained special momentum since the financial crisis of 2008. Economic downturn, the rise in public debt and the imposition of budget constrictions have pushed governments to look for alternative sources of revenue. With value creation moving online, the Internet has become a primary target.[87]

Internet taxation, or the taxation of the digital economy, usually involves the taxation of economic activities that make intense use of information and communication technologies, including the provision of the service of access to the Internet. It also encompasses both direct and indirect taxation, that is to say, the direct taxation of income and wealth and the intermediary taxation of general economic transactions.[88]

85 Reuters (2013) *It's not just Google…*; EurActiv (2014) 'Google, Apple and Amazon under fire in OECD war on tax evasion'; Corkery *et al* (2015) 'Taxes, the Internet and the digital economy', p. 3ff.

86 On the most common tax planning strategies in the digital economy: OECD (2015) *Addressing the Tax Challenges of the Digital Economy*, p. 167ff.

87 UN (2014) *The Mapping of International Internet Public Policy Issues*, p. 37–38.

88 The taxes that apply to the digital economy are the same as those applied to other economic sectors and industries. The most common are: (i) valued-added or general sales taxes, (ii) corporate income taxes and (iii) withholding taxes on the cross-border transfer of specific items of income, such as dividends, interest and royalties. The specific provision of the service of access to the Internet is usually taxed in the same way as other telecommunications services. In the EU, for example, according to Article 24(2) of Council Directive 2006/112/EC of 28 November 2006 and Article 6a(1)(g) of Council Implementing Regulation (EU) No 282/2011 of 15 March 2011, access to

The OECD has been particularly engaged in framing the international agenda in the field. Initially, the focus was more concentrated on the issues of indirect taxation. The Ottawa Taxation Framework Conditions for electronic commerce, approved by a ministerial conference of the organization in 1998, has served as a sort of benchmark for the taxation of economic transactions conducted through computer networks.[89] It establishes a principle of neutrality, advocating the equal tax treatment of electronic commerce and traditional forms of commerce, which should all be submitted to the same levels of taxation and the same value-added or general sales taxes.[90] It also advises countries to apply the destination principle to cross-border trade, taxing the transaction in the place of consumption whenever possible.[91]

Regarding specifically the cross-border trade of digital goods and services, which do not have a material dimension and consist, basically, in electronic transmissions, since 1998 the World Trade Organization (WTO) has periodically re-affirmed the informal agreement among its member states about the non-imposition of customs duties on electronic transmissions.[92] This creates, in practice, a sort of "duty-free cyberspace" for electronically delivered products, whose eventual cross-border nature would be very difficult to assess by customs authorities anyway, given the predominantly borderless functioning of the Internet.

The most promising initiative of international cooperation, however, comes from the recent coalition between the OECD and the G20 on an action plan to tackle the general issues of base erosion and profit shifting at the global level, which was agreed upon in 2013 and is commonly referred to as the "BEPS Project".[93] The project is very ambitious and contains a set of proposals to

the Internet is considered a telecommunications service for tax purposes. In the US, however, the Internet Tax Freedom Act exempts the service of access to the Internet from taxation, and also prohibits the imposition of discriminatory taxes on e-commerce by state and local governments. See: Congressional Research Service (2016) *The Internet Tax Freedom Act.*

89 OECD (1998) *Electronic Commerce.*

90 OECD (1998) *Electronic Commerce*, p. 4.

91 OECD (1998) *Electronic Commerce*, p. 5.

92 WTO (1998) *Declaration on Global Electronic Commerce.* The informal agreement was recently confirmed by a decision adopted in the last Ministerial Conference of the WTO, which took place in Buenos Aires in December 2017. According to the WTO (2017) *Work Programme on Electronic Commerce*: "We agree to maintain the current practice of not imposing customs duties on electronic transmissions until our next session which we have decided to hold in 2019". From the perspective of customs authorities, the cross-border e-commerce of physical goods is not different from other forms of international trade in goods, since physical goods are usually submitted to the same tariffs and customs duties independently of the medium of communication used to conduct the transaction.

93 OECD (2013) *Action Plan on Base Erosion and Profit Shifting.* According to the broad definition of the OECD (2013) *Addressing Base Erosion and Profit Shifting*, p. 39: "BEPS focuses on moving profits to where they are taxed at lower rates and expenses to where they are relieved at higher rates."

close the legal loopholes currently exploited by TNCs in order to avoid taxes worldwide, especially the direct taxation of corporate income. It acknowledges that real sovereignty over tax policies requires international cooperation and agreement on common tax rules and principles. A sovereignty that may not be reasonably exercised unilaterally or in isolation from the international community.[94]

Action 1 of the BEPS Project is specifically dedicated to address the tax challenges of the digitalization of the global economy.[95] It recognizes that, while the issues of base erosion and profit shifting are not unique to the digital sector, the risks of tax avoidance are exacerbated by the spread of digitalization.[96] The high mobility of income derived from the exploitation of intangible assets and the remote sale of goods and services is a special feature of big TNCs of the Internet economy that poses serious challenges to the tax capabilities of nation states.[97]

According to BEPS' Action 1, the main challenges are to establish a territorial nexus for tax purposes with the main business operations of digital TNCs, as well as to properly characterize the income derived from innovative business models, which tend to make intensive use of data collected directly from customers.[98] The initial proposals focus on changing the concept of what constitutes the permanent establishment of a business enterprise that triggers the state's right to collect taxes from income supposedly generated in its territory (the so-called "PE status").[99] New rules for the assessment of transfer prices, especially in intra-company transfers of intellectual property, are also suggested in order to guarantee that profits are attributed to the places where value is effectively created.[100]

The EU is also trying to develop its own common approach to the tax challenges of the digital economy. Google's aggressive tax planning on the continent, as well as the reactions thereto, provide a good illustration of these challenges.

94 OECD (2013) *Addressing Base Erosion and Profit Shifting*, p. 28ff. On the current implementation of the original action plan agreed upon in 2013: OECD (2018) *OECD/G20 Inclusive Framework on BEPS – Progress Report July 2017–June 2018.* Besides the review of existing guidelines, best practices and other soft law instruments on international taxation, the BEPS Project has also produced a multilateral convention to reform existing international tax rules that are currently spread around a complex network of bilateral tax treaties. The convention entered into force on 1 July 2018 among the parties that had already ratified it. See: OECD (2016) *Multilateral Convention to Implement Tax Treaty Related Measures to Prevent Base Erosion and Profit Shifting.*

95 OECD (2015) *Addressing the Tax Challenges of the Digital Economy.* The interim report on BEPS' Action 1 was published in 2018 and the final report is expected to be published in 2020. See: OECD (2018) *Tax Challenges Arising from Digitalisation – Interim Report 2018.*

96 OECD (2015) *Addressing the Tax Challenges of the Digital Economy*, pp. 11–12.

97 OECD (2015) *Addressing the Tax Challenges of the Digital Economy*, p. 85ff.

98 OECD (2015) *Addressing the Tax Challenges of the Digital Economy*, p. 97ff.

99 OECD (2015) *Addressing the Tax Challenges of the Digital Economy*, p. 88.

100 OECD (2015) *Addressing the Tax Challenges of the Digital Economy*, p. 90ff.

3.2.2 Searching for Google's mobile and stateless income

Like other big TNCs of the digital economy, Google has been engaging in very aggressive tax planning strategies both worldwide and in the territory of the EU.[101] The mobility and immateriality of the company's extremely valuable intangible assets, as well as of its ubiquitous digital products and services, has been exploited in order to avoid taxes and generate huge amounts of stateless income.[102]

Google wields considerable financial power. Its worldwide gross revenues in the year of 2018, in the order of US$137 billion, were higher than the GDP of many EU Member States.[103] Being present in multiple locations, the company is able to shift its flows of money for tax avoidance purposes with the help of the manipulation of the flows of technology and information that make up most of its revenues. And it seems to be very proud of its capacity to artificially reduce its tax liabilities in order to maximize the return to its shareholders, allegedly without formally breaking the law.[104]

Google's overall tax strategy in Europe consists mainly in avoiding the payment of corporate income taxes, and related withholding taxes, by shifting the profits made in the continent, as well as in Africa and the Middle East, to the small North Atlantic island of Bermuda, which, like other UK overseas territories, is a famous tax haven. The tax structure, also used by other big TNCs, especially of the digital sector, has been baptized the "Double Irish Dutch Sandwich". It basically involves the creation of shell companies and the manipulation of intra-group transactions in Ireland and the Netherlands to

101 The general problem of tax avoidance by big US TNCs of the digital sector has been officially recognized on many occasions by the European Commission itself. According to the European Commission (2015) *A Digital Single Market Strategy for Europe*, p. 93: "There is broad and rising public and political concern over the fact that some multinationals currently succeed in paying very little corporate income tax in the EU. Several of the high profile public examples concern digital companies such as Apple, Google or Amazon. Aggressive tax planning strategies concern all industries. Increased mobility through digitalisation merely exacerbates the scale of it for purely digital companies". Not only is tax avoidance more frequent and intense in the case of digital companies, it also tends to disproportionally affect their non-US earnings. See: European Commission (2014) *Report of the Commission Expert Group on Taxation of the Digital Economy*, pp. 24 and 54–55.

102 Bloomberg (2010) 'Google 2.4% rate shows how $60 billion is lost to tax loopholes'; Bloomberg (2012) 'Google revenues sheltered in no-tax Bermuda soar to $10 billion'; Bloomberg (2019) 'Google cuts taxes by shifting billions to Bermuda—again'.

103 More specifically, it is higher than the GDP of ten EU Member States, considering the year of 2018: Slovakia, Luxembourg, Croatia, Bulgaria, Slovenia, Lithuania, Latvia, Estonia, Cyprus and Malta. Financial data on the performance of Alphabet Inc., Google's holding company, is available on the website: https://abc.xyz/investor. Statistical data on the economy of the EU and its Member States is available on the website of Eurostat: http://ec.europa.eu/eurostat.

104 *Telegraph* (2012) 'Google's tax avoidance is called "capitalism", says Chairman Eric Schmidt'.

intermediate the transfer of Google's profits in Europe to Bermuda. It works as described below.[105]

The first step: transferring technology to a hybrid entity. Google's parent company and main holding of the corporate group (originally Google Inc., now Alphabet Inc.), which is headquartered in Mountain View, California, is the owner of the company's most valuable intellectual property: its search engine and online advertising technologies. The right to exploit these technologies in the EMEA area (Europe, Middle East and Africa) was transferred in 2003 to Google Ireland Holdings, which, besides making a buy-in payment, has also entered in a cost-sharing agreement with the parent company for the further development and improvement of the technologies.

Google Ireland Holdings has a dual residence structure. It is headquartered in Ireland, but, according to specific provisions of Irish tax law, it has its tax residence in Bermuda because it is formally managed and controlled from an office there. This is the first and most important "trick": while the rest of the world, including Europe, sees only an Irish company, Ireland itself treats the company as being resident in Bermuda for tax purposes. Although the Irish corporate income tax rate of 12.5 percent is already one of the lowest in the whole world, Bermuda, as a tax haven, does not tax corporate profits at all.

Google has also established another Irish company: Google Ireland Limited. In contrast to Google Ireland Holdings, which is only an assets management firm with almost no real activity, this second company is the one really engaged in concrete economic transactions. It owns physical assets, employs people and pursues the remote sales of online advertising and other digital products and services to customers in Ireland and the rest of Europe. Google has also other subsidiaries in the territory of the EU involved in local marketing and customer relations activities, but most sales are automatically conducted over the Internet, allegedly from Ireland. Google Ireland Limited, then, operates the real business, at least in theory, and the other European subsidiaries are remunerated based on the auxiliary and preparatory services provided to it.[106]

105 The following brief description is based on: Kleinbard (2011) 'Stateless income', p. 706ff; Darby III and Lemaster (2007) 'Double Irish more than doubles the tax savings'; OECD (2015) *Addressing the Tax Challenges of the Digital Economy*, p. 171ff.

106 The objective of this arrangement is to concentrate the conclusion of contracts for the sale of digital products and services, mainly online advertising, in Ireland, so that the company can avoid the status of having a permanent establishment for tax purposes in other European countries. According to international tax rules, the activities carried out by these other subsidiaries are, then, classified as "auxiliary" or "preparatory" and do not create a tax link to the main business operations conducted by the Irish company. The exclusion of "auxiliary" and "preparatory" activities from the definition of permanent establishment for tax purposes is provided for by both Article 5(4)("e" and "f") of the OECD (2014) *Model Tax Convention on Income and on Capital*, and Article 5(4) ("e" and "f") of the UN (2011) *Model Double Taxation Convention between Developed and Developing Countries.* In the context of the BEPS Project referred to above, these model conventions were both reviewed in 2017 in order to close some of the most prominent legal loopholes that have been used by TNCs for tax avoidance purposes,

The second step: manipulating transfer prices and routing profits through a shell company. Google has also established a shell company in the Netherlands, Google Netherlands BV, in order to intermediate the intra-group payment of royalties. The hybrid company, Google Ireland Holdings, licenses the technology, originally received by the US parent company, to the Dutch shell company, which, for its part, sublicenses the technology to the European hub located in Ireland, Google Ireland Limited.

By the manipulation of transfer prices, royalties are set in a way that the profits effectively made in Europe end up being routed to Bermuda, where they are not taxed. The real and economically active Irish company reduces its already low-taxed European-wide profits by paying overvalued royalties to the Dutch company, which, after retaining a small spread, pays back the overvalued royalties to the other Irish company, the hybrid one. That is when the second "trick" comes in to play.

According to EU tax rules, no withholding taxes are levied on the payment of royalties between the Irish and Dutch companies. However, if the royalties were paid directly to Bermuda – for example, by the real Irish company to the hybrid one – withholding taxes would be charged. The Dutch shell company, then, allows the arbitrage of tax laws. When it pays royalties to the hybrid company, Dutch law sees only an intra-European transaction. Irish law, instead, sees the hybrid company, which is tax resident in Bermuda, receiving income from outside Ireland, an income that is not submitted, therefore, to Irish taxes.[107]

The result: multiple non-taxation and stateless income. The strategy is, then, twofold. On the one hand, by concentrating its business operations in Ireland, operations that basically involve flows of data and information through the Internet in the remote provision of online advertising services, Google is able to avoid the status of having a permanent establishment for tax purposes in other European countries with higher corporate income tax rates. On the other hand, by manipulating the transfer prices related to the rights to exploit its technologies and by taking advantage of loopholes in national and international tax rules, the company

including the concept of "permanent establishment", whose new definition may now make it more difficult, at least in theory, to exclude these kind of "auxiliary" and "preparatory" activities. See: OECD (2017) *Model Tax Convention on Income and on Capital*; UN (2017) *Model Double Taxation Convention between Developed and Developing Countries.*

107 According to Kleinbard (2011) 'Stateless income', p. 712: "Google BV exists because royalties paid directly from an Irish company to a Bermuda company (that is, from Ireland Limited to Ireland Holdings) would be subject to an Irish withholding tax. That tax does not apply to royalties paid to a company resident in an EU member state, even one that is an affiliate and that apparently serves no purpose but the elimination of Irish withholding tax. The Netherlands does not impose withholding tax on the outbound royalties paid to Ireland Holdings, and contents itself with collecting a small tax (essentially a fee for the use of its tax system) on the modest 'spread' between the royalties Google BV receives and those it pays on to Ireland Holdings. It is normal in Dutch tax practice to negotiate this sort of spread in advance with the Dutch tax authorities."

artificially shifts its profits to Bermuda, where it pursues no relevant economic activity at all. Profits originally made in Europe are, therefore, routed to a tax haven, where they are retained as long as possible in order to escape the normal taxation in the event of repatriation to the US.[108]

Different tax systems are combined and played against each other. US, Irish, Dutch and other European countries' national tax rules, as well as EU rules on intra-European transactions, international rules contained in bilateral tax treaties and the "exceptional" rules of a very small island are all exploited in a worldwide strategy of tax avoidance. The transnationality of the company and the mobility of its income end up overtaking the territorial logic of existing forms of taxation. That is stateless income in action, an income simultaneously generated in various states, but taxed in none of them.

This specific strategy of aggressive tax avoidance, which is not particular to a single company, shows some of the political and legal (to a certain extent, also constitutional) limits of the project of European integration. The EU provides supranational protection in the form of the fundamental freedoms of movement, and even a supranational currency, to facilitate economic transactions at the continental level. However, it does not provide a common fiscal policy strong enough to deal with the disturbing consequences of the enhanced liberalization. Fiscal consolidation and restrictions on public spending are not enough if the revenue side remains almost untouched.

The result is that global and continental flows of wealth become even more immune to still nationally based and fragmented systems of taxation, accelerating the process of interstate competition for mobile capital, as well as the related trends toward sovereign indebtedness. With the restrictions imposed by supranational rules on the internal market and the increased tax competition between Member States, fiscal policy loses its already limited ability to influence economic cycles and to provide for some form of redistribution of income. National public finances are, consequently, trumped by the enhanced intracontinental mobility of transnational capital.[109]

108 The legal formalities exploited in order to avoid taxation in the US, which usually taxes the worldwide profits of its TNCs, are also complex and intricate, involving the artificial manipulation of transfer prices, corporate structures and multiple legal personalities. According to Kleinbard (2011) 'Stateless income', pp. 712–713: "from a U.S. tax point of view, neither Ireland Limited nor Google BV exists at all. The United States sees only an Irish (not Bermuda) company (Irish Holdings) with a Bermuda branch, where most of its net income comes to rest. The end result is a near-zero rate of tax on income derived from customers in Europe, the Middle East, and Africa that is attributable to the high-value intangibles that encompass the bulk of Google's economic factors of production, and a very low rate of tax on returns attributable to the services of Google's Irish-based sales force."

109 On the absence of fiscal integration in the EU and the acceleration of tax competition between Member States, with its negative effects in terms of democratic and redistributive politics: Ganghof and Genschel (2008) 'Taxation and democracy in the EU'; Genschel and Jachtenfuchs (2011) 'How the European Union constrains the state';

In theory, Member States are relatively free to design their own national systems of taxation, provided that they respect the supranational principles and rules of free movement, non-discrimination and market competition. The EU itself has very limited formal competence in the area of taxation, with an explicit mandate to harmonize indirect taxes, and an implicit mandate to provide for the approximation of laws in the field of direct taxes, always with a view to improving the functioning of the internal market and avoiding the distortion of competition.[110]

Even in the absence of a fiscal union, the EU has progressively moved its initially restricted focus on the removal of obstacles to the functioning of the internal market toward a more active approach in the provision of coordination and cooperation in order to tackle the common problems of "harmful" tax competition and the fight against tax fraud, tax evasion and tax avoidance.[111] Nevertheless, while some progress has been achieved in the harmonization of value-added taxes, convergence in the field of corporate income taxes still lags behind, which itself tends to constitute an additional obstacle to the very process of integration.[112]

The lack of a common approach to the taxation of corporate income may be seen as a cause, as well as a consequence, of the increasing tax competition in the territory of the EU. With the rules on capital mobility and market competition

Genschel, Kemmerling and Seils (2011) 'Accelerating downhill'; Wasserfallen (2014) 'Political and economic integration in the EU'.

110 For a brief overview of the EU competences and policies in the field of taxation: European Commission (2015) *Taxation*; European Parliament (2015) *Tax policy in the EU*; Aujean (2010) 'Tax policy in the EU'. Articles 113 and 115 of the TFEU contain, respectively, the legal bases for the harmonization of indirect taxes and the approximation of laws in the field of direct taxation. Both provide for a special legislative procedure that requires unanimity in the Council and on which the Parliament is only consulted, which reflects the preference for the intergovernmental method to deal with such a nationally sensitive issue. For a critique of the common assumption of the limited tax powers of the EU, stressing the significant ways in which the EU constrains the tax policy of Member States by means of the secondary legislation of the Council and the case law of the CJEU: Genschel and Jachtenfuchs (2011) 'How the European Union constrains the state'.

111 European Parliament (2015) *Tax policy in the EU*, pp. 26–27. On some recent EU policy initiatives in the field of taxation, especially in the fight against tax avoidance and evasion: European Commission (2009) *Taxation and good governance: the European Commission proposes actions to improve transparency, exchange of information and fair tax competition*; European Commission (2012) *Clamping down on tax evasion and avoidance: Commission presents the way forward;* European Commission (2015) *Combatting corporate tax avoidance: Commission presents Tax Transparency Package*; European Commission (2016) *Fair taxation: Commission presents new measures against corporate tax avoidance*; European Commission (2016) *European Commission proposes public tax transparency rules for multinationals.*

112 Aujean (2010) 'Tax policy in the EU', p. 12. According to Scharpf (2010) 'Legitimacy in the multi-level European polity', p. 93, the EU's "notorious inability to regulate competition over taxes on company profits and capital incomes" is an example of its lack of capacity to promote some form of common good that nation states alone cannot promote, which may be seen as a deficit of republican legitimacy.

already established at the supranational level, and given the absence of a common fiscal policy, nation states naturally resort to tax measures in order to attract private investment. The original lack of fiscal integration stimulates tax competition, which, in turn, tends to block concrete and significant measures of supranational convergence and coordination.[113]

One of the many contradictions and paradoxes of the European politics of integration, and of the global initiatives of economic liberalization more generally, is that tax competition is itself praised and condemned at the same time. It is praised for allegedly increasing efficiency in the allocation of resources. Countries that offer more benefits may get more investments,[114] but when companies, acting "rationally", as is expected of them, take advantage of these benefits and plan their worldwide activities with a view to maximizing their profits, states proclaim the need to fight "aggressive" tax avoidance. Paradoxically, tax competition is accepted and even stimulated, notwithstanding all the outrage that comes to the fore when it produces its "normal" results.

As usual, the paradox is hidden with the help of distinctions. Tax competition may be "fair", but it may also be "harmful".[115] It is normal to expect companies to take taxation into consideration when planning their activities, but they should, nonetheless, be frowned upon when they become too knowledgeable and "aggressive" in the art of avoiding taxes.[116] Something has to be done in order to tackle the disturbing effects of tax havens, but one should be extremely careful when pointing the finger at the UK for the internal affairs of its overseas territories, or when demanding incisive action from the EU, given the respectful status of Luxembourg as one of its founding members, as well the privileged economic relations between the EU and countries like Switzerland and Lichtenstein. Member states clearly have sovereignty over their taxes, but the fact that

113 For evidence indicating that the decline in statutory corporate tax rates and the spread of preferential tax regimes has taken a more accelerated pace in the EU than in the rest of the world: Genschel, Kemmerling and Seils (2011) 'Accelerating downhill', p. 590ff. On the failure of fiscal integration in the EU and the resistance against tax harmonization from low-tax countries: Wasserfallen (2014) 'Political and economic integration in the EU'.

114 For an unapologetic defense of the benefits of tax competition and international tax planning: Hong and Smart (2010) 'In praise of tax havens'; Trovato (2014) 'La tassazione dell'economia digitale'.

115 The OECD has a long-standing coordination work in the area of "harmful tax competition", which is also the objective of a specific action in the current BEPS Project. See: OECD (1998) *Harmful Tax Competition*; OECD (2015) *Countering Harmful Tax Practices More Effectively, Taking into Account Transparency and Substance.*

116 The OECD (2011) *OECD Guidelines for Multinational Enterprises*, p. 60, exhorts companies to "comply with both the letter and spirit of tax laws and regulations". The very distinction between the "letter" and the "spirit" of the law is an old strategy of legal doctrine to deal with the paradoxes of "creative" judicial interpretation. In the field of taxation, this distinction itself may be very difficult to manage. In the case of the "Double Irish Dutch Sandwich" structure, for example, what would be the "spirit" of national laws, such as the Irish and Dutch ones, which allows the creation of hybrid and shell companies, if not to stimulate tax avoidance itself?

companies start making "tax sandwiches" with their laws is perhaps too much to put up with.

In connection with the common international framework provided by the G20/OECD's BEPS Project, the EU has also been trying to come up with a common approach to tackle the specific tax challenges of the digitalization of the global economy. While promoting its digital single market, it also aims to curb the excessive leeway with which TNCs like Google have been avoiding taxes in the continent. The obstacles, however, are the same as those to the development of a common fiscal and tax policy: tax fragmentation and interstate competition, especially in the field of the direct taxation of corporate income.[117]

A report delivered by an expert group in 2014 summarized some of the main policy concerns over the taxation of the digital economy in the EU.[118] According to the report, there would be no need for a special tax regime for "digital companies", which should be submitted to the same tax rules already applied to any other company.[119] However, a general simplification of existing tax systems and the reduction of the current fragmentation of national laws would be welcome in order to boost the digital single market and to allow small and medium companies to take advantage of digitalization in the expansion of their cross-border activities.[120]

While praising the EU current approach of gradually extending the destination principle to all transactions subject to VAT, the report makes the already known case for more coordination and convergence in the direct taxation of business profits, which would be a necessary step in the fight against tax avoidance in the continent.[121] Regarding the BEPS Project specifically, it suggests the consolidation of a common EU position around three main topics: (i) the need to counter "harmful" tax competition between nation states by closing legal loopholes and hybrid mismatches; (ii) the need to review the current rules on transfer pricing, especially in transactions involving intangibles; and (iii) the need to review the rules on the definition of the status of a permanent establishment for tax purposes, taking into consideration the innovative business models typical of the digital economy.[122]

117 For an overview of recent initiatives at the EU level, as well as initiatives adopted or proposed by specific Member States: Bernardi (2015) 'Internet and taxation in the European Union'.

118 European Commission (2014) *Report of the Commission Expert Group on Taxation of the Digital Economy.*

119 European Commission (2014) *Report of the Commission Expert Group on Taxation of the Digital Economy*, pp. 5 and 41.

120 European Commission (2014) *Report of the Commission Expert Group on Taxation of the Digital Economy*, pp. 5 and 26–27.

121 European Commission (2014) *Report of the Commission Expert Group on Taxation of the Digital Economy*, pp. 31ff and 41ff.

122 European Commission (2014) *Report of the Commission Expert Group on Taxation of the Digital Economy*, p. 43ff. Some measures specifically designed to counter "harmful tax practices" have been recently adopted by the so-called "Anti-Tax Avoidance Directives": *Council Directive (EU) 2016/1164 of 12 July 2016 laying down rules*

In the area of indirect taxation, the EU has made significant progress in the harmonization of national laws on value-added taxes in order to address the main concerns over digitalization. The main achievement has been the progressive extension of the destination principle to the taxation of most economic transactions. This prevents companies from choosing their location based only on VAT rates, since the rate applied to the transaction is determined by the location of the customer. The high mobility of the digital economy and the possibility of conducting transactions over the Internet are, then, neutralized for VAT purposes.

Since January 2015, the provision of telecommunications, broadcasting and electronic supplied services to final consumers has also been submitted to the destination principle. This principle was already applied to most business-to-business transactions and the business-to-consumer supply of goods. The business-to-consumer supply of services, however, was generally taxed in the place of residence of the supplier. With the changes that entered into force in January 2015, all these "e-services", which make up most of the main activities of the digital economy, are taxed in the place of residence of the consumer, thus neutralizing the main risks of digital tax avoidance in the field of VAT.[123].

against tax avoidance practices that directly affect the functioning of the internal market; Council Directive (EU) 2017/952 of 29 May 2017 amending Directive (EU) 2016/1164 as regards hybrid mismatches with third countries. Other legislative instruments have also been recently enacted in order to increase tax transparency and the exchange of information among Member States: *Council Directive (EU) 2016/881 of 25 May 2016 amending Directive 2011/16/EU as regards mandatory automatic exchange of information in the field of taxation; Council Directive (EU) 2018/822 of 25 May 2018 amending Directive 2011/16/EU as regards mandatory automatic exchange of information in the field of taxation in relation to reportable cross-border arrangements.*

123 The progressive extension of the destination principle to all transactions submitted to VAT has been accompanied by a simplified system for the collection of the tax known as "Mini One Stop Shop" (MOSS), which allows taxpayers to register for VAT and pay the tax in one Member State only, thus reducing administrative costs and bureaucratic burdens. The destination principle and the MOSS system had applied to non-EU suppliers of electronic services since 2003. Their extension to all business-to-consumers transactions involving telecommunications, broadcasting and electronically supplied services was agreed upon in 2008, but only entered into force in January 2015 in order to grant an adequate window period for Member States to adapt to the new rules. See: European Commission (2002) *VAT: Commission welcomes Council adoption of rules for application of VAT to electronically delivered services*; European Commission (2014) *Taxation: countdown to simpler and fairer VAT system*; European Commission (2014) *Questions & Answers: VAT changes from 2015.* One particularity of EU tax law, provided for in Articles 14 and 24 of *Council Directive 2006/112/EC of 28 November 2006 on the common system of value added tax*, is that almost all products that do not have a physical and tangible dimension are treated as services, which is the case of software applications and digital media content, such as music, video and books downloaded from the Internet. Therefore, most digital products and services transacted through the Internet are classified simply as "electronically supplied services". According to the definition provided for by Article 7 of *Council Implementing Regulation (EU) No 282/2011 of 15 March 2011*: "'Electronically supplied services' … shall include services which are delivered over the Internet or an electronic network and the nature of which renders their supply essentially automated and involving minimal human intervention,

However, the impact on Google has not been significant. Most of the company's profits are made from the provision of online advertising services in business-to-business transactions, which were already taxed based on the destination principle.[124] The sale of digital products, such as software applications and digital media content, to final consumers through its online platform, "Google Play Store", has, nonetheless, been affected by the 2015 legislative changes. As the platform owner, Google is responsible to charge and collect VAT, the rate of which is now determined by the place of residence of the consumer.[125]

and impossible to ensure in the absence of information technology". A detailed list of these services is contained in Annex I to *Council Implementing Regulation (EU) No 282/2011 of 15 March 2011*, which specifically includes the provision of the online search and advertising services that constitute the main business activities of Google. Given the relatively borderless nature of the Internet, identifying the precise location of the supply of "e-services" may prove to be very "tricky", though, as the complex and detailed rules governing the presumptions on the location of customers demonstrate (Articles 24a, 24b, 24d, 24f, 25 and 31c of *Council Implementing Regulation (EU) No 282/2011 of 15 March 2011*). On the recent policy initiatives at EU level to modernize the common system of VAT, taking into consideration the "digital market strategy": European Commission (2016) *VAT Action Plan: Commission presents measures to modernise VAT in the EU.*

124 Google's activities in online advertising intermediation involve both publishers and advertisers. On the one hand, publishers sell advertising space to Google on their own websites and other digital locations (software applications, online videos, etc.) through the platform AdSense. For tax purposes, publishers are the suppliers of electronic services and Google Ireland Limited is the customer. So, following the destination principle, the transaction is submitted to Irish VAT, which shall either be charged to Google by publishers established in Ireland or directly paid by Google itself when publishers are established in other countries, according to the reverse charge mechanism. On the other hand, advertisers buy advertising space from Google through the platform AdWords. The space may be the property of Google, like its search engine pages, or the property of Google's AdSense network of partner publishers. For tax purposes, Google Ireland Limited is the supplier of electronic services and advertisers are the customers. Following the destination principle, the transaction is submitted to the VAT of the place of residence of the advertiser. When advertisers are established in Ireland, Google charges them the Irish VAT. When advertisers are established in other countries, they are responsible for paying the corresponding VAT according to the reverse charge mechanism. The reverse charge mechanism, provided for in Articles 195 and 196 of *Council Directive 2006/112/EC of 28 November 2006 on the common system of value added tax*, is a rule which states that in business-to-business transactions in which the supplier and the customer are not established in the same Member State, the customer is responsible to pay and collect the VAT. Information on the application of VAT to Google's transactions with publishers is available on the website: https://support.google.com/adsense/answer/1322028?hl=en&ref_topic=1727162&rd=1. Information on the application of VAT to Google's transactions with advertisers is available on the website: https://support.google.com/adwords/topic/3121938?hl=en&ref_topic=3119101,3181080,3126923.

125 Information on the application of VAT to transactions conducted through Google Play Store is available on the website: https://support.google.com/googleplay/answer/2850368?hl=en.

The aggressive tax planning strategies of companies like Google are mainly focused on the avoidance of corporate income taxes and related withholding taxes. Therefore, what is really needed in order to tackle the problem of digital tax avoidance in Europe is a greater degree of convergence in the field of direct taxation of business profits. But that is exactly where fragmentation, interstate competition and unintended, as well as intended, legal loopholes and mismatches tend to prevail, as the "Double Irish Dutch Sandwich" structure used by Google clearly illustrates.

The EU itself has more than once tried to address the problem of corporate income taxation, ranging from the proposition of some minor and specific palliative measures to the much more ambitious project of a broad corporate tax reform.

One of the first initiatives was the Code of Conduct for Business Taxation, adopted by the Economic and Financial Affairs Council in 1997.[126] It is a non-binding, soft law instrument that establishes a mechanism of peer-review among Member States on their practices and measures related to the taxation of corporate income. While acknowledging the positive effects of "fair" competition, the Code of Conduct recognizes that tax competition may also be "harmful" and have a negative impact on the location of business activities in the territory of the EU, especially when Member States adopt measures that give preferential treatment to non-residents or to companies without a significant economic presence in their territory (so-called "Preferential Tax Regimes", or PRTs). Member States have thus made the political compromise of refraining from adopting new "harmful tax measures" (standstill clause), as well as re-assessing and possibly eliminating existing ones (rollback clause).[127]

126 EU (1997) *Council Resolution of 1 December 1997 on a Code of Conduct for Business Taxation.*

127 For an overall assessment of the Code of Conduct and other EU initiatives related to the coordination of corporate taxes: Genschel, Kemmerling and Seils (2011) 'Accelerating downhill', p. 595ff. The European Commission has recently taken a more active approach in the assessment of some aspects of these preferential tax regimes and harmful tax practices. It has launched specific investigations into tax rulings adopted by tax authorities in Luxembourg, Ireland, the Netherlands, Belgium, the UK and Gibraltar that allegedly grant selective advantages to specific companies, in violation of EU rules on state aid. It has already decided that advantages granted to specific TNCs by some Member States are illegal under EU state aid rules, issuing a very interesting order to these Member States, according to which they shall recover the unpaid taxes, that is to say, a sort of "sanction" that may end up increasing public revenues. These decisions regard the following companies and Member States: (i) Apple in Ireland (case number SA.38373); (ii) Starbucks in the Netherlands (case number SA.38374); (iii) Fiat in Luxembourg (case number SA.38375); (iv) Amazon in Luxembourg (case number SA.38944); (v) Engie in Luxembourg (case number SA.44888); (vi) various TNCs in Belgium (case number SA.37667); (vii) various TNCs in Gibraltar (case number SA.34914). The Commission is also currently conducting the following investigations: (i) IKEA in the Netherlands (case number SA.46470); (ii) Nike in the Netherlands (case number SA.51284); (iii) various TNCs in the UK (case number SA.44896). Furthermore, in a case related to MacDonald's in Luxembourg (case number SA.38945), the Commission concluded that there was no irregularity. Official information on all the investigations and proceedings is available at: http://ec.europa.

In addition to soft law instruments and political commitments, the EU has also campaigned for the adoption of a Common Consolidated Corporate Tax Base (CCCTB). The CCCTB was originally proposed by the European Commission in 2011 and was later re-launched in 2015. On the one hand, the proposal would introduce a common tax base to harmonize the taxation of corporate income in the territory of the EU. While Member States would still be able to offer different tax rates, there would be uniform rules for the definition of the tax base, which would potentially reduce existing loopholes and mismatches that create opportunities for tax avoidance. On the other hand, it would remove the need for the complex assessment of transfer prices in intra-group transactions. The tax base of the whole corporate group would be consolidated at EU level and, then, shared among the Member States according to a specific formula to measure economic activities and value creation based on the distribution of assets, labor and sales.

The project itself is too ambitious and the specific proposal on consolidation has not gathered enough consensus. This has led the European Commission to adopt a more graduated approach, focusing in the short-term on the harmonization of tax bases and the introduction of specific measures agreed upon in the framework of the BEPS Project.[128]

With specific reference to the case of Google, after much international pressure, at the end of 2014, the Irish government announced a change in its tax rules to put an end to the "Double Irish" structure.[129] According to the new rules, from January 2015 onward, all companies incorporated in Ireland are also required to have their tax residence there. The creation of hybrid entities, which are incorporated in Ireland, but are tax resident elsewhere (usually, in a tax haven), is no longer allowed. However, existing arrangements in place before January 2015 have a generous deadline of five years to adapt to the new rules.

However, after this five year window period, profits formally made in Ireland will continue to be taxed according to the very low Irish corporate income tax, whose standard rate is 12.5 percent. Moreover, nothing prevents Ireland from offering general tax breaks for income derived from intellectual property. Even if

eu/competition/state_aid/register. The investigations themselves, especially the ones targeting Luxembourg, seem to have gained special momentum after the revelation of secret documents about Luxembourg's tax rulings at the end of 2014, rulings that have contributed to the tax avoidance strategies of many TNCs in Europe and worldwide. The "Luxleaks", as the episode became known, have probably caused the EU some embarrassment, since the then President of the European Commission, Jean-Claude Juncker, was the incumbent Prime Minister of Luxembourg when the tax rulings were negotiated. See: *Guardian* (2014) 'Dane investigating EU tax deals says Luxleaks trail will lead to fair pay'.

128 On the original proposal of the CCCTB in 2011: European Commission (2011) *European corporate tax base: making business easier and cheaper*. On its re-launch in 2015 in the context of a broader action plan on corporate taxation: European Commission (2015) *Commission presents Action Plan for Fair and Efficient Corporate Taxation in the EU*.

129 Forbes (2014) 'Ireland declares "double Irish" tax scheme dead'; *New York Times* (2014) 'Ireland to phase out "double Irish" tax break used by tech giants'.

"harmful" in practice, low tax rates and general tax breaks for R&D and technology are both forms of "fair" tax competition. Without further and effective convergence and coordination at EU level, the current vain search for Google's mobile and stateless income will probably continue.

The lack of an effective international and EU-wide response to the problem of tax avoidance in general, and digital tax avoidance in particular, has led many countries to start acting on their own. Tax authorities in the UK,[130] France,[131] Italy[132] and Spain[133] have all initiated investigations and proceedings against Google for alleged failure to comply with their respective tax laws, some of them demanding high compensation in the order of a billion euros or more.

In addition to the recovery of unpaid taxes from digital companies like Google, proposals have also been made to collect additional revenues from the Internet economy. The Hungarian government made official plans to impose a specific tax on access to the Internet based on the volume of data "consumed" by users, but had to roll it back at the end of 2014 after thousands of protesters took to the streets in Budapest.[134] An Italian legislative initiative to collect extra revenues from the digital economy, especially from the provision of online advertising services, known as the "web tax", was also abandoned at the end of 2014 because of legal difficulties.[135] Germany and Spain have managed, instead, to impose an obligatory fee on news aggregators, such as "Google News", which is not exactly a tax, but an extra-fiscal revenue destined to increase the leverage of their respective publishing industries against Google and other online media companies.[136]

One of the most innovative, as well as most controversial, proposals, however, was made in 2013 by a taskforce on the taxation of the digital economy in a specific report commissioned by the French government.[137] The main argument of the report is that value creation in the digital economy is derived mainly by the exploitation of the flows of data generated in the interaction between companies

130 *Wall Street Journal* (2014) 'U.K. details 'Google tax' plans'; *Guardian* (2016) 'Google agrees to pay British authorities £130m in back taxes'.

131 *Le Monde* (2016) 'Une vaste perquisition menée dans les locaux de Google à Paris'; *Guardian* (2016) 'France to seek €1.6bn in back taxes from Google, says official'.

132 *Repubblica* (2016) 'Google, fisco italiano all'attacco'; *Corriere della Sera* (2016) 'Google e il fisco italiano'.

133 *El Pais* (2016) 'Hacienda busca en Google Spain y Google Ireland indicios de fraude fiscal'.

134 *The Economist* (2014) 'Hungary's Internet tax'; Interdisciplinary Internet Institute (2015) 'Taxing Internet use'.

135 *Corriere della Sera* (2014) 'L'iter (finito) della Web Tax'.

136 Msoftnews (2013) 'German parliament passes "Google tax" law, forcing royalty payments for news snippet's; Business Insider (2014) 'Spain just passed an insane law taxing Google for linking to news'. The European Commissions' proposal for a directive on copyright in the digital single market, whose legislative process was still under way at the beginning of 2019, provides for a similar "link tax" in the form of a remuneration to be paid by news aggregators to press publications. See: European Commission (2016) *Proposal for a Directive of the European Parliament and of the Council on Copyright in the Digital Single Market*, p. 29 (Article 11).

137 Collin and Colin (2013) *Mission d'expertise sur la fiscalité de l'économie numérique.*

and users, especially the personal data supplied by users, as well as the content directly created by them (the so-called user-generated content).[138]

According to the report, the new task of fiscal policy in the digital economy would be to establish a link between the taxation of business profits and the collection and use of online data. This would have to be achieved by international cooperation, the main goal of which should be to re-define the concept of a permanent establishment for tax purposes in such a way that a company's income would be taxable in a specific state if its business activities are significantly related to the collection and use of data from users resident in that state.[139] In the meantime, the report also proposes the creation of a national transitory tax on the collection of user's data, the purpose of which would not be the increase of fiscal revenues per se, but the enforcement of privacy rules. Like the "polluter pays" principle in environmental taxes, this data tax would be designed to encourage the promotion of data protection rights.[140]

These basic ideas of: (i) substituting digital presence for physical presence, and (ii) recognizing the role of personal data and user generated content in value creation are also behind the latest proposals of the European Commission to promote the "fair taxation" of the digital economy, even if the proposals have no explicit connection with the enforcement of privacy and data protection.

In March 2018, the Commission proposed new legislative measures to be adopted by the Council of the EU in the form of two specific directives. One would lay down rules allowing Member States to tax corporate income based on the "significant digital presence" of a company, which would not require the physical existence of a permanent establishment, but only the existence of a significant degree of interaction between the company and the users who are physically present in the territory of the Member State and who contribute to the value creation process by means of their personal data and the content autonomously generated by them. This would be a long-term solution designed to be eventually incorporated in the larger framework of the CCCTB. Until this solution is effectively adopted, the other directive proposed by the Commission would create an interim indirect tax ("digital services tax") on the revenues resulting from the provision of digital services that also make intensive use of personal data and online content generated by Internet users.[141]

138 Collin and Colin (2013) *Mission d'expertise sur la fiscalité de l'économie numérique*, p. 35ff.

139 Collin and Colin (2013) *Mission d'expertise sur la fiscalité de l'économie numérique*, p. 121ff.

140 Collin and Colin (2013) *Mission d'expertise sur la fiscalité de l'économie numérique*, p. 130ff. For an overall assessment of the proposals contained in the report: De Filippi (2013) 'Taxing the cloud'. The case for the use of taxes to enforce privacy rules is also made by Larnier (2014) 'Whoever owns our data will determine our fate'. Moreover, the policy option of introducing a specific tax, or "equalizing levy", on the collection and use of personal data was also briefly considered by the OECD (2015) *Addressing the Tax Challenges of the Digital Economy*, p. 115ff.

141 European Commission (2018) *Digital taxation: Commission proposes new measures to ensure that all companies pay fair tax in the EU*; European Commission (2018)

Besides promoting "fair taxation" and ensuring a "level playing field" between "digital companies" and traditional ones, this recent set of proposals is also designed to avoid the risk of the fragmentation of the "digital single market" represented by the uncoordinated unilateral measures adopted by Member States.[142] Moreover, by advancing these proposals, the EU also aims to shape the debate currently going on at the G20/OECD level.[143]

In general terms, taxation is itself connected with the broad principles of democracy and fundamental rights. The organization and functioning of the state, as well as the protection and promotion of individual rights, always demand a considerable degree of funding by means of taxes.[144] Re-establishing (or re-constituting) the public power to collect taxes on corporate income in an ever more digitalized global economy is, therefore, an issue of great constitutional relevance, even if not always perceived as so. If rights have their costs, tax avoidance has its price. A negative price in terms of equality, income distribution and the quality and effectiveness of public policies in society at large.[145]

Whether or not data flows can work as a proxy for business profits in the taxation of corporate income is certainly a controversial question, which probably deserves much deeper consideration, research and public debate. The very analogy, however, between environmental taxes and an eventual data protection tax is quite revealing. If the natural environment of society is endangered by the normal consequences of the regular productive processes of an industrial economy, the autonomy and integrity of its "human environment" seem to be disturbed by the accelerated data flows of an information economy.[146] In the latter case, Google would certainly be a prominent "polluter".

Questions and Answers on a Fair and Efficient Tax System in the EU for the Digital Single Market. It is interesting to note that this new set of proposals go against the "expert advice" given to the European Commission a couple of years earlier. According to the European Commission (2014) *Report of the Commission Expert Group on Taxation of the Digital Economy*, pp. 7 and 47: "There is no convincing argument why the collection of data via electronic means in a country should in itself create a taxable presence in that country".

142 However, given the small prospect of the adoption of a EU-wide solution in the short-term, France has already introduced its own version of the "digital services tax", and Austria has announced it intends to do the same. See: *Le Figaro* (2018) 'Taxe GAFA: la France imposera les géants du numérique à partir du 1er janvier 2019'; Deutsche Welle (2018) 'Austria to implement digital tax for tech giants'.

143 The very alternative of the introduction of an interim tax on digital services by specific states, at least while the debates on a global solution to the tax challenges of the digital economy are still under way, was expressly acknowledged by the participants in the BEPS Project. See: OECD (2018) *Tax Challenges Arising from Digitalisation – Interim Report 2018*, p. 177ff.

144 Holmes and Sustein (2000) *The Cost of Rights.*

145 Tax Justice Network (2015) *Ten Reasons to Defend the Corporation Tax*; Christensen and Murphy (2004) 'The social irresponsibility of corporate tax avoidance'.

146 On the idea of human beings, their bodies and minds, as the environment of the system of society, an idea that is based on the very distinction system/environment: Luhmann (2002) *Theories of Distinction*, p. 169ff; Luhmann (2012 [1997]) *Theory of Society*, p. 28ff.

The EU has developed a strong legal framework for the protection of privacy and personal data, which has been recently applied by its Court of Justice in cases directly or indirectly affecting Google, as well as other big TNCs of the Internet economy. The next and final chapter of the book addresses some recent conflicts between Google and the EU in the field of privacy and human rights more generally.

4 Privacy, social memory and global data flows

Jorge Luis Borges' often-quoted short story about a man who is incapable of forgetting is a nice allegory for our current relationship with digital technologies:

> For nineteen years he had lived as one in a dream: he looked without seeing, listened without hearing, forgetting everything, almost everything. When he fell, he became unconscious; when he came to, the present was almost intolerable in its richness and sharpness, as were his most distant and trivial memories. Somewhat later he learned that he was paralyzed. The fact scarcely interested him. He reasoned (he felt) that his immobility was a minimum price to pay. Now his perception and his memory were infallible. ... I thought that each of my words (that each of my movements) would persist in his implacable memory; I was benumbed by the fear of multiplying useless gestures.[1]

It is in the nature of a literary genius to grasp in fiction the reality we are not always able to convey. Borges probably did not have any specific technology in mind when he wrote in 1942 about the mysteries and paradoxes of remembering and forgetting. One who remembers everything and forgets nothing is barely able to think, because to think is "to forget differences, generalize, make abstractions".[2] Funes, "el memorioso", is not capable of engaging in reflexive thinking.[3] Paradoxically, he has little or no memory at all, because memory is the unity of remembering and forgetting. It is not a sum or a storehouse, but "a disorder of indefinite possibilities".[4]

There is, of course, a great deal of difference between the memory of individuals and specific groups and the memory of society as a whole. With the progressive differentiation of society, and the co-related process of the individualization of individuals, social memory has evolved along a path that is increasingly

1 Borges (1962 [1942]) 'Funes the memorious', p. 151ff.

2 Borges (1962 [1942]) 'Funes the memorious', p. 154.

3 "In remembering, one faces the world; in forgetting one faces oneself" (Esposito (2008) 'Social forgetting', p. 182).

4 "La memoria del hombre no es una suma; es un desorden de posibilidades indefinidas" (Borges (1983) *La Memoria de Shakespeare*).

autonomous from individual and collective memory.[5] Beyond both the physical-chemical and psychic processes that are particular to each individual, and the day-to-day interactions among restricted and relatively small sets of people, social memory is mainly dependent on media, on the technologies and systems available for the diffusion of communication and for the storage, processing and transmission of information. These technologies and systems entail a wide, complex and unpredictable network of communication and information processing that is beyond the reach of any human mind or group interaction.[6]

Notwithstanding these obvious differences, society too is able to selectively remember and forget. As already shown in Chapter 2, digital technologies in general, and search engines in particular, do have a quantitative, as well as a qualitative impact on social memory. Besides being able to remember, and also to forget, more information, our contemporary society has changed its default memory value: remembering is now the rule and forgetting is the exception that requires constant social and technological effort, and in some circumstances, even legal protection.

Google's search engine, for instance, is so good not just because it remembers everything, being able to store and index the whole visible Web in its powerful computers for later retrieval. The main reason for it being outstanding is because of its dynamic ability to forget, to apply its ranking algorithm in the selection of different sets of data from one search to the other, thus providing the precise information that is relevant to someone, while simultaneously hiding an ocean of data that might otherwise be potentially informative.

The main problem with digital technologies and search engines like Google is that they create a specific kind of power imbalance. Individuals become ever more exposed to the inevitable arbitrariness of public and private bureaucracies, as well as to the casual surveillance of their peers. The wide circulation of their personal data, from the most intimate to the most trivial, increases the risk that they may be negatively affected and discriminated against by a variety of concrete measures and decisions, which in some cases they (or eventually anybody) may not even be aware of. In the environmental analogy, it is as if the digitalization and acceleration of global data flows began to generate a sort of "pollution" that is rather dangerous in the "human environment" of society.[7]

5 Esposito (2001) *La Memoria Sociale*; Esposito (2008) 'Social forgetting', p. 183ff. From a different perspective, Aleida Assmann and Jan Assmann also speak of the difference between the communicative memory of specific groups and the cultural memory of society at large. See: Assmann (2008) 'Canon and archive'; Assmann (2008) 'Communicative and cultural memory'.

6 Luhmann (2012 [1997]) *Theory of Society*, p. 348ff. In Kittler's famous words: "What remains of people is what media can store and communicate" (Kittler (1999 [1986]) *Gramophone, Film, Typewriter*, p. xl).

7 This environmental analogy is curiously used by many authors with different theoretical backgrounds, be it in the context of the already mentioned proposals to tax global data flows, be it in the assessment of the potential harms posed by digital technologies to the privacy and autonomy of individuals. Concepts such as risk regulation and the precautionary principle are borrowed from environmental law in order to be applied in

This final chapter begins by addressing some critical aspects of the global flows of data and information enabled by our contemporary digital technologies (4.1) that have an impact on our conceptualization of human rights such as privacy and data protection (4.2). Google is at the center of these debates. The EU, especially its Court of Justice, has developed a legal framework for the protection of personal data that may set (or is already setting) the global agenda for the imposition of constitutional limits on companies such as Google, as well as on the intelligence services with which they closely cooperate (4.3).

From the case law of the Court of Justice of the European Union (CJEU), it is possible to thematically select two main sets of concerns that deserve further analysis: one regarding the widespread publication and processing of general content online that may contain personal data (4.3.1), and the other regarding the intentional collection and worldwide transfer of personal data specifically for classification, discrimination and surveillance purposes (4.3.2). These different, but interrelated concerns, as well as the solutions provided by the court to address them, are, then, critically assessed with reference to the "two indexes of Google"[8] and their respective global (or transnational) scope (4.4).

While the right to be forgotten recently recognized by the court is addressed mainly to the more well-known and publicly available "first index" of Google (4.4.1), its decisions to invalidate both the Data Retention Directive and the Safe Harbour Agreement seem to be addressed mainly to the more secret and opaque "second index" of Google and other "digital bureaucracies" (4.4.2). The decisions themselves may serve as precedents to deal with the increased privacy risks of exposure and discrimination generated by the "profiling" of people (4.4.3). Moreover, these decisions may have (or are already having) wide consequences for world society beyond Europe that deserve especial attention, consequences for both society and the self, for social memory and the private sphere of individuals.

the field of data protection law. See: Collin and Colin (2013) *Mission d'expertise sur la fiscalité de l'économie numérique*, p. 130ff; Rodotà (2014) *Il Mondo nella Rete*, e-book 34%; Albers (2014) 'Realizing the complexity of data protection', p. 232; Solove (2006) 'A taxonomy of privacy', p. 559. The growing popularity of this analogy in the background of the current acceleration of global flows of data, information and communication more generally would seem to vindicate one of the most controversial theses of systems theory, according to which modern society is a global system of communication whose environment is constituted by natural phenomena, as well as by people themselves. Individuals are not "parts" of the system of society, but elements of its environment. See: Luhmann (1995 [1984]) *Social Systems*, p. 176ff; Luhmann (2012 [1997]) *Theory of Society*, p. 28ff. On the continuing relevance of the distinction system/environment in the current situation of the rapid spread of technologically enhanced environments (or "smart environments"): Esposito (2017) 'An ecology of differences'.

8 Stalder and Mayer (2009) 'The second index'.

4.1 The media of data and the forms of information

The words data and information are generally used as synonyms to denote, in a rather simplified way, the facts about society and the world that constitute the basic object or content of communication. It is possible, however, to draw a distinction between these two concepts in order to shed some light on the particular dynamics of digital technologies and their impact on modern society. Data may be described as the medium, and information as the form.

The distinction medium/form has its origins in the psychology of perception.[9] It describes the relationship between two sets of elements based on their internal structures and their modes of interconnection. The medium is a set of loosely coupled elements, while the form is a set of tightly coupled ones. The form impresses itself onto the medium by tightening the connectivity of its elements. As the form presupposes a previous medium, it may also serve as a medium itself for the generation of ulterior forms. In the context of physical phenomena, for instance, images are forms produced on the medium of light, and sounds are forms produced on the medium of air. Images may, nonetheless, be condensed for the production of pictograms, and sounds may be articulated in the development of language.

Information and communication technologies may also be described from the perspective of this distinction. Writing, the printing press and computers are all media of communication that allow the emergence of ever more complex, abstract and differentiated communicative forms. With every new technological change, the elements of communication may be combined, re-combined, stored and transmitted in new, different and rather unpredictable ways.[10]

With the invention of writing, communication detaches itself from face-to-face interactions, so that the elements of language may be decoupled from concrete situations and, then, re-connected in the production of a multiplicity of texts, which may be read in the most varied contexts and interpreted by sets of people that have never known each other. The printing press, in its turn, introduces more malleable and flexible forms for the organization of the elements of a text, as well as the possibility of its serial and standardized reproduction and diffusion to the growing portions of a literate population.[11]

As already discussed in Chapter 2, digital technologies go one step further and turn the generation and management of information into an autonomous process that detaches itself from the other elements of communication. Information is decoupled from both utterance and understanding and is reduced to the most basic elements of binary data. The intentions of the emitter and the comprehension of the receiver lose (or loosen) their connection to the information that is

9 Heider (2017 [1926]) *Chose et médium*. On the appropriation by systems theory of the distinction medium/thing from the theory of perception and its re-elaboration as the distinction medium/form in the description of sociological phenomena of communication: Luhmann (2012 [1997]) *Theory of Society*, p. 113ff.

10 Esposito (2004) 'The arts of contingency', p. 9ff.

11 Esposito (2004) 'The arts of contingency', p. 12ff.

communicated, which is, then, treated as data. Data work as the medium, whose elements may be constantly combined and re-combined for the purposes of "in-forming".

Information has been defined in a number of different ways. Most of them tend to stress its elements of novelty, as well as its ephemeral nature. From a more technical and engineering perspective that has become classic in information theory, information is a measure of entropy, a quantitative element that defines the potential variability of the content of a message.[12] In economics, it has also been defined as a reduction in uncertainty, an economic commodity that alters the perception of market agents about uncertain events in the future.[13]

Beyond quantification and commodification, some branches of cybernetics and systems theory have put the focus on the more dynamic or relational aspects of information. In the famous definition of Gregory Bateson, information is "any difference which makes a difference in some later event".[14] An event is perceived as a difference by an agent (or system), who (or which) processes the event and, as a result, changes (or differentiates) its own internal state (or structure). In the case of individuals and social systems, information is an element of communication: something is uttered by someone and, then, understood (or misunderstood) by someone else. A difference in perception, such as the one caused by the utterance of a message, produces a difference in understanding: the utterance is understood beyond its mere external manifestation (a sound that is listened, an image that is seen or a text that is read), as the act of conveying some meaningful information about the world.[15]

Information, then, is the ephemeral element of novelty in communication. As stressed by Luhmann, any news read twice is no longer informative.[16] Data, in its turn, is the material and quantifiable element whose informative potential may vary from time to time and from context to context. Properly speaking, the semantic element of novelty is so ephemeral and complex that it can never be recorded in its entirety, unless drastically reduced into the rather meaningless materiality of data, such as letters in a book, analogical marks in a tape or digital signals in a computer. Google, for instance, organizes the world's information by treating it as data that may be automatically stored and retrieved in the constant production and reproduction of novel information.

The acceleration of time so characteristic of modernity already creates a specific "hunger" for, or "addiction" to, information and data that is inscribed in the very structure of most social systems. The routine changes in legislation and judicial interpretation, the day-to-day mood of a public opinion oriented toward periodic elections, the idiosyncratic movements of prices and market positions, the high expectations associated with scientific discoveries and technological innovations are

12 Shannon and Weaver (1964) *The Mathematical Theory of Communication.*

13 Arrow (1996) 'The economics of information'.

14 Bateson (1972) *Steps to an Ecology of Mind*, p. 386.

15 Luhmann (2002) *Theories of Distinction*, p. 155ff.

16 "A news item run twice might still have its meaning, but it loses its informative value" (Luhmann (2000 [1996]) *The Reality of the Mass Media*, p. 19).

all constantly feeding, as well as being fed, by rapid flows of information that have to be dealt with by the legal, political, economic and scientific systems, which are themselves relentlessly being pushed and "irritated" by the selective memory of the mass media.[17]

Further uncoupling the elements of communication, digital technologies increasingly accelerate the production and the global flows of information by treating it as data that can be stored, processed and transmitted with the help of machines. Complex and ephemeral semantic elements are reduced to discrete digital sequences. Communication and information are captured and uncoupled into the medium of binary data, whose elements may be automatically combined and re-combined for the constant production of new forms that are potentially informative.

More than wide accessibility and diffusion, the overall possibility of combining and re-combining data to produce information, to uncouple and re-couple the elements of the medium in the creation of ever new forms, is what seems to be really revolutionary about the Internet and digital technologies more generally.[18] Users are not only isolated points of emission and diffusion of previously established content, but active and productive factors in the very manipulation of data for the generation of information.[19]

It has become commonplace to talk about our contemporary "data deluge" or "information overload" now that the structural inclinations of modern society toward information and novelty have met the known (and yet unknown) potentialities of digital technologies for the automation of the management of data.[20] Information captured as data may now be stored, processed and transmitted on an industrial scale and by automatic means. The medium of data itself can be constantly programmed (and increasingly self-programmed) in the form of logical structures and commands (software and algorithms) to automatically deal with large quantities of unstructured and loosely coupled elements of data, or "raw data", in order to produce insightful, useful and very profitable information. To quote Heidegger, it seems to be the "essence" of digital technologies to decompose reality in the form of data and, then, treat these data as "standing reserve", as a sort of constant "energy supply" that feeds the relentless need for novelty of an "information society".[21]

17 Luhmann (2000 [1996]) *The Reality of the Mass Media*, p. 20ff. On the "shortening life spans of information" in our contemporary society inundated by data, where updating also implies outdating: Kallinikos (2009) 'The making of ephemeria'.

18 Esposito (2004) 'The arts of contingency', p. 22ff.

19 This is the very meaning of the "generativity" of the Net stressed by Zittrain (2008) *The Future of the Internet*, p. 7ff. According to Balkin (2004) 'Digital speech and democratic culture', p. 6ff, this generativity of the medium, the widespread possibility of combining and re-combining, creating and innovating, "routing around" and "glooming on", is exactly what characterizes the "digital revolution".

20 *The Economist* (2010) *Data, Data Everywhere*; World Economic Forum (2011) *Personal Data*.

21 Heidegger (1977) *The Question Concerning Technology and Other Essays*, p. 3ff.

Rather inflated expectations have been associated with the perceived novel potential of so-called "big data", or "open big data", to inform and produce value.[22] New branches of knowledge (or technology) focused specifically on data have emerged, such as data science and analytics, made up of engineers, software programmers and statisticians, whose work is to sift through large amounts of data in search of correlations, patterns and trends that would supposedly lift the "veil of reality" and allow us to de-code its deeper layers, discovering "secrets" until now hidden.[23]

The decomposition of reality into the medium of data, however, is always a selective process.[24] The reality of the world, the functioning of society and especially the identities and preferences of individuals are never captured in their entirety, complexity and transient nature. Even the most powerful computers and the most sophisticated algorithms are only able to record and process fragments of this reality. The information, thus, generated is always biased in some way or another. It is dependent on the medium in which it has condensed its forms. Especially when the medium is made up of a variety of fragments of data that are constantly being exchanged among different machines, which, for their part, are increasingly autonomous from each other and whose algorithms are able to "learn", to dynamically change their states and structures from one operation to the next. A process that itself adds a growing element of unpredictability (and uncontrollability) to the ever more accelerated production of information out of data.

Notwithstanding all the selectivity of data and the multiple (and inevitable) biases of information, the contemporary enthusiasm for big data tends to forge a specific kind of "data determinism", or "data behaviorism", which consists of praising the aura of neutrality and objectivity with which society, the world and even people might now be researched and "mined" with the help of artificial intelligence and self-learning algorithms.[25] It seems that the old "book of nature" that was once supposed to be read by modern science – in itself, a metaphor for

22 Kallinikos (2013) 'The allure of big data'. The term big data usually refers to the dimensions of volume, variety and velocity of the large amounts of data that are routinely collected, analyzed and combined by contemporary information systems and technologies. Beyond the distinctions big/small and open/closed, the concept of "open big data" stresses the dimensions of relationality and ex-post ordering that characterizes the current technological and social practices of data management, the fact that data become ever more valuable because of the capacity to combine different databases in the flexible ordering of data, an ordering that does not depend on predetermined categories and classifications, but is dynamically generated *ex-post*. See: Marton, Avital and Jensen (2013) 'Reframing open big data'.

23 Kallinikos (2013) 'The allure of big data', p. 42; Kuner *et al* (2012) 'The challenge of "big data" for data protection', p. 48; Davenport and Patil (2012) 'Data scientist'; Anderson (2008) 'The end of theory'.

24 Kallinikos (2009) 'On the computational rendition of reality'.

25 Anderson (2008) 'The end of theory'; Pentland (2012) 'Reinventing society in the wake of big data'; *The Economist* (2010) *Data, Data Everywhere*; *Wall Street Journal* (2012) 'So, what's your algorithm?'

the golden age of the printing press[26] – is now supposed to run on software code and to be deciphered by computers and technology experts. This fascination with the alleged "superior wisdom" of data tends to revive old dreams about the possibility of a detached and external, and thus more neutral and objective, observation of the world. These dreams make their entry (or re-entry) in the world of the machine, paradoxically generating new sorts of "digital prophecies", in which predictive analytics seems to substitute for ancient oracles and divinatory methods traditionally used to deal with the future.[27]

Computers and algorithms are supposed to take the place of the hidden observer that paradoxically tries to detach itself from the world within the world. They (and their multiple uses) cannot escape, however, from the well-known consequences associated with both the open future that characterizes modern society and the inevitable double contingency of every social action (or operation), including the most basic one of simply "observing the world".[28] To observe the world is to act upon it, to draw a distinction that guides the observation by putting a mark or value that did not exist before and that further influences the observation without being able to be observed by it, unless in the paralyzing form of a tautology or paradox.[29]

When we observe the automated observation of the world made possible with the help of computers – a special form of "second-order observation"[30] – it is not some deeper and hidden reality that is suddenly revealed by the objectivity of data, but the reflexivity, performativity and circularity of these same data, as well as the ways through which they are programmed and used. In our contemporary situation of ubiquitous computing and widespread digital networking, data science and analytics strive to extract knowledge and information about a world that is increasingly shaped by data science and analytics. Computers and algorithms are

26 Gumbrecht (2003) 'Why intermediality – if at all?', p. 174ff.

27 On the curious similarity between the current frenzy over data and old forms of divinatory rationality, a similarity that is itself paradoxical since this attitude of "data determinism" does not fit well with the basic assumptions of modernity and its open future: Esposito (2013) 'Digital prophecies and Web intelligence'; Esposito (2011) 'A time of divination and a time of risk'.

28 Contingency itself is opposed to the idea of necessity and implies that every experience of, and action upon, the world may be different from that expected because it cannot be completely pre-determined. The concept of double contingency is used in the social sciences to explain the particularity of the social dimension, in which multiple agents and systems must not only orient their actions and operations toward the inevitable contingency of the external world, but must also take into consideration the contingency of the actions and expectations of each other. It implies an element of circularity and performativity: one orients one's expectations toward the actions and experiences of others knowing that they will do the same. See: Luhmann (1995 [1984]) *Social Systems*, p. 103ff; Vanderstraeten (2002) 'Parsons, Luhmann and the Theorem of Double Contingency'. On the concept of performativity in the social sciences in general and in economics in particular: Esposito (2013) 'The structures of uncertainty'.

29 Luhmann (2002) *Theories of Distinction*, p. 79ff.

30 Luhmann (2002) *Theories of Distinction*, p. 94ff.

programed to interpret a reality that is itself, to a large extent, created and shaped by them. The world of big data is not necessarily a world of neutral, objective and "big knowledge", but a world of "big feedback loops".

Notwithstanding the use of "smart" devices and "intelligent" artefacts, the act of creating models, interpreting data and making predictions about society, as well as profiles about the behavior of people, is always a reflexive or performative act, an act that changes the very "reality" in which the models, interpretations, predictions and profiles are supposed to work.[31] Google, for instance, organizes and makes available information about a world that is increasingly shaped by Google itself. The company not only acknowledges this fact, but it also takes advantage of it, of its reflexive, performative and circular relationship with its users. As already discussed in Chapter 2, the way it dynamically ranks the information available on the Web is determined, to a large extent, by the way people have searched for the information in the past and reacted to the results provided by the search engine.

The naïve attitude toward data, and the so-called "unleashed potential of big data", may fit well with the marketing strategies and public relations campaigns of large companies of the digital economy, companies that thrive in the abundance and availability of data, exploiting the profitable ways of putting them to productive and commercial use. This attitude, however, should be de-mystified (or deconstructed) if the wide impact of digital technologies and global data flows on society and individuals is to be taken seriously.

To exert control over the medium is to influence the arrangement and configuration of its forms. In order to counterbalance the negative effects of the concentration of the power over global flows of data and information by public and private bureaucracies, it is necessary to consider how traditional human rights such as privacy are evolving in reaction to the challenges of the online environment.

4.2 Privacy and data protection online

From a constitutional perspective, the most problematic issue with the digitalization and acceleration of global data flows is one of power, especially economic and media power that may be politically exploited. Big transnational corporations of the digital economy such as Google exert control over large portions of the flows of data and information that circulate globally, usually providing (voluntarily or not) malicious and well-hidden "backdoors" to law enforcement and intelligence agencies. Besides creating opportunities for the monopolization of markets and the avoidance of taxes, this power over data and information has major

31 While computers may be able to deal with the "simple contingency" of the world, calculating risks and providing probabilistic models of the future, they are not able to calculate the effects of their own calculations and models on the social world because of its inherent indeterminacy, which is the indeterminacy of the situation of double contingency itself. See: Esposito (2013) 'Digital prophecies and Web intelligence', p. 133ff.

geopolitical relevance, as well as negative effects on the autonomy of democratic institutions and the fundamental rights of individuals.[32]

As already discussed in Chapter 2, the Snowden revelations have shed some light on the pervasive practices of mass surveillance online carried out by the US, its closest allies and some major transnational corporations of the ICT sector. Practices that are also shared by other governments and companies around the world. The close relationship between technological innovation and the industrial-military complex seems to generate a common pattern of promiscuity between private companies and government organizations for the purposes of widespread surveillance and industrial espionage.

The commodification of data and its geopolitical exploitation have huge consequences for both society and the self. Statistical trends and patterns about the day-to-day functioning of society may be extracted by means of the automated (or semi-automated) analysis of its global data flows, from city traffic to health emergencies, from market movements to the changes in mood of public opinion. When turned into information, these data are extremely relevant not exactly to predict the future, but to act upon the present in order to influence and potentially change its course.[33]

The same is valid for individuals. A large part of so-called big data is personal data, that is to say, data that may potentially inform something about someone.[34] From trivial details to intimate secrets, everything that is recorded about someone's life is available, almost by default, to be analyzed in order to generate classifications, categorizations and discriminations of the most varied sorts. More than unveiling their past or allegedly controlling or pre-determining their future, it is the present of people that is at stake. Besides the serious risk of having their lives

32 The recent scandal at the beginning of 2018 about a "data breach" involving Facebook and the political marketing company Cambridge Analytica has clearly demonstrated the risks of the exploitation of data, especially personal data, in terms of the involuntary exposure of people and the manipulation of electoral processes. See: *Guardian* (2018) 'Revealed: 50 million Facebook profiles harvested for Cambridge Analytica in major data breach'.

33 Google, for instance, makes available on its "Google Trends" website (https://www.google.com/trends) aggregated data on search terms that searchers around the world use when making their searches. The analysis of these data may produce a lot of real-time information about the functioning of society based on the behavior of online searchers. On the potential use of Google aggregated data on search behavior for scientific research and policy-making: Askitas (2015) 'Google search activity data and breaking trends'.

34 According to Article 4(1) of the GDPR (*Regulation (EU) 2016/679 of the European Parliament and of the Council of 27 April 2016 on the protection of natural persons with regard to the processing of personal data and on the free movement of such data, and repealing Directive 95/46/EC*): "'personal data' means any information relating to an identified or identifiable natural person ('data subject'); an identifiable natural person is one who can be identified, directly or indirectly, in particular by reference to an identifier such as a name, an identification number, location data, an online identifier or to one or more factors specific to the physical, physiological, genetic, mental, economic, cultural or social identity of that natural person".

exposed without their consent, of losing any control over their social identities, people may be negatively affected and discriminated against by means of automated (or semi-automated) measures and decisions that are not clear to them or even to anyone. From security checks to price discounts, from police investigations to access to credit, employment and social benefits.[35]

The concentration of the control over, and the ownership of, global flows of data tend to create new information asymmetries, as well as to increase the existing ones. The collection, combination, re-combination and diffusion of the fragments of reality that have a performative effect on this same reality are increasingly recognized as an element of power and wealth. The "data divide" is one of the most critical dimensions of the "digital divide", the general inequality in the access to digital technologies. Unequal access to data and information also means enhanced political and economic inequality among nation states, among corporations and also among individuals and groups.[36]

Transnational corporations like Google record and organize all sorts of data about society and its physical and human environments, secretly sharing large parts of them with the intelligence and law enforcement agencies of their nation states of origin. Whatever information is generated out of these data, it is asymmetrically distributed for the advantage of more powerful states and dominant or monopolistic companies. As already stressed above, the main issue at stake is not one of simply unveiling the past in order to predict and determine the future, but one of framing our present reality, of decomposing and re-combining its elements in order to reflexively act upon it, "in-forming" and "per-forming" concrete actions and decisions that have a direct impact on society and its environment.

It is precisely in order to counterbalance these new configurations (or re-configurations) of political, economic and media power that human rights are as important "online" as they are "offline".[37] In their function of constitutional artefacts of modern society, they too have a critical message to "impress" over the digital medium: the counter-factual protection of the autonomy of democratic institutions and different spheres of communication, as well as the integrity of individuals and their social identities. Since the main risks and threats do not come

35 Solove (2001) 'Privacy and power'; Citron (2008) 'Technological due process'; Barocas (2014) 'Data mining and the discourse on discrimination'; Barocas and Selbst (2016) 'Big data's disparate impact'.

36 Newman (2014) 'The costs of lost privacy', p. 853ff; Kallinikos (2013) 'The allure of big data', p. 43; Marton, Avital and Jensen (2013) 'Reframing open big data', p. 10.

37 The equal enforceability of human rights both online and offline has been recognized by the UN on many occasions, especially with regard to the enforcement of the rights to privacy and freedom of expression on the Internet. See: UNCCPR (2011) *General comment No. 34*; UNGA (2011) *Report of the Special Rapporteur on the promotion and protection of the right to freedom of opinion and expression*; UNHRC (2012) *Resolution on the promotion, protection and enjoyment of human rights on the Internet*; UNGA (2013) *Resolution on the right to privacy in the digital age*; UNGA (2014) *Report of the Special Rapporteur on the promotion and protection of human rights and fundamental freedoms while countering terrorism*; UNHRC (2014) *Report on the right to privacy in the digital age*.

from the state alone, but rather from disruptive global flows of wealth and information – in this case, wealth and information generated out of data – the "horizontal effect" of human rights is just as important as, or even more important than, their traditional "vertical" one.[38]

As was the case with the printing press, digital technologies have an immense potential to disrupt and re-configure both public communication and private lives. Therefore, the very distinction between the public and private spheres seems to be at stake, with new risks emerging in terms of the privatization of the public and the compression of the private. To keep the distinction alive and to keep the present open toward the future, two basic human rights, particularly in relation to the media and forms of communication, tend to gain increased relevance: freedom of expression and privacy.

Some of the new challenges to freedom of expression and access to information posed by the rise and spread of the Internet, as well as the limitations on market mechanisms and competition law to properly address them, have already been discussed in the first section of Chapter 3. Although communication and information may now flow with more autonomy from the centralizing influence of traditional mass media, they are more dependent on the technical configuration of the medium, especially its network infrastructure. Network neutrality, therefore, becomes a relevant condition for the protection and promotion of media pluralism and freedom of expression online.

The particular significance of the neutrality debate for Google has already been addressed. Search engines are not simply neutral platforms for the circulation of information, nor are they autonomous editors with complete discretion over what is to be remembered and forgotten on the Web. Beyond their common and opposing descriptions as either "objective conduits" or "subjective editors", search engines are also, to a certain extent, "speech engines", artefacts for the articulation and diffusion of communication and information in society at large. As stressed by James Grimmelmann, a function that has more similarities with the role of an advisor than with that of a passive platform or an active news agency.[39] Their very conceptualization has an impact on the proper definition of their responsibilities and liabilities for the violation of rights that may take place in (or make use of) cyberspace.[40]

38 The very distinction between vertical and horizontal effects seems rather old-fashioned, since it is reminiscent of a hierarchical description of society centered on its political system. As stressed by Teubner (2012) *Constitutional Fragments*, p. 124ff, the main function of human rights is to protect institutional and individual autonomy against the expansive and "totalitarian" rationalities of functional systems in general and not only politics.

39 Grimmelmann (2014) 'Speech engines'.

40 The EU's Directive on electronic commerce states, as a general rule, that intermediary service providers are not liable for the content uploaded and circulated on their networks, servers and platforms by third parties. See: Articles 12–15 of *Directive 2000/31/EC of the European Parliament and of the Council of 8 June 2000 on certain legal aspects of information society services, in particular electronic commerce, in the Internal Market.* Although search engines like Google may, in theory, qualify for this general

Search engines like Google have certainly contributed to the expansion of the possibilities of producing and accessing information, of publishing and finding content online. These gains in terms of freedom of expression are usually associated, however, with a loss in terms of privacy. In order to get the benefits of the wide and free access to information, one has to provide more information about oneself. The benefits of enhanced free speech come, then, with an inevitable privacy cost. One pays with one's own data in order to get wide and free access to global data flows.[41]

From a constitutional perspective, though, it is also possible to stress the mutual interdependence between privacy and freedom of expression beyond their seemingly obvious and inevitable economic trade-offs. Human rights activists and practitioners usually refer to this as the "indivisibility of human rights", the fact that human rights presuppose and depend on each other, having a mutually reinforcing effect.[42]

In order to freely express oneself in public, one needs to have the guarantee of a private space that is not subjected to constant public scrutiny. In the same way, in order to effectively protect one's private sphere, one needs access to information and the freedom to express oneself and take part in public life. Without privacy there is no public communication and without transparency, accountability and free speech there is no protection of privacy at all. Privacy and freedom of expression may be understood, then, as two sides of the same coin (or distinction). The distinction itself is more important than any of its sides, especially because each side presupposes and cannot exist without the other.[43]

While dissolving rigid hierarchical orders and loosening the ties between fixed social position, the functional differentiation of modern society also poses new threats to the then autonomous individuals, to the integrity of their "bodies and minds". The growing bureaucratization of social life and the increasing dependence of society on its formal organizations require some institutional counterbalances in the form of rights that protect the individual against impersonal

exemption of liability, its applicability to concrete cases may give rise to numerous situations in which freedom of expression may be restricted without legitimate grounds. On the lack of adequate legal protection for search engines in Europe against request for removal of search results: Hoboken (2009) 'Search engine law and freedom of expression'. On the more general risks of censoring search: Grimmelmann (2014) 'Speech engines'.

41 Downes (2010) 'A market approach to privacy policy'; Muth (2009) 'Googlestroika'; Newman (2014) 'The costs of lost privacy. On the limits of the traditional law and economics approach to privacy: Pasquale (2013) 'Privacy, antitrust, and power'.

42 Clapham (2006) *Human Rights Obligations of Non-State Actors*; Alston (ed) (2005) *Non-State Actors and Human Rights.*

43 Habermas would speak here of the co-originality and co-evolution of the public and private spheres: Habermas (1991 [1962]) *The Structural Transformation of the Public Sphere*; Habermas (1996 [1992]) *Between Facts and Norms.* Arendt (1998 [1958]) *The Human Condition*, p. 68ff, in her turn, refers to the "discovery of intimacy" as a sort of reaction to the blurring of boundaries between public and private that would be typical of mass society.

communicative processes, that is to say, against the autonomous functioning of social systems. First of all, against politics and its "totalitarian tendencies", but also against the economy and the mass media.[44]

Privacy is probably the best example of a right that aims to protect individual consciousness from the "immaterial" and "moral" risks stemming directly from social communication and its invasive tendencies.[45] It may be described as a sort of paradoxical right to inclusion by means of exclusion. It provides a boundary that excludes some aspects of private life from public consideration. The aim is to ensure that the general inclusion of people in society and its organizations remains open and independent from specific elements that are particular to the self. It somehow immunizes the self against the selectivity of social systems and their specialized mechanisms of inclusion and exclusion. One may, then, choose one's own way of life without necessarily pre-determining one's prospects of political participation, opportunities of employment, access to justice and the possibility of engaging in social interactions more generally.

By protecting a space of social indifference regarding one's own personality, privacy allows the differentiation of society to cope with the individualization of individuals.[46] In other words, privacy gives people some say about their social identity, about which (individual) differences should make a (social) difference, which elements of their lives, elements that they may be able to control, may legitimately influence decisions about their lives, decisions that they may not be able to control. It entails an element of freedom and dignity that reinforces equality, working as a fundamental guarantee that one may be different without being discriminated against.

The traditional understanding of the right to privacy as the "right to be let alone", as formulated in the second half of the nineteenth century, was a reaction to the evolution of the mass media and the spread of new technologies for the storage and diffusion of data such as photography.[47] Since its consolidation, the freedom of the press has also implied some form of freedom from the press, that is to say, freedom from mass communication and mass surveillance.[48]

The evolution of privacy during the twentieth century may be read in the context of the evolution of the language of rights more generally, the dynamic and often turbulent "plot of rights" that constitutes one of the central elements of

44 Luhmann (2002 [1965]) *I Diritti Fondamentali come Istituzione*; Verschraegen (2002) 'Human rights and modern society'; Teubner (2012) *Constitutional Fragments*, p. 124ff.

45 Warren and Brandeis (1890) 'The right to privacy', p. 197, had already stressed the seriousness of the immaterial "injuries to the feelings" against which the right to privacy should offer protection.

46 On role of privacy in the protection of the "situated practices of boundary management through which the capacity for self-determination develops": Cohen (2013) 'What privacy is for', p. 1905ff.

47 According to Kittler (1999 [1986]) *Gramophone, Film, Typewriter*, p. 16ff, this was the time of the emergence and spread of technical media.

48 The classical reference in the legal literature is still Warren and Brandeis (1890) 'The right to privacy'.

constitutional democracy. A historical process in which the re-configuration of politics comes together with the re-configuration of law. As the masses struggle for the rights to political participation and economic welfare, these struggles also entail a redefinition of the right to privacy, a redefinition, indeed, of the very boundaries between the public and private spheres.

From an alleged bourgeois privilege claimed mainly by the propertied classes against the indiscretions of the "gossip press", the right to privacy comes to be perceived as a general condition of freedom, equality and dignity. It comes to be perceived not just as a synonym for the intimacy and sanctity of the home, as a sort of extension of private property, restricted, then, to those who can afford it. It goes beyond that and comes to entail the overall claim that one should be treated with equal respect and consideration by public and private organizations whose decisions may directly affect one's private life, social identity and social inclusion more generally. Organizations that are increasingly opaque to people, while people and their data are increasingly transparent to them.[49]

Organizational and technological changes certainly pose new challenges to privacy and to the very distinction between public and private. Instead of the often-announced "end of privacy",[50] these changes entail a re-birth of privacy itself, its very re-conceptualization, even if in more difficult conditions.[51]

One such re-birth or re-conceptualization, probably the major one, was caused by the invention and spread of computers. The "computational turn" has generated since its beginnings a specific form of privacy risk.[52] As already discussed above, computers reduce not only the reality of society and the world in which we live to binary data, but also people and their social identities, whose digital fragments may be constantly collected, combined, re-combined and diffused by automatic means. Their private lives and social identities become ever more exposed and available for economic, administrative and political manipulation.

Nevertheless, as organizations and people move online, so does privacy. Law has reacted to these new challenges by introducing a new dimension (or meaning) to the right to privacy, providing it with an adapted form to the digital medium:

49 On the evolution and re-configuration of privacy in the context of the "plot of rights": Rodotà (2005) *Intervista su Privacy e Libertà*, p. 7ff; Rodotà (2012) *Il Diritto di Avere Diritti*, p. 378ff; Rodotà (2014) *Il Mondo nella Rete*, e-book 24%ff. Rodotà (2005) *Intervista su Privacy e Libertà*, p. 55ff, mentions the interesting and rather paradoxical example of Italy, where the right to privacy, previously undermined as a sort of "bourgeois relic", was first formally introduced in Italian law by the Labour Act of 1970 (*Statuto dei Lavoratori*) to protect employees from the discriminatory surveillance of employers. On the complexity and multiple dimensions of the right to privacy: Solove (2006) 'A taxonomy of privacy'; Cohen (2013) 'What privacy is for'; Nissenbaum (2004) 'Privacy as contextual integrity'; Nissenbaum (2010) *Privacy in Context*; Nissenbaum (2011) 'A contextual approach to privacy online'.

50 *The Economist* (1999) 'The end of privacy'; *Guardian* (2010) 'Privacy no longer a social norm, says Facebook founder'; Baker (2010) 'The privacy problem'.

51 Solove (2008) 'The end of privacy?'; Zimmer (2010) 'Privacy protection in the next digital decade'.

52 Hildebrandt and Vries (eds) (2013) *Privacy, Due Process and the Computational Turn.*

the right to the protection of personal data. The main purpose of this right is not to simply block the circulation of personal data, but to insist on the same sort of "boundary management" that is typical of privacy.[53] Regulating the collection and use of personal data is a means of guaranteeing some form of informational self-determination, to give people some control over how information about them is used by others, a sort of control over their "electronic bodies".[54]

The use of computerized databases by public and private organizations was already a matter of concern during the 1970s and 1980s, when specific legislation and judicial decisions started to be adopted in European countries such as France and Germany, and the first international legal instruments dealing with the automatic processing of personal data were negotiated at the level of the OECD and the Council of Europe.[55]

In order to unify and give more consistency to the fragmented legislation of its Member States, in 1995 the EU adopted its famous Data Protection Directive (DPD), which set an important precedent for the legislative protection of personal data around the world.[56] It was later complemented in 2002 by the so-called ePrivacy Directive, which lays down specific rules for the protection of the privacy of the users of electronic communications services.[57]

Both directives have always had the dual goal of protecting individuals while also promoting the internal market. They have established a common regulatory framework for the collection, processing and use of personal data in the EEA, which Member States had to internalize in order to "approximate" their laws and, then, reduce the obstacles to the movement of data across their borders. They have added up a new dimension to the four fundamental freedoms of the internal market: the "free movement of data", which is supposed to be enhanced by means of a more or less uniform set of rules.

The right to the protection of personal data is also listed in the Charter of Fundamental Rights of the European Union of 2000 just after the traditional right to "respect for private and family life". These two formally differentiated rights may be seen together as elements of privacy in its broader sense, as the protection of the private sphere of individuals both offline and online.[58]

53 Cohen (2013) 'What privacy is for', p. 1905ff.

54 Rodotà (2014) *Il Mondo nella Rete*, e-book 27%ff.

55 OECD (2013) *The OECD Privacy Framework*; Council of Europe (1981) *Convention for the Protection of Individuals with Regard to Automatic Processing of Personal Data*. The issue of data protection also made its entry on the agenda of the UN: UNGA (1990) *Guidelines for the Regulation of Computerized Personal Data Files*.

56 EU (1995) *Directive 95/46/EC of the European Parliament and of the Council of 24 October 1995 on the protection of individuals with regard to the processing of personal data and on the free movement of such data*.

57 EU (2002) *Directive 2002/58/EC of the European Parliament and of the Council of 12 July 2002 concerning the processing of personal data and the protection of privacy in the electronic communications sector*.

58 According to Articles 7 and 8 of the Charter: "Article 7 – Respect for private and family life: Everyone has the right to respect for his or her private and family life, home and communications. Article 8 – Protection of personal data: 1. Everyone has the right

If privacy in its more traditional sense demands respect, restraint, the absence of intrusion or intervention, the protection of personal data has a more active and procedural meaning. It demands the existence of a more detailed set of rules and procedures to regulate the collection, processing and use of personal data in order to guarantee that these activities will be carried out in a fair and limited way, based on the consent of individuals or another previously established legal basis. It gives people the right to access their data and to take part in their processing, providing for an independent authority to control compliance with the applicable rules and regulations.[59]

To a certain extent, data protection has more to do with due process and access to information than with the liberal conceptualization of privacy as a "negative freedom".[60] It is, indeed, both negative and positive, private and public. It requires restraint by providing for constraint. In an attempt to counter-balance and re-distribute power over "data objects", it demands transparency from organizations and technologies while conferring rights and prerogatives upon "data subjects". The exclusion of the private is matched by an inclusion in the public. The protection of the private sphere is achieved by the further "publicization" of economic, administrative and digital bureaucracies.[61]

to the protection of personal data concerning him or her. 2. Such data must be processed fairly for specified purposes and on the basis of the consent of the person concerned or some other legitimate basis laid down by law. Everyone has the right of access to data which has been collected concerning him or her, and the right to have it rectified. 3. Compliance with these rules shall be subject to control by an independent authority". The right to the protection of personal data is also mentioned in the founding treaties of the EU: (i) Article 16 of the TFEU deals with the general right to data protection and provides for the use of the ordinary legislative procedure to regulate its application to activities that fall within the scope of EU law; and (ii) Article 39 of the TEU contains an exception to this general clause, providing for the use of a special legislative procedure in which the Council alone shall regulate issues of data protection that fall within the scope of the common foreign and security policy. The right to privacy in its more traditional form is also protected by international treaties which the Member States of the EU are a party to, such as the UN International Covenant on Civil and Political Rights (Article 17) and the Council of Europe's European Convention on Human Rights (Article 8). For an overview on the main laws, regulations and legal precedents in the field of European data protection law: FRA and Council of Europe (2014) *Handbook on European Data Protection Law*.

59 Rodotà (2014) *Il Mondo nella Rete*, e-book 28%ff; Albers (2014) 'Realizing the complexity of data protection'.

60 Vries (2013) 'Privacy, due process and the computational turn'; Kerr (2013) 'Prediction, pre-emption, presumption'; Rouvroy (2013) 'The end(s) of critique'. According to Albers (2014) 'Realizing the complexity of data protection', p. 224: "Data protection aims at regulating data processing, but precisely also at regulating the generation of information and knowledge, at influencing the decisions based on such generation, and at preventing adverse consequences for the individuals affected."

61 Koops (2013) 'On decision transparency, or how to enhance data protection after the computational turn'; Hildebrandt (2013) 'Profile transparency by design?'. Even those who seem to strategically despise the right to privacy as a "reactionary defense of the status-quo" vis-à-vis the essential security services provided by the state and its intelligence agencies acknowledge that some degree of transparency and

This concern with the growing power of bureaucracies and centralized databases is, indeed, at the root of the new configuration of privacy and its "re-birth" as data protection. The problem is not simply that one's private life and intimate secrets may be uncovered and exposed in public, which is, indeed, a constant risk that has to be taken seriously. An even more serious problem, though, is that of losing any control of how, and to what extent, the processing of one's own personal data has an impact on concrete measures and decisions that directly affect one's private life, social identity and general prospects of inclusion.[62]

This is not a brand-new problem. It is, instead, the result of the intensification of the particular risks that the progressive functional differentiation and bureaucratization of social life create to the "human environment" of society. Digital technologies and digital bureaucracies intensify the risks of modern technology and modern bureaucracy more generally, the risks of people being constantly affected by the arbitrary consequences of decisions taken by others without their consent, participation or even awareness.[63] Social differentiation and personal individualization bring about new possibilities for autonomy and self-determination, but also new risks in terms of blind automation and the general disempowerment of individuals.

The spread of the Internet during the 1990s, together with the current frenzy over big data, have brought the "plot of privacy" to a new level or "chapter", one that is currently being written in the context of a wide transatlantic and transnational conflict, in which the European strong privacy legislation tends to collide with the main practices and business models of the "data-driven economy" dominated by big transnational corporations of US origin such as Google.[64]

Artefacts for data collection, storage, processing and transmission are now ubiquitous and interconnected. Compounding the problem of surveillance by bureaucratic organizations with centralized databases, the new possibilities of decentralized eavesdropping of people on their peers pose new risks and dilemmas for the protection of privacy.[65] Computers have become smaller and more

accountability may be legitimately demanded from agents and agencies with access to the bulk collection of data, so that the necessary discretion (or indiscretion) of governments may be balanced by some sort of "technological audit". See: Baker (2010) 'The privacy problem'.

62 Solove (2006) 'A taxonomy of privacy', p. 487ff; Solove (2001) 'Privacy and power', p. 1426ff; Magnani (2013) 'Abducting personal data, destroying privacy', p. 78ff.

63 Luhmann (2005 [1991]) *Risk*.

64 On the transatlantic and transnational conflict between the EU and the US over the interrelated issues of freedom of expression and privacy online: Whitman (2004) 'The two Western cultures of privacy'; Kobrin (2004) 'Safe harbours are hard to find'; Bernal (2014) 'The EU, the US and right to be forgotten'; De Busser (2014) 'Privatization of information and the data protection reform', p. 141ff.

65 Zittrain (2008) *The Future of the Internet*, p. 200ff, refers to the new risks of widespread and decentralized mass surveillance posed by the very generativity of the Net as a problem of "Privacy 2.0", which would compound the earlier problem of "Privacy 1.0", related to the risks of abuse of personal data by centralized databases owned by governments and corporations, the "Big Brother" and the "Little Brother" respectively. On the privacy risks posed by databases in general: Solove (2001) 'Privacy and

powerful, while databases have grown bigger and more decentralized, as different machines are now constantly "talking to each other" and exchanging data over a global network. To a certain extent, we may even say these digital artefacts are "talking about us", as profiles of people get richer and more detailed, generating real-time information that may be permanently acted upon in the form of automatic (or semi-automatic) measures and decisions that have a concrete effect on our lives.[66]

The EU has set one of the main stages of the "plot". Connected with its overall strategy to enhance the competitiveness of its "digital single market", in April 2016 the EU adopted two new pieces of legislation on the protection of personal data in order to modernize its legal framework and address the new challenges posed by the Internet: the General Data Protection Regulation (GDPR),[67] which substituted the DPD of 1995, and a directive on the processing of personal data for the purposes of law enforcement and criminal prosecution.[68] Both of them entered into force in May 2018.[69]

Moreover, the EU has recently adopted a new regulation on data protection applicable specifically to its own institutions and bodies.[70] It is also currently discussing the adoption of an ePrivacy Regulation to substitute the ePrivacy Directive

power'. On the current risks posed by the emergence of big data and analytics: Tene and Polonetsky (2012) 'Privacy in the age of big data'.

66 On the growing use of profiling techniques for security, administrative and business purposes and the consequent risks to privacy and data protection: Bechmann (2013) 'Internet profiling'; Otterlo (2013) 'A machine learning view on profiling'; Kerr (2013) 'Prediction, pre-emption, presumption'; Hildebrandt (2013) 'Profile transparency by design?'.

67 EU (2016) *Regulation (EU) 2016/679 of the European Parliament and of the Council of 27 April 2016 on the protection of natural persons with regard to the processing of personal data and on the free movement of such data, and repealing Directive 95/46/EC.*

68 EU (2016) *Directive (EU) 2016/680 of the European Parliament and of the Council of 27 April 2016 on the protection of natural persons with regard to the processing of personal data by competent authorities for the purposes of the prevention, investigation, detection or prosecution of criminal offences or the execution of criminal penalties, and on the free movement of such data, and repealing Council Framework Decision 2008/977/JHA.*

69 On the main reasons that a reform in EU data protection law was called for: European Commission (2012) *Commission proposes a comprehensive reform of data protection rules to increase users' control of their data and to cut costs for businesses*; European Commission (2014) *Inspiring trust: stronger data protection rules to boost the Digital Single Market*; Gutwirth, Leenes and De Hert (eds) (2014) *Reloading Data Protection*. The very option of the use of regulations instead of directives is meant to provide more unity and consistency and to avoid unnecessary fragmentation in the legal framework, since regulations have "general application" and are "binding in [their] entirety and directly applicable in all Member States", while directives are binding only in regard to "the result to be achieved", leaving "to the national authorities the choice of form and methods" (Article 288 of TFEU).

70 EU (2018) *Regulation (EU) 2018/1725 of the European Parliament and of the Council of 23 October 2018 on the protection of natural persons with regard to the processing of personal data by the Union institutions, bodies, offices and agencies and on the free movement of such data, and repealing Regulation (EC) No 45/2001 and Decision No 1247/2002/EC.*

of 2002 in order to deal with the new trends of the market for electronic communications, since more and more people are using Internet-related alternatives for communication, such as voice over IP and instant messaging, in the place of traditional telephony.[71]

Besides this new regulatory framework, recent decisions of the CJEU are also contributing to framing the global debate over privacy and data protection online. A debate in which Google is again a central actor or player.

4.3 The case law of the CJEU

From the large and complex case law of the CJEU, two recent decisions already mentioned in the introduction to the book are particularly relevant to the activities of Google and to the protection of privacy in the context of the increasingly accelerated global flows of data and information: (i) the decision on the so-called "right to be forgotten", or "right to delist" (from now on, *Google Spain*),[72] which directly affects Google and its global activities of intermediation and provision of information online, and (ii) the decision on the "Safe Harbour Agreement" (from now on, *Schrems*),[73] which affects the company indirectly by forcing, in practice, a change in the rules for cross-border transfer of personal data between the EU and the US. The following subsections, as well as the next section, focus mainly on these two cases, even if other cases are referred to in order to better understand and contextualize them.[74]

4.3.1 Publishing, searching and forgetting content online

Before *Google Spain*, the applicability of the DPD to the Internet was first put to test in the *Bodil Lindqvist* case in 2003.[75] Bodil Lindqvist was a Swedish woman who had published on her personal website information about people who were voluntarily working with her in a parish of the Swedish Protestant Church. The information published was mostly trivial, regarding the day-to-day activities of the parish and its parishioners.[76] She was being, nonetheless, criminally prosecuted for the processing of personal data by automatic means and their transfer to a third country without legal authorization and without the consent of the subjects involved, which constituted a criminal offence according to Swedish law. After

71 European Commission (2017) *Commission proposes high level of privacy rules for all electronic communications and updates data protection rules for EU institutions.*

72 CJEU (2014) *Case C-131/12: Google Spain SL, Google Inc. v Agencia Española de Protección de Datos, Mario Costeja González.*

73 CJEU (2015) *Case C-362/14: Maximillian Schrems v Data Protection Commissioner.*

74 Information about the facts and arguments of the cases is based on the official documents of the court.

75 CJEU (2003) *Case C-101/01: Criminal Proceedings against Bodil Lindqvist.*

76 The most "serious" piece of information published seems to have been about the foot injury of one of her colleagues that led to part-time sick leave, something that constitutes, nevertheless, a sensitive category of personal data according to Article 8 of the DPD, since it relates to a person's health.

being fined by the District Court, she appealed against the sentence. The Court of Appeal (*Göta hovrätt*), then, stood the proceedings and referenced the case to the CJEU for a preliminary ruling on the applicability of the DPD.

The main conclusions of the CJEU were threefold. First, the publication of even trivial information about people on the Internet may be qualified as a "processing of personal data wholly or partly by automatic means".[77] Second, the mere fact that the information may be accessed from other countries does not constitute, however, a "transfer of personal data to a third country". Otherwise, every uploading of personal data on the Internet would be considered as a sort of worldwide transfer, since, once published, the data might be accessed by any computer in the world with an Internet connection.[78] Third, Member States have a "margin of maneuver" in the implementation of the DPD and it is the obligation of the national authorities to ensure a fair balance between privacy and freedom of expression in concrete cases, as well as between the free movement of data in the EU and the protection of private life. In other words, instead of considering whether the conduct of the defendant might be covered by the right to freedom of expression, the CJEU left the final conclusion about the criminal nature of the conduct to the Swedish courts.[79]

The case is interesting because it concerns the potential privacy harms stemming from the actions of ordinary citizens who publish information about their peers without the use of any particularly complex technology besides the setting up of a

77 A wide definition of the activity of "processing" is provided by both Article 2(b) of the DPD and Article 4(2) of the GDPR.

78 The court has based its reasoning here on the unreasonable nature of the legal consequences of the opposing interpretation: "If Article 25 of Directive 95/46 were interpreted to mean that there is 'transfer [of data] to a third country' every time that personal data are loaded onto an internet page, that transfer would necessarily be a transfer to all the third countries where there are the technical means needed to access the internet. The special regime provided for by Chapter IV of the directive would thus necessarily become a regime of general application, as regards operations on the internet. Thus, if the Commission found, pursuant to Article 25(4) of Directive 95/46, that even one third country did not ensure adequate protection, the Member States would be obliged to prevent any personal data being placed on the internet" (CJEU (2003) *Case C-101/01: Criminal Proceedings against Bodil Lindqvist*, p. 13020).

79 Since the preliminary ruling only concerns the interpretation of EU law, the application of the norms, as interpreted by the CJEU, to the concrete facts of the case is a task for the national courts, which dispose of a "margin of maneuver" to interpret themselves the interpretation of the CJEU. This division of tasks, as well the recognition of this "margin of maneuver", is a common strategy of self-restraint that allows the European courts to provide for some degree of uniformity in the application of EU law, while at the same time leaving some space for national accommodations. To a certain extent, it is a paradoxical strategy for combining unity with diversity, or, in systems theory terms, redundancy with variety. The European Court of Human Rights uses a similar strategy, which is known as the doctrine of the "margin of appreciation". See: Greer (2000) *The Margin of Appreciation*; Rosenfeld (2008) 'Rethinking constitutional ordering in an era of legal and ideological pluralism', p. 33ff. On the management of the distinction redundancy/variety by legal argumentation in general: Luhmann (1995) 'Legal argumentation'; Luhmann (2008 [1993]) *Law as a Social System*, p. 305ff.

webpage. There is no centralized database, no complex algorithm, no government or corporate power involved, no malicious intent, no relevant public scandal. The case is about common people writing about common people on the Internet. It is also about the autonomy of one specific Member State to impose its own rigid standards on privacy and data protection upon its own citizens (or residents).[80]

A decade later, the court again had to face a major and certainly much more relevant issue of data protection on the Internet in *Google Spain.* By then, the important role of search engines in cyberspace, the dominant presence of Google in the European market and the details about the US widespread policy of mass surveillance online were part of the landscape. The European Commission had already proposed the introduction of a specific "right to be forgotten", or "right to erasure", when launching the debate about the reform of its data protection legislation.[81] A right that remains controversial even after its formal recognition by the CJEU.

In *Google Spain*, the now "unforgettable" Mario Costeja Gonzáles, a Spanish citizen resident in Spain, lodged a complaint with the Spanish Data Protection Authority (*Agencia Española de Protección de Datos – AEPD*) against the newspaper *La Vanguardia* and both Google Spain and its parent company Google Inc. on 5 March 2010. The main cause of the complaint was that a search on Google for his name showed links to pages of two old printed editions of the newspaper from 1998 which contained an announcement of a real-estate auction connected with attachment proceedings taken by the Spanish Ministry of Labour and Social Security against him for the recovery of social security debts.

Mr. Gonzáles argued that the pages contained information about him that was related to old legal proceedings that had already been resolved and were no longer

80 The EU legal tolerance for this kind of "Nordic sensitivity" does not seem to be acceptable in terms of the US tradition of free speech. See: Garcia (2005) 'Bodil Lindqvist'.

81 European Commission (2012) *Commission proposes a comprehensive reform of data protection rules to increase users' control of their data and to cut costs for businesses.* After many iterations and changes in wording, the GDPR of 2016 contains an explicit reference to the right to erasure as a "right to be forgotten" in its Article 17, which reads as follows: "Article 17 – Right to erasure ('right to be forgotten') 1. The data subject shall have the right to obtain from the controller the erasure of personal data concerning him or her without undue delay and the controller shall have the obligation to erase personal data without undue delay where one of the following grounds applies: (a) the personal data are no longer necessary in relation to the purposes for which they were collected or otherwise processed; (b) the data subject withdraws consent on which the processing is based according to point (a) of Article 6(1), or point (a) of Article 9(2), and where there is no other legal ground for the processing; (c) the data subject objects to the processing pursuant to Article 21(1) and there are no overriding legitimate grounds for the processing, or the data subject objects to the processing pursuant to Article 21(2); (d) the personal data have been unlawfully processed; (e) the personal data have to be erased for compliance with a legal obligation in Union or Member State law to which the controller is subject; (f) the personal data have been collected in relation to the offer of information society services referred to in Article 8 (1) [child's consent]."

relevant. He asked the newspaper to delete the pages from its online database and asked Google to no longer show the links to the pages when a search was made for his name. The claim was legally based on his fundamental right to data protection, which comprised his right to object to the processing of his personal data and demand its erasure and blocking, since the processing was allegedly no longer adequate and relevant and there was no legitimate basis for its further processing.

On 30 July 2010, the Agencia Española de Protección de Datos (AEPD) rejected the complaint against the newspaper, since the personal data contained on its webpages were all related to public and official information that had been lawfully published. However, it upheld the claim against Google and ordered the company to no longer make available the links to the pages when a search was made for the name of the complainant. Google appealed against the decision to the Spanish court with competence over the decisions of high administrative authorities (*Audiencia Nacional*). The court then referred the case to the CJEU for a preliminary ruling on the application of the DPD to search engines on 27 February 2012.[82]

The CJEU published its ruling on 13 May 2014. It revolves around three main issues: (i) the territorial scope of application of the DPD regarding Google Spain and its parent company; (ii) the material scope of application of the Directive regarding the interpretation of the concepts of "processing of personal data" and "data controller" in the context of the activities carried out by search engines; and (iii) the nature and extent of the right claimed by the Spanish citizen.

Regarding the territorial scope, the court considered that the local advertising and commercial activities carried out by Google Spain are closely connected to the operation of the search engine by its parent company, Google Inc., since the "free services" offered by the latter are remunerated by means of the selling of advertising that is facilitated by the former. Independently of the physical place where the data is effectively processed, whether in Spain, the US or another third country, there is a clear link between the collection and processing of the data and the commercial and advertising activities carried out by the Spanish establishment in relation to the residents of Spain.

The alleged "extraterritoriality" of the global data flows operated and managed by Google was, then, "re-territorialized" based on a realistic economic assessment of its business model. Since its advertising services are always targeted to a certain public, taking into consideration relevant elements such as national language and territorial location, a public whose personal data is constantly collected, processed and transmitted by computers and networks around the world, this public may enforce their rights against the company where the relevant activities of data collection and targeted advertising are presumed to take place. The court then concluded that the collection and processing of personal data by Google in relation to the Spanish citizen were carried out in the context of the activities of its Spanish

82 Audiencia Nacional del Reino de España (2014) *Procedimiento Ordinario 725/2010: Google Spain SL, Google Inc. v Agencia Española de Protección de Datos, Mario Costeja González.*

establishment, so that the DPD and the related Spanish implementing legislation were perfectly applicable to the case.[83]

Regarding the material scope, the court had already established in *Bodil Lindqvist* a broad interpretation for the concept of "processing of personal data", an interpretation that matches the broad definition of the term by the DPD. Hence, there was no difficulty in applying the concept either to search engines or to professional webpublishers such as a well-established newspaper. Since ordinary citizens who publish trivial information about their peers on the Internet may be considered to "process personal data" for the purposes of the Directive, so does a company whose mission is to organize and make this information available worldwide.

The court also considered that Google was not only a "data processor", but also a "data controller", the one that determines the "purposes and means" of the processing.[84] It drew a distinction between the processing carried out by webpublishers and the one carried out by search engines. If the webpublisher is the one that originally uploads the data on the Web, the search engine is the one responsible for collecting the data, aggregating and organizing them according to specific criteria and making them available to be found by a much larger audience.

The latter processing is not only different from the former, it is also much more relevant and potentially disturbing to data subjects. It allows a vast amount of information to be generated about them out of previously scattered, unrelated and unstructured data. Small pieces of data may then be automatically gathered and combined in order to provide a detailed profile about someone, with increased risks to one's rights to privacy and data protection. If these rights were to be

83 One year later, the same reasoning of *Google Spain* was used as a precedent by the court in the *Weltimmo* case, in which a company registered in Slovakia that ran a property dealing website concerning Hungarian properties forwarded personal data about its Hungarian clients to debt collection agencies without their consent. See: CJEU (2015), *Case C-230/14: Weltimmo s. r. o. v Nemzeti Adatvédelmi és Információszabadság Hatóság*. The general issue of territorial jurisdiction on the Internet had already been dealt with by French courts back in 2001 in a famous and often-quoted "leading case" in which Yahoo! was ordered to implement geolocation and geoblocking technology in order to prevent people located in France from accessing websites that auction Nazi memorabilia. See: Reidenberg (2002) 'Yahoo and democracy on the Internet'; Goldsmith and Wu (2006) *Who Controls the Internet?*, p. 1ff.

84 The definitions of "data controller" and "data processor" are provided by Article 2(d)(e) of the (DPD), as well as by Article 5(7)(8) of the GDPR. Contrary to the court, the Advocate General argued that in his opinion, in relation to the processing of content originally published on third-party websites, Google should not be considered a "data controller", since the "purposes and means of the processing" were not specifically determined by it. See: CJEU (2014) *Case C-131/12: Google Spain SL, Google Inc. v Agencia Española de Protección de Datos, Mario Costeja González*, Opinion of the Advocate General, p. 16ff. The same opinion had already been stated long before the case by the so-called "Article 29 Data Protection Working Party", an influential advisory body composed of representatives of European data protection authorities, according to which search engines should not be considered "data controllers" when acting as "pure intermediaries" in the provision of content online. See: WP29 (2008) *Opinion 1/2008 on data protection issues related to search engines*, p. 13ff.

widely and effectively protected, such as intended by the Directive, the obligations and duties of a data controller had to be imposed on search engines like Google.[85] Having clarified the territorial and material scope of the Directive and its applicability to the case, the court, then, assessed the nature and extent of the right at stake.

In their activities of crawling the Web, indexing and ranking its content and making it available for further retrieval, search engines do not establish any particular relationship with the people whose data are collected and processed. They neither get their consent – which would not be possible anyway, given the wide range of people affected – nor act to perform a specific contract or legal obligation of any sort. Data on the Web is automatically collected, stored, processed and diffused whether they are personal or not. In the case of personal data, the legal basis on which they are processed is the legitimate business interests of search engines themselves, as well as the interest that the general public may have in the availability of these data for online search.

In this situation, data subjects have both the right to object at any time to the processing of data relating to them, as well as the right to demand the erasure of the data or the blocking of the processing activity when the processing is incompatible with the provisions of the DPD, especially when the data are incomplete and inaccurate.[86] The Directive itself sets high standards for the processing of personal data in the form of "principles of data quality", according to which, among other criteria, data must be: "adequate, relevant and not excessive in relation to the purposes for which they are collected and/or further processed", as well as "accurate and, where necessary, kept up to date".[87]

The facts Mr. Gonzáles wanted to be "forgotten" were not intimate, fake or defamatory in nature. They were public and official facts, facts related to legal proceedings that had been regularly taken against him. They had been originally published by the newspaper following a legitimate request made by an official state authority. The information was accurate and complete. There was, moreover, a

85 According to the court (CJEU (2014) *Case C-131/12: Google Spain SL, Google Inc. v Agencia Española de Protección de Datos, Mario Costeja González*, p. 17): "processing of personal data, such as that at issue in the main proceedings, carried out by the operator of a search engine is liable to affect significantly the fundamental rights to privacy and to the protection of personal data when the search by means of that engine is carried out on the basis of an individual's name, since that processing enables any internet user to obtain through the list of results a structured overview of the information relating to that individual that can be found on the internet — information which potentially concerns a vast number of aspects of his private life and which, without the search engine, could not have been interconnected or could have been only with great difficulty — and thereby to establish a more or less detailed profile of him. Furthermore, the effect of the interference with those rights of the data subject is heightened on account of the important role played by the internet and search engines in modern society, which render the information contained in such a list of results ubiquitous."

86 Articles 12(b) and 14(a) of the DPD.

87 Article 6 of the DPD.

clear public interest in the newspaper making its old printed editions available online for the purposes of historical research and the preservation of social memory.[88]

According to the reasoning of the court, even if the information published by the newspaper about Mr. Gonzáles was lawful and true, its further processing by a search engine was not necessarily legitimate. As already mentioned, the two forms of processing are different. They have different legal bases and different purposes, as well as different impacts on the private sphere of the data subject.[89]

The court concluded that, in such cases, the rights of the data subject take precedence over the economic interests of the search engine, as well the interest of the public in having the information easily available for an online search. Any balance to be struck in a concrete situation would have to take this *prima facie* precedence into consideration. One of the main elements to be assessed should be the time that has elapsed since the original publication of the facts, as well as its sensitivity to the data subject. Other criteria, though, would also have to be evaluated, such as the eventual role played by the data subject in public life, which would, indeed, weigh in favor of its wide availability online and against its restriction on privacy grounds.

In the end, the court did not expressly mention some new and specific "right to be forgotten", or even a supposed "right to delist".[90] It presented its decision in more traditional terms, as an interpretation of the rights and legal provisions already contained in the DPD, as well as in the EU Charter of Fundamental Rights. Summing up: independently of the truthfulness and lawfulness of the information originally published and of the concrete disadvantages eventually stemming from its wide availability, data subjects have a right to demand search engines to remove links to data related to them from the list of results generated by a specific search for their name when these data are "inadequate, irrelevant or

88 Article 9 of the DPD provides for exemptions and derogations related to freedom of expression.

89 According to the court (CJEU (2014) *Case C-131/12: Google Spain SL, Google Inc. v Agencia Española de Protección de Datos, Mario Costeja González*, p. 18): "it must be stated that not only does the ground, under Article 7 of Directive 95/46, justifying the publication of a piece of personal data on a website not necessarily coincide with that which is applicable to the activity of search engines, but also, even where that is the case, the outcome of the weighing of the interests at issue to be carried out under Article 7(f) and subparagraph (a) of the first paragraph of Article 14 of the directive may differ according to whether the processing carried out by the operator of a search engine or that carried out by the publisher of the web page is at issue, given that, first, the legitimate interests justifying the processing may be different and, second, the consequences of the processing for the data subject, and in particular for his private life, are not necessarily the same."

90 The misleading label "right to be forgotten" has been stressed by both critics and supporters of the judgment: Kulk and Borgesius (2014) '*Google Spain v. González*', p. 12; Kuner (2015) 'The Court of Justice of the EU judgment on data protection and Internet search engines', p. 7; Lynskey (2015) 'Control over personal data in a digital age', p. 528ff.

no longer relevant, or excessive in relation to the purposes of their original processing".[91]

Later on, on 29 December 2014, when applying the preliminary ruling to the facts of the case, the referring court upheld the original decision of the Spanish Data Protection Authority and decided that Mr. Gonzáles had the right to have the links to the newspaper's webpages removed from the list of results generated after a search for his name.[92] Paradoxically, as a quick search for his name on Google shows, he is already remembered, and will probably always be, as the first individual to ever get the right to be forgotten.[93]

The CJEU's ruling has generated a lot of controversy and has been the target of fierce criticism for its alleged deficit in terms of legal reasoning and argumentation, for its limited balancing approach, since the fundamental rights to freedom of expression and access to information were barely considered (or not considered at all) by the court, and also for the questions that have remained open about its future implementation. These and other issues related to the case will be analyzed in the next section.[94]

91 The fourth item of the dispositive part of the ruling reads as follows (CJEU (2014) *Case C-131/12: Google Spain SL, Google Inc. v Agencia Española de Protección de Datos, Mario Costeja González*, p. 21): "Article 12(b) and subparagraph (a) of the first paragraph of Article 14 of Directive 95/46 are to be interpreted as meaning that, when appraising the conditions for the application of those provisions, it should inter alia be examined whether the data subject has a right that the information in question relating to him personally should, at this point in time, no longer be linked to his name by a list of results displayed following a search made on the basis of his name, without it being necessary in order to find such a right that the inclusion of the information in question in that list causes prejudice to the data subject. As the data subject may, in the light of his fundamental rights under Articles 7 and 8 of the Charter, request that the information in question no longer be made available to the general public on account of its inclusion in such a list of results, those rights override, as a rule, not only the economic interest of the operator of the search engine but also the interest of the general public in having access to that information upon a search relating to the data subject's name. However, that would not be the case if it appeared, for particular reasons, such as the role played by the data subject in public life, that the interference with his fundamental rights is justified by the preponderant interest of the general public in having, on account of its inclusion in the list of results, access to the information in question."

92 Audiencia Nacional del Reino de España (2014) *Procedimiento Ordinario 725/2010: Google Spain SL, Google Inc. v Agencia Española de Protección de Datos, Mario Costeja González*, Sentencia.

93 This is a typical case of the so-called "Streisand effect": asking the media to "forget" something usually has the contrary effect of attracting more public attention to the facts that one would like to be "forgotten". It is a manifestation, at the social level, of one famous paradox of memory: while one may strive to remember that one has to remember something, it is not possible to remember to forget, because this would increase remembrance, not forgetting. See: Eco (1988) 'An *ars oblivionalis*?'; Esposito (2017) 'Algorithmic memory and the right to be forgotten on the Web', pp. 6–7. This does not change the fact that Mr. Gonzáles is now remembered not only as a social security debtor, but as a sort of "champion" of the right to privacy online, that is to say, in a more positive light.

94 For a critical assessment of the ruling: Kulk and Borgesius (2014) '*Google Spain v. González*'; Kuner (2015) 'The Court of Justice of the EU judgment on data protection

However, one specific aspect of the case deserves further consideration here. The law may require that certain pieces of information about someone no longer be easily "remembered" on the Web, nonetheless, they will remain "forgotten as data"[95] in some private or public database, or probably both, since the public/private boundary among digital bureaucracies is very tenuous – at least in times of mass surveillance and bulk data collection, which are, by the way, our times.

These databases are not available to the public, even if they "inform" a large number of measures and decisions that are taken about this same public. Besides the vast amounts of content that are constantly being published by people and organizations on the Web, companies like Google also collect, store and process the most varied types of "transaction data" about their users, who usually give their formal "consent" to that when they agree to the company's general terms of use and privacy policies: search history, emails sent and received, instant messages exchanged, websites visited, applications used, advertisements clicked on, videos watched, music listened to, books read, location data, traffic data and all sorts of other data about data (or metadata) that is generated by means of a simple access to the Internet.[96]

These are more restricted kinds of global data flows. The data involved are originally collected from the traces left by people when they access the open Internet, but they are further processed mainly through closed intranets, that is to say, the internal and more protected networks of large organizations. And since intranets are much more secret and opaque, "forgetting" may be, at least to a certain extent, even more difficult to enforce on them. Even if databases become more decentralized and start moving into the "cloud" in order to interact more easily with each other, large parts of them remain controlled and classified. Moreover, the algorithms that sift through and dynamically organize their data are usually treated as business secrets and protected by intellectual property rights.

This situation generates its own sorts of privacy risks. Risks that have also been recently dealt with by the CJEU.

and Internet search engines'; Lynskey (2015) 'Control over personal data in a digital age'; Stute (2015) 'Privacy almighty?'; Esposito (2017) 'Algorithmic memory and the right to be forgotten on the Web'; Derecho a Leer (2014) *The unforgettable history of the seizure to the defaulter Mario Costeja Gonzáles that happened in 1998*. The CJEU is soon expected to provide further clarifications on the territorial scope of the right recognized in *Google Spain* in a case referred to it by the French *Conseil d'État*, in which the main question is whether the links objected to by the data subject should be made inaccessible for searchers worldwide or only in a specific territorial area, be it the state of residence of the data subject or all the Member States of the EU. See: CJEU (2017) *Case C-507/17: Google Inc. v Commission nationale de l'informatique et des libertés.*

95 Marton (2011) 'Forgotten as data – remembered through information'.

96 On the differentiation of the data processing activities of search engines and their two different roles with regard to personal data, as providers of service and as mere providers of content: WP29 (2008) *Opinion 1/2008 on data protection issues related to search engines*, p. 4ff. The distinction between "content data" and "transaction data" is further elaborated in the next section with regard to the "two indexes" of Google.

4.3.2 Collecting, transferring and spying on personal data

In the aftermath of the Snowden revelations and only one month before its ruling on *Google Spain*, the CJEU invalidated the controversial Data Retention Directive of 2006[97] in the *Digital Rights Ireland* case.[98]

The Data Retention Directive was adopted in order to harmonize the legislation of Member States on the mandatory retention of metadata generated in the provision of electronic communications services.[99] It established that companies that provide telecommunications services, as well as "value added services", such as fixed and mobile telephony, Internet telephony (voice over IP), electronic mail and access to the Internet in general were required to retain, for a minimum of six months and a maximum of two years, depending on the specific option of each Member State, "traffic and location data" related to the subscribers of their services. Data that should be made available on request to public authorities for the purposes of the investigation and prosecution of "serious crimes".[100]

The Directive expressly prohibited the retention of the content of the communications or the information accessed, but the sorts of metadata subjected to this form of "mandatory remembering" were wide in scope and very invasive: the source, destination, date, time and duration of the communication, the type of service provided, the equipment used, as well as the identification of the users and their respective locations. Even if the "what" was allegedly to be "forgotten", the "who", "when", "where", "how" and "in which circumstances" were all to be actively "remembered" by the companies in order to be further available to the "competent national authorities".[101]

In *Digital Rights Ireland*, questions about the validity and interpretation of the Directive were referred to the CJEU for a preliminary ruling by the Irish High Court and the Austrian Constitutional Court (*Verfassungsgerichtshof*). Both courts

97 EU (2006) *Directive 2006/24/EC of the European Parliament and of the Council of 15 March 2006 on the retention of data generated or processed in connection with the provision of publicly available electronic communications services or of public communications networks and amending Directive 2002/58/EC.*

98 CJEU (2014) *Joined Cases C-293/12 and C-594/12: Digital Rights Ireland and Seitlinger and Others.*

99 According to the definition provided by Article 2(c) of *Directive 2002/21/EC of the European Parliament and of the Council of 7 March 2002 on a common regulatory framework for electronic communications networks and services (Framework Directive)*, electronic communication services include, generally, the transmission of signals over networks that allow communication to take place at a distance, and do not include services that provide content or that involve any "editorial control" over the content of the communication. The more general concept of "information society services", in its turn, is currently provided by Article 1(b) of *Directive (EU) 2015/1535 of the European Parliament and the Council of 9 September 2015 laying down a procedure for the provision of information in the field of technical regulations and of rules on Information Society services (codification)*: "any service normally provided for remuneration, at a distance, by electronic means and at the individual request of a recipient of services".

100 Article 1 of the Data Retention Directive.

101 Article 5 of the Data Retention Directive describes in detail the data that should be mandatorily retained.

had to stay legal proceedings about legislative and administrative measures involving data retention, since the laws that were being challenged had been adopted in order to transpose the Directive into their respective national legal orders.

The main argument for the invalidation of the Directive by the CJEU was that it violated the general principle of proportionality. The Directive was not invalidated simply because of the incompatibility of mandatory data retention, per se, with the fundamental rights to privacy and data protection. The real problem, according to the court, was that the Directive went too far. The measures were adequate, in theory, to protect the general interest on public security. They were, however, more invasive than strictly necessary to attain this legitimate purpose. When put on the scales, then, the fundamental rights to privacy and data protection weighed more than the public interest in security.[102]

The very analytical and straightforward reasoning of the court may be summarized as follows: (i) the data retention provided for by the Directive constituted a wide-ranging and serious interference in the rights to privacy and to the protection of personal data; (ii) the interference did not adversely affect the essence of these rights, because the Directive prohibited the retention of the content of the communication and mandated the respect for certain principles of data protection and data security; (iii) the interference also satisfied an objective of general interest related to public security and the fight against terrorism and other serious crimes; (iv) given the seriousness of the interference, however, the discretion of the EU legislature was restricted by the principle of proportionality; (v) data retention might be considered an adequate means to attain an objective of general interest related to public security; (vi) the measures adopted by the Directive were not strictly necessary, given the widespread scope of the interference, the general absence of limits to the retention of data and the lack of objective criteria, as well as substantive and procedural conditions, regulating the access and use of the retained data by public authorities; (vii) finally, given its incompatibility with the principle of proportionality, the court did not find it necessary to assess the compatibility of the Directive with the fundamental rights to freedom of expression and access to information.[103]

102 The principle of proportionality is commonly used in order to solve collisions between different fundamental rights or between fundamental rights and "collective needs", allowing a sort of "balancing" of the different rights and interests involved in the conflict. On the mainstream legal doctrine of the "balancing method": Alexy (2003) 'Constitutional rights, balancing and rationality'. For a critical assessment of the method of balancing rights based on the principle of proportionality, which would tend to diminish the effectiveness of fundamental rights by submitting them to the imperative needs of politics and economics: Habermas (1996 [1992]) *Between Facts and Norms*, p. 253ff.

103 More recently, at the end of 2016, the CJEU re-affirmed its reasoning in *Digital Rights Ireland* by ruling that the authorization given by the ePrivacy Directive for the adoption of national legislation on data retention (Article 15(1) of Directive 2002/58/EC) does not allow the general and indiscriminate retention of all traffic and location data of all users of electronic communications services. See: CJEU (2016) *Joined Cases*

To a certain extent, the invalidation of the Data Retention Directive set the stage (or precedent) for a significantly bolder move a year and a half later: the invalidation, in *Schrems*, of the Safe Harbour Agreement between the EU and the US.

The Data Retention Directive itself had a more limited applicability to Internet companies such as Google, since its main focus was on companies that provide electronic communication services such as traditional telephony and Internet access. The provisions on data retention related to Internet telephony and especially electronic mail were applicable, nonetheless, to Google and other similar companies that provide the same services.[104]

The Safe Harbour Agreement, on the other hand, was the general legal framework regulating the cross-border transfer of personal data between the EU and the US, especially the global flows of data between big transnational corporations of the digital economy with a presence on both sides of the North Atlantic.

By invalidating the Data Retention Directive, the CJEU exercised its normal powers of judicial review over acts and decisions adopted by the EU institutions and bodies. By invalidating the Safe Harbour Agreement, it formally did just that, but its powers had, in theory, a much more direct and significant impact on the other side of the North Atlantic, in a sort of transnational (or transatlantic) imposition of checks and balances on the wide and intrusive power over global data flows of the US and its transnational corporations.

The DPD contained specific rules on the transfer of personal data to third countries, that is to say, to countries outside the territory of the European Economic Area (EEA). Basically, it stipulated that such transfers may take place only if the third country provides an "adequate level of protection", which is presumably a level of protection similar to the that provided by the European privacy standards.[105] The Directive itself contained a number of derogations to this clause. Derogations that may be triggered, among other conditions, by the "unambiguous consent" of the data subject to the transfer, or the provision of appropriate legal safeguards by the data controller in the form of contractual clauses and/or binding corporate rules.[106]

Besides these exceptions that are usually applied on a case-by-case basis, the Directive also provided that the "adequate level of protection" in a third country may be generally attested by the European Commission after negotiations with the third country.[107] Instead of counting either on the rather unpredictable interpretation of what constitutes an "adequate level of protection" by multiple European courts and data protection authorities, or on specific derogations applicable on a case-by-case basis, the assessment of the Commission, which is

C-203/15 and C-698/15: Tele2 Sverige and Secretary of State for the Home Department v Post- och telestyrelsen and Others.

104 Besides the provision of electronic mail services by its known platform "Gmail", Google also provides other communication services such as instant messaging, video chat and voice over IP through its platform "Google Hangouts".

105 Article 25(1)(2) of the DPD.

106 Article 26 of the DPD.

107 Article 25(6) of the DPD.

binding on the Member States, provides a much more stable and predictable framework for the cross-border data flows between the EU and the third country, which is in the clear interest of companies operating in both.

The rise and spread of the Internet and the consequent acceleration and, to a certain extent, decentralization of global data flows have made the cross-border protection of personal data much more difficult and complex. Not only are large and transnational organizations automatically exchanging data between themselves on a day-to-day basis, but people too are now a central part of the game, as both "subjects" and "objects", with their personal computers, mobile telephones and other wearable devices globally "communicating with each other".

According to the precedent set in *Bodil Lindqvist*, the mere publication on the Internet of content that contains personal data and that is globally accessible does not constitute, by itself, a cross-border transfer of data that would need special legal protection. However, most data generated out of these data do. The digital traces that people leave online and that are "transacted" with companies like Google in exchange for their "free" data services do qualify for this especial protection. In other words, they need "safe harbors".

On the one hand, information and content published on and circulated through the Internet are usually accessible to anyone who is willing to pay with either money or data, and money itself is increasingly treated as data, "monetary data" that may need to be placed in "havens" that are safe from taxes. On the other hand, personal data that are not meant for publication and that are "transacted" over the Internet, and additionally circulate through multiple intranets, are not and should not be accessible to everyone. Access in this case is an exclusive right of "data subjects", whose personal data is constantly being "processed" by different public and private "controllers". The problem, though, as shown by the Snowden revelations and acknowledged by the CJEU itself, is that when these data flow globally, and they do it all the time, "safe harbors" are increasingly hard to find.[108]

Such an (un)safe harbor was agreed upon by the European Commission and the US government at the beginning of the millennium: the "Safe Harbour Agreement".[109]

The agreement provided a mechanism for the self-certification of US companies regarding the observation of privacy and data protection principles that was supposed to provide an "adequate level of protection" to the processing of personal data transferred from the EU to the US. It was a sort of compromise between the comprehensive and rigorous European data protection legislation and the more flexible and fragmented US sectoral approach to privacy. The aim was to provide a

108 On the complex issues of territoriality, jurisdiction and enforceability related to the regulation of global data flows: Kobrin (2004) 'Safe harbours are hard to find'; Svantesson (2014) 'The extraterritoriality of EU data privacy law'; Kuner (2011) 'Regulation of transborder data flows under data protection and privacy law'.

109 EU (2000) *Commission Decision 2000/520/EC of 26 July 2000 pursuant to Directive 95/46/EC of the European Parliament and of the Council on the adequacy of the protection provided by the safe harbour privacy principles and related frequently asked questions issued by the US Department of Commerce.*

stable and predictable framework for transatlantic data flows, facilitating, therefore, trade and commerce between the EU and the US.[110]

The agreement worked as follows: (i) the US Department of Commerce issued a set of privacy principles, the "Safe Harbor Privacy Principles", as well as further guidance on their application in the form of "Frequently Asked Questions", which stipulated general norms and standards of data protection such as notice and consent, data security, data integrity and right of access; (ii) US companies could, then, voluntarily adhere to the arrangement through a process of self-certification in which they had to disclose a public commitment to comply with the norms and standards, as well as submit themselves to the supervisory authority of a government body in the US, which was either the Federal Trade Commission or the Department of Transportation, depending on the case; (iii) since both the Privacy Principles and the FAQs were approved by the European Commission, self-certified companies would be automatically presumed to provide an "adequate level of protection" to the processing of personal data of citizens and residents of the EU; (iv) finally, the national authorities of the Member States retained the power to suspend data flows to non-compliant organizations in certain specific circumstances.[111]

This rather convoluted legal arrangement was controversial from the outset. The so-called "Article 29 Data Protection Working Party", an influential advisory body composed of representatives of European data protection authorities, raised a number of concerns about the safeguards contained in the arrangement, especially regarding its unclear and rather weak enforcement mechanisms.[112] The European Commission, moreover, approved the arrangement without the express consent of the European Parliament, which had its justified doubts about the "adequate level of protection" provided in the US.[113]

More than a decade later, the Snowden revelations of June 2013 would somehow vindicate these original hesitations. The main problem was not the lack of a comprehensive and more rigorous legislation for data protection applicable to the private sector in the US, which was the reason behind the complex system of self-certification provided for by the agreement. The outrage, instead, was directed toward the absence of safeguards against, and limitations on, the access by public

110 Kobrin (2004) 'Safe harbours are hard to find'. On the differences between the US and the EU approach to privacy: Whitman (2004) 'The two Western cultures of privacy'.

111 These provisions were contained in Articles 1 and 3 of Commission Decision 2000/520/EC.

112 WP29 (2000) *Opinion 4/2000 on the level of protection provided by the "Safe Harbor Principles"*. Other opinions issued by the advisory body on the Safe Harbour Agreement are listed on recital 10 of Commission Decision 2000/520/EC. As its very name indicates, Article 29 Data Protection Working Party was set up by Article 29 of the DPD. With the entrance into force of the GDPR on May 2018, it was replaced by the European Data Protection Board. See: Article 68ff of the GDPR.

113 European Parliament (2000) *Report on the draft Commission decision on the adequacy of the protection afforded by the 'Safe Harbor Privacy Principles' and related frequently asked questions issued by the United States Department of Commerce.*

authorities to the personal data transferred to the US. US national security seemed to have made the safe harbor unsafe for Europe.[114]

To a certain extent, it is possible to say that, in the middle of a new round of transatlantic negotiations to review the agreement and "rebuild trust" among the parties, the invalidation of the original decision of the European Commission was somewhat expected.[115]

In *Schrems*, the privacy advocate and then law student Maximillian Schrems lodged a complaint against Facebook with the Irish Data Protection Commissioner. Although the complainant was an Austrian citizen resident in Austria, the complaint was lodged in Ireland because, like Google, the subsidiary of Facebook in Ireland acts as a sort of European hub for the company. It was lodged on 25 June 2013, just a couple of weeks after the National Security Agency's (NSA's) secret documents started to be leaked to the international press. Mr. Schrems asked the Commissioner to order the suspension of the transfer of his personal data by Facebook Ireland to the US. His argument was that, given the revelation of the US policy of bulk data collection and mass surveillance online, the country did not provide an "adequate level of protection" to the processing of his personal data, which was subjected to wide and indiscriminate access by the law enforcement and intelligence agencies of the US and its closest allies.

The Data Protection Commissioner rejected the complaint on the grounds that the European Commission had already determined that the level of data protection in the US was adequate to meet the EU standards, a decision that was binding on the Member States. Moreover, Mr. Schrems would not have been able to specifically assert that his personal data had been unduly accessed by US public authorities – something, by the way, that would be almost impossible for a common citizen to prove. Mr. Schrems then challenged this decision by bringing an action to the Irish High Court. While reproaching the policy of mass surveillance online, which would violate fundamental rights protected by the Irish Constitution, the Irish High Court referred the case to the CJEU for a preliminary ruling on whether the Safe Harbour Agreement prevented national authorities from investigating a complaint against the transfer of personal data to the US on the basis of the lack of an adequate level of protection.

The CJEU's decision to invalidate the agreement – or, which is the same thing, to invalidate the Commission's decision that approved the agreement – was articulated according to the following argumentative steps: (i) the Commission's decision on the adequate level of protection does not eliminate or reduce the powers of the national authority to examine complaints against the transfer of personal data to a third country in order to enforce the fundamental rights to

114 Annex I to Commission Decision 2000/520/EC, which contained the privacy principles issued by the US Department of Commerce, indicated that the adherence to the principles might be limited "to the extent necessary to meet national security, public interest, or law enforcement requirements".

115 European Commission (2013) *Rebuilding Trust in EU-US Data Flows.*

privacy and to the protection of personal data; (ii) only the court itself, though, can invalidate a decision of the Commission, so that cases in which the validity of such a decision is questioned must be referred to the court for a preliminary ruling; (iii) the Commission had failed by not ascertaining that the level of protection in the US is equivalent to that of the EU, but only that the arrangement, which depends on the voluntary self-certification of companies, provides an adequate level of protection; (iv) since the arrangement itself is not binding on US public authorities, even self-certified companies are bound to disregard the privacy principles in cases of data requests by these authorities on grounds of national security and public interest; (v) the agreement, therefore, allows undue interference by US public authorities in the fundamental rights of European citizens and the Commission did not address this issue in its decision; (vi) widespread and unrestricted collection of, and access to, personal data, even for reasons of public security, are not compatible with fundamental rights; (vii) because of its binding nature on Member States, the Commission's decision may unduly restrict the power of national authorities to protect personal data; (viii) finally, with the invalidation of the decision, the proceedings should be brought back to the consideration of the Irish Data Protection Commissioner, which should assess the original complaint and decide on the request for the suspension of the transfer of personal data to the US.[116]

In a press conference held on the same day the judgment was published, members of the European Commission praised the court's ruling, considering it to be important in order to uphold the fundamental rights of European citizens and

116 Besides the violation of the rights to privacy and data protection, the CJEU also found a violation of the fundamental right to an effective remedy (CJEU (2015) *Case C-362/14: Maximillian Schrems v Data Protection Commissioner*, p. 23): "legislation permitting the public authorities to have access on a generalised basis to the content of electronic communications must be regarded as compromising the essence of the fundamental right to respect for private life .... Likewise, legislation not providing for any possibility for an individual to pursue legal remedies in order to have access to personal data relating to him, or to obtain the rectification or erasure of such data, does not respect the essence of the fundamental right to effective judicial protection, as enshrined in Article 47 of the Charter". In the follow-up of the CJEU's decision, the Irish High Court referred the case again to the CJEU, now for a preliminary ruling on the validity and binding nature of the "Standard Contractual Clauses" used by Facebook, as well as other companies, as a legal basis for the transfer of personal data of European users to the US. The Irish High Court has also questioned the validity and binding nature of the new agreement on transatlantic data flows, the "EU-US Privacy Shield", which is briefly analyzed below. The case is already being called "Schrems II". See: CJEU (2018) *Case C-311/18: Data Protection Commissioner v Facebook Ireland Limited, Maximillian Schrems*. In another recent case involving Mr. Schrems and Facebook, the CJEU ruled that: (i) Mr. Schrems has the right, as a consumer, to sue Facebook in his country of domicile, which is Austria; and (ii) he does not have the right to sue Facebook in his country of domicile in relation to claims assigned to him by other consumers, in a sort of class action. See: CJEU (2018) *Case C-498/16: Maximilian Schrems x Facebook Ireland Limited.*

to reinforce the Commission's stance on the then current negotiations of a new agreement.[117]

Since "safe harbors" are really hard to find, the EU and the US have agreed to establish a new and allegedly stronger "shield" for privacy in order to address the legal issues raised in *Schrems*, especially the lack of enforceability of the privacy principles in relation to US public authorities. On 12 July 2016, less than a year after the judgment, the European Commission approved the new agreement on transatlantic data flows, now re-branded as the "EU-US Privacy Shield".[118]

The new arrangement is similar to the old one, even if its provisions are much more detailed in the form of multiple letters, annexes, attachments and commitments. The core mechanism of voluntary self-certification is retained, with additional instruments for enforcement included, such as company complaints, arbitration procedures and the explicit obligation of companies to cooperate with European data protection authorities.[119]

Regarding access requests by US public authorities, the agreement provides for an "Ombudsperson" to somehow oversee the work of the US "intelligence community" in the collection of "signals intelligence".[120] There is a paradoxical commitment that the bulk collection and processing of personal data will be as "targeted" and "focused" as possible.[121] A commitment that does not seem to

117 European Commission (2015) *First Vice-President Timmermans and Commissioner Jourová's press conference on Safe Harbour following the Court ruling in case C-362/14 (Schrems).*

118 EU (2016) *Commission Implementing Decision (EU) 2016/1250 of 12 July 2016 pursuant to Directive 95/46/EC of the European Parliament and of the Council on the adequacy of the protection provided by the EU-U.S. Privacy Shield.* Following the approval of the Judicial Redress Act by the US at the end of 2015, which extends to European citizens some privacy remedies already guaranteed to US citizens, the EU and the US also signed a comprehensive agreement on the protection of personal data in the context of law enforcement cooperation, the so-called "Umbrella Agreement", which entered into force in February 2017 ("Agreement Between the United States of America and the European Union on the Protection of personal information Relating to the Prevention, Investigation, Detection and Prosecution of Criminal Offences", approved by Council Decision (EU) 2016/2220 of 2 December 2016). In the area of law enforcement and the fight against terrorism, the EU and the US had already signed two other agreements on the exchange of data related to financial transactions and airline transport: "Agreement between the European Union and the United States of America on the processing and transfer of Financial Messaging Data from the European Union to the United States for the purposes of the Terrorist Finance Tracking Program", approved by Council Decision 2010/412/EU of 13 July 2010; and "Agreement between the United States of America and the European Union on the use and transfer of passenger name records to the United States Department of Homeland Security", approved by Council Decision 2012/472/EU of 26 April 2012.

119 Provisions about enforcement are contained in Annex 2 (Annex I and Annex II(III)(11)) of Commission Implementing Decision (EU) 2016/1250.

120 The access requests by public authorities are regulated by Annex 2 (Annex II(III)(16)) of Commission Implementing Decision (EU) 2016/1250, and the activities of the "Ombudsperson" by its Annex A.

121 This paradoxical commitment is contained in Annex VI of Commission Implementing Decision (EU) 2016/1250.

have generated much enthusiasm among European data protection authorities and the Members of the European Parliament, who again reacted with skepticism to the agreement, raising concerns about the effectiveness of the new safeguards and guarantees for the protection of the privacy of European citizens and residents, whose personal data will continue to flow indiscriminately through the networks and databases of US public and private bureaucracies.[122]

It remains to be seen how this new agreement will work in practice, as well as how the "right to be forgotten" recently recognized by European courts and legislators will be enforced in future cases across the continent. What is certain is that these new legal developments will have (or are already having) an impact that goes well beyond Europe and its transatlantic relationships. An impact on the way modern society conceives of its ever more accelerated global data flows and the constitutional questions raised by them.

4.4 Remembrance, forgetting, surveillance

In a world of accelerated global flows of data, information and communication more generally, legislative and judicial decisions tend to spread beyond their original settings. Courts, parliaments and administrative agencies are compelled to keep one eye on their constituencies and the other on each other. Common problems arise and each specific solution delivered to address them ends up having an "irritating" effect in different contexts and situations, generating both convergence and divergence, more redundancy and more variety, the reinforcement of already existing patterns, as well as the stimulus for further differentiations.

The worldwide spread of digital technologies and digital media create worldwide risks to the "human environment" of society. They disturb traditional forms of mass communication, re-configuring the inner mechanisms of social memory and posing new challenges to privacy and data protection. The global reach of transnational corporations such as Google, a reach that feeds back into the US power of mass surveillance, transcends national borders, generating transnational privacy problems.

The EU is trying to come up with its own supranational answers to these problems in the form of new legislation, political pressure and judicial decisions with a strong constitutional dimension. Decisions that widen both the territorial and

122 WP29 (2016) *Opinion 01/2016 on the EU–U.S. Privacy Shield draft adequacy decision*; EDPS (2016) *Opinion on the EU-U.S. Privacy Shield draft adequacy decision*; EU Parliament (2017) *Resolution on the adequacy of the protection afforded by the EU-US Privacy Shield*; EU Parliament (2016) *Resolution on transatlantic data flows.* Besides being currently the object of judicial proceedings at EU level in so-called "Schrems II" (CJEU (2018) *Case C-311/18: Data Protection Commissioner v Facebook Ireland Limited, Maximillian Schrems*), the legal validity of the "EU-US Privacy Shield" has also been the object of two actions directly brought before the CJEU by civil society organizations. One of them was dismissed based on the absence of legal standing (CJEU (2017) *Case T-670–16: Digital Rights Ireland v Commission*). The other is still pending before the court (CJEU (2016) *Case T-738/16: La Quadrature du Net and Others v Commission*).

material scope of fundamental rights, invalidating current laws and pushing for new transnational (or transatlantic) negotiations on the regulation of global data flows.

These conflicts and solutions reverberate through world society. On the one hand, the so-called right to be forgotten has made its entry into the agenda of multiple national and transnational constituencies beyond the EU.[123] On the other hand, the eventual merits and failures of the current European attempts to impose some checks and balances on global powers of mass surveillance, both public and private, will certainly influence the future evolution of privacy and data protection online. Even with the improvement of technologies for geolocation and geoblocking and the correlated, and somewhat exaggerated, fears of the "balkanization" and "fragmentation" of the Internet, mandatory changes to the code of cyberspace in Europe tend to spread to other locations around the world.[124]

The main legal, political and constitutional issues addressed by the rulings of the CJEU that were the object of the previous section may be further analyzed with the help of a distinction between two forms of global data flows. A distinction that has already been drawn in the previous section and that may be better illustrated by the "two indexes" of Google.[125]

Let us call the first index the "content data index" (or "first-order index"). It comprises all the content that is available online and that Google is constantly crawling through, collecting, storing, ranking and retrieving in reply to specific searches. This is either general content that has been published on the Web by others, such as the multitude of webpages, images, videos, music and documents that organizations and people are constantly uploading, or specific content that Google itself has decided to publish, like maps, satellite photos and scanned copies of printed books. When "processed" by means of a simple search, these data may provide all sorts of information about society and the world in which we live. Therefore, they may also provide lots of information about people. In other words, they also contain large amounts of personal data.

Let us call the second index the "transaction data index" (or "second-order index"). This mainly consists of data generated in the search for and interaction with content data. More specifically, data generated when people produce, distribute and get access to content online, or even when they merely make use of, or

123 *New York Times (2015)* '"Right to be forgotten" online could spread'; *Wall Street Journal (2016)* 'Indonesia's "right to be forgotten" raises press freedom issues'; JOTA (2014) 'STF vai julgar direito ao esquecimento em repercussão geral'; Derecho a Leer (2014), 'The unforgettable history of the seizure to the defaulter Mario Costeja Gonzáles that happened in 1998'.

124 On the influence and impact of European law and regulations on the global framing of privacy issues: Kurbalija (2014) *An Introduction to Internet Governance*, p. 182ff; Kuner (2011) 'Regulation of transborder data flows under data protection and privacy law'; Svantesson (2014) 'The extraterritoriality of EU data privacy law'.

125 This distinction was originally drawn by Stalder and Mayer (2009) 'The second index'. The main forms of data collection used by Google are briefly described in its privacy policy: https://www.google.com/policies/privacy.

get into contact with, digital artefacts.[126] These interactions leave traces and these traces are transacted with search engines like Google in exchange for their "free services". The second index is almost entirely about people and their profiles, what they have done and what they will probably do. It is a vast and diversified index (or database) of personal data.

Data from the first index flow through the Internet and are generally available to the public on the huge, decentralized and rather chaotic database called the Web – the "mother of all lists", as Umberto Eco once put it.[127] Data from the second index, on the other hand, run mostly through secret and proprietary intranets and are the object of further economic transactions, besides being available to governments, especially the US government, on "bulk demand".

Even if their respective data flows usually follow different paths (or networks), the two indexes are constantly overlapping, interacting and "re-entering" into each other by means of circular and reflexive feedback loops. The "production" and "consumption" of content data by people generates transaction data about them, which is further used to organize, rank and distribute content that generates further transactions and so on. Search engines like Google mediate these overlaps, interactions and "re-entries". They organize and sort content (or the first index) for people and organize and sort people (or the second index) for advertisers.[128]

The second index has a double function. On the one hand, it helps organize and sort the first index based on the transaction data produced by the interaction of people with content data. Google and other search engines extract from these transaction data a valuable sort of "virtual contingency", the sort of contingency that people constantly generate when they interact with content, as well as with each other, online, and which computers and algorithms strive to "decipher".[129] This "virtual contingency" is fed back into the machine. The automatic organization, ranking and retrieval of content do not depend primarily on pre-defined categories and rules. They usually come *ex-post* and are based on the way people are dynamically searching for and interacting with content. Searches and interactions that generate a reserve of contingency in the form of transaction data. The predictability and calculability of the machine is thus enriched by the very contingency and indeterminacy of people.[130]

On the other hand, beyond this reflexive function in relation to the first index, the second index, as a big and centralized database of personal data, is also a

126 According to Koops (2011) 'Forgetting footprints, shunning shadows', these include people's "digital footprints" and "digital shadows", data they themselves leave behind, as well as information gathered about them by others.

127 Eco (2009) *Vertigine della Lista*, p. 360.

128 Stalder and Mayer (2009) 'The second index', p. 99.

129 Esposito (2014) 'Virtual contingency'.

130 According to Esposito (2017) 'Algorithmic memory and the right to be forgotten on the Web', p. 5: "The machine works without abstraction and without reference to meaning. Merely calculating, algorithms manage to produce intelligent and significant results not because they operate in an intelligent way, but because they 'parasitically' exploit the intelligence and the attribution of meaning by the users of the web, in a process that continuously feeds on itself."

valuable source of information about people. A source especially praised by advertisers and intelligence agencies. The transaction data it contains may be further exploited for economic and political purposes, informing organizations about people and influencing the adoption of various measures and decisions that have an impact on them: from targeted advertising online to price discriminations more generally, from security checks in airports to official investigations by the police.

As the cases discussed in the previous section show, each index, with its particular global flows of data, generates specific privacy concerns. Concerns that have been associated with remembrance, forgetting and surveillance.

4.4.1. The first index and the right to be forgotten

The "right to be forgotten" recognized in *Google Spain* is a right related (or opposed) to the first index, whose global data flows run in a more decentralized way through the open Internet. Here, personal data are usually generated out of content data in the absence of a specific authorization from, or legal relationship with, data subjects. Data are collected in bulk from the content available on the Web. Google and other search engines must process the data based on their own "legitimate interests", as well as the interests of the general public in having easy access to the data by means of an online search.

The main risk posed by the first index seems to be related, first and foremost, to the more traditional dimension (or meaning) of privacy. The risk of being exposed to the "indiscrete gaze" of others, of having one's own life scrutinized not only by corporate and government bureaucracies, but also by a wide and unknown mass audience. An audience that, thanks to the Internet and to search engines, may easily get updated, as well as outdated, information about almost anyone by means of a simple search, which is able to provide a "detailed profile" of people out of vast amounts of pieces of previously scattered and unrelated data.

The "right to be let alone", as well as the right to exercise some form of "informational self-determination", to have some control over the flows of data that constantly shape one's own social identity, how "the one" is perceived by "the others", is thus challenged by the first index of Google.

This is certainly not the only side of the problem. Losing control over personal data that flow through the Web also means losing control over how these data will inform concrete measures and decisions that directly impact one's life. Not only the more prosaic prospects of a casual date, but one's job and career also may be put at risk by what Google shows on its lists of results.[131] The existence of such a risk, however, is not a necessary condition of the exercise of the right to be

131 Mr. Gonzáles himself was probably worried about how widely available information related to his past debts would have an influence on his professional life as a lawyer and calligrapher. The potential negative impact of the wide circulation of personal data on the Web on people's professional lives had already been demonstrated by the often-quoted "Drunken Pirate" case: Ars Technica (2008) 'Court rejects appeal over student-teacher drunk MySpace pics'. For evidence of the risks of racial discrimination in online advertising: Sweeney (2013) 'Discrimination in online ad delivery'.

forgotten, since the CJEU itself has stated that it is not necessary "in order to find such a right that the inclusion of the information in question in that list causes prejudice to the data subject".[132] The risk does not come from the publication of the information itself, which may even remain available on the Web. It comes from the increased exposure of the data subject when the information (or data) is processed by search engines.[133]

Furthermore, this is a more decentralized and distributed kind of risk. The "detailed profiles" generated by search engines are publicly available. Searches may be made by anyone about anyone. Anyone, in theory, may "google" anyone else. It is not a typical problem of mass surveillance by some large and threating bureaucratic organization. It is mainly a problem of mass surveillance by the masses themselves. A sort of "mass self-exposure". In the language of cyberspace, with its fixation on serial versions and periodic updates, it is a problem of "Privacy 2.0" created by the "Web 2.0".[134]

The right to be forgotten, as recognized by the CJEU in *Google Spain*, is especially tailored to deal with this problem. It is basically a right against digital media and their automatic processing of personal data, just as the right to privacy was first recognized against the more traditional mass media and their invasive use of new "mechanical devices".[135] Nowadays, with "free access" to search engines and social media, one may easily satisfy one's curiosity without the "gossip press".

From the perspective of the legal system, when remembering becomes the rule, forgetting becomes a right, a sort of fundamental right to privacy and freedom online. A right to be able to free oneself from the past that is constantly inundating the present in the form of ever more data and ever more accelerated data flows. A right to re-open one's own future, to "start again".[136]

132 CJEU (2014) *Case C-131/12: Google Spain SL, Google Inc. v Agencia Española de Protección de Datos, Mario Costeja González*, Judgment of the Court, p. 21.

133 According to the taxonomy developed by Solove (2006) 'A taxonomy of privacy', the main privacy problems stemming from the first index would be related to "aggregation", "identification" and "increased accessibility".

134 Zittrain (2008) *The Future of the Internet*, p. 205ff. The term "Web 2.0" usually refers to the growth of user-generated content available on the Web, due mainly to the spread of platforms such as blogs, social media, social networks, wikis and other software applications that count on the active participation of users for the generation and ranking of content. See: O'Reilly (2007) 'What is Web 2.0'; Zimmer (2007) 'The panoptic gaze of Web 2.0'.

135 In the words of Warren and Brandeis (1890) 'The right to privacy', p. 195: "Instantaneous photographs and newspaper enterprise have invaded the sacred precincts of private and domestic life; and numerous mechanical devices threaten to make good the prediction that 'what is whispered in the closet shall be proclaimed from the housetops'".

136 On the evolution of the right to be forgotten from the specific right of ex-cons to have their criminal records cleared to the more general dimension of freedom online: Rouvroy (2007) 'Réinventer l'art d'oublier et de se faire oublier dans la société de l'information'; Rodotà (2014) *Il Mondo nella Rete*, e-book 37%ff; Rodotà (2012) *Il Diritto di Avere Diritti*, p. 404ff; Bernal (2014) 'The EU, the US and right to be forgotten'; Tamò and George (2014) 'Oblivion, erasure and forgetting in the digital age'. Besides the right to

This is not exactly a right against memory, or against social memory. It is a right against automatic remembrance, against this new sort of "remembrance by default". Properly speaking, the right does not provide for forgetting, for the "erasure" or "deletion" of personal data. Its purpose is only to make remembrance, or "mass remembrance", more difficult. Neither webpublishers, nor search engines are necessarily compelled to erase or delete the data from their databases. The data remain on the "first index". They remain on the Web. They only become more difficult to find because they are dissociated from the data subject's name for the purposes of automatic retrieval. "Remembering" them remains, at least in theory, possible, even if it requires much more effort.

The CJEU's decision seems to have raised many more questions than provided definitive answers.[137] This should not necessarily be regretted, though, since every "leading case" is also a "hard case". It deals with sensitive situations and complex legal principles, whose interpretation cannot be fixed once and for all. It marks the beginning, not the end, raising new normative meanings that need to be further concretized. Especially in the context of the European multilevel legal system, in which the CJEU is not exactly in a hierarchical position in relation to national courts, in a position to simply dictate from above rigid rules to be uniformly applied around the continent. Being more "discrete" and "evasive", answering only what has been strictly asked and taking care not to go further than necessary may also be seen as a judicial strategy of self-restraint, a strategy to attain a certain level of unity without renouncing diversity.

Three main concerns have been raised over the ruling that will probably influence the future implementation of the right and the stabilization of its normative meaning (or meanings): (i) the concerns over territoriality and jurisdiction, (ii) the concerns over enforcement, or private enforcement, and (iii) the concerns over the effects on freedom of expression and access to information.

Regarding territoriality and jurisdiction, the first reaction of Google was to apply the ruling only to the European versions of its website. Jurisdiction was interpreted, then, not in territorial terms, but in "digital" terms.

Besides the general domain name "google.com", which is the original US version,[138] Google offers many different nationally customized versions of its website,

be forgotten as recognized by the CJEU, an alternative to enforcing forgetting online would also consist in the multiplication of information online with the purpose of making filtering and ranking more difficult. It would not aim at the "erasure of memories", but at their multiplication. See: Brunton and Nissenbaum (2013) 'Political and ethical perspectives on data obfuscation'; Esposito (2017) 'Algorithmic memory and the right to be forgotten on the Web', p. 6ff.

137 This fact seems to be regretted by some authors, who expected the court to give more definitive solutions to the enforcement of the right: Kuner (2015) 'The Court of Justice of the EU judgment on data protection and Internet search engines'; Kulk and Borgesius (2014) '*Google Spain v. González*'.

138 Google, like most Internet companies, does not have a country specific domain name for the US version of its website, such as "google.us". It takes the US for the whole, or the whole for the US, and offers only its general commercial domain name in the US: "google.com".

such as "google.it" for Italy, "google.hu" for Hungary and "google.es" for Spain. These versions may be further customized by language,[139] as well as by location.[140] Indeed, territorial location does not determine which national versions may be accessed, since all versions are accessible, at least in theory, from everywhere.[141]

According to Google's initial interpretation of the judgment, European privacy requests for search removals had no specific territorial effect at all. Since most people, by simple inertia, usually access the national version of the website that is customized to the country where they are located, it would be enough to implement the removals only on the European versions of the website. The ruling of a European court would thus have effect on the European versions of the website that are customized by the company to people in Europe. The fact that everyone in Europe would still be able to search and find the same results as if nothing had happened just by accessing another version of the website – "google.com", for instance – would not be relevant, because only a small percentage of people choose to change the default national version of the website.[142]

This particular interpretation proved to be unacceptable to European data protection authorities, which demanded Google apply the judgment globally to all versions of its website, so that nobody, no matter where they were located, would be able to search and find results that were legitimately requested to be removed. After all, most companies, Google included, apply worldwide restrictions when they limit access to content that allegedly violates intellectual property rights. If property is enforced globally, so should privacy be.[143]

Google then came up with a sort of compromise. Instead of either restricting "personal searchability" only on the European versions of its website, with no concrete effect on territory, or on all its versions, with a global effect on territory, the company adopted a mixed solution. When a request for search removal is granted, in addition to restricting "personal searchability" on all the European versions of its website, the restriction is also applied to all other versions whenever they are accessed from the country of residence of the requester. The effects of the

139 Local languages, as well as English, are usually available for each national version of Google's website. The Spanish version ("google.es"), for instance, may be accessed in five different languages: English, Spanish, Catalan, Galician and Basque.

140 Location may be either customized by default, based on technologies of geolocation online, or chosen by the user. Search results will be shown with proper consideration given to the place where the user is located.

141 Territorial location, nationality and language are independent variables. For instance, a Brazilian national may access the Italian version of Google ("google.it") in English from Hungary.

142 Google (2015) 'Implementing a European, not global, right to be forgotten'.

143 CNIL (2015) 'CNIL orders Google to apply delisting on all domain names of the search engine'; WP29 (2014) *Guidelines on the implementation of the Court of Justice of the European Union judgment on "Google Spain and Inc v. Agencia Española de Protección de Datos (AEPD) and Mario Costeja Gonzáles" C-131/12*, p. 9. The Advisory Council instituted by Google to provide independent advice on the enforcement of the CJEU's ruling recommended, instead, that the removal should be implemented only on the European versions of Google's website. See: Google (2015) *The Advisory Council to Google on the Right to be Forgotten*, p. 20.

restriction are, then, Europe wide on digital domains and country specific on territorial domains. Physical space makes its "re-entry" into cyberspace in order to provide some territorial scope for the protection of privacy online.[144]

The issue, however, is far from settled. After Google appealed against a decision of the French Data Protection Authority (*Commission Nationale de l'Informatique et des Libertés (CNIL)*) that ordered the company to enforce the right globally in all versions of its website, the French highest administrative tribunal (*Conseil d'État*) referred the case to the CJEU in July 2017. Thus, the court will soon have to further specify the territorial scope of its recent ruling.[145]

Both corporations and governments are increasingly using geolocation and geoblocking technologies in the provision of services and the regulation of content online. The privacy conflict, however, has already moved from the technological layer to the constitutional (or transnational constitutional) layer. While European data protection authorities claim that their privacy laws should be globally applied, US companies and public authorities do not accept such a claim to global enforcement, raising the rather legitimate concern over the risk of a "run to the bottom" in terms of free speech. A "run to the bottom", though, that does not seem to worry these same companies and authorities when the global effects of US intellectual property law are at stake.[146]

Territoriality and jurisdiction are also related to the issue of private enforcement, that is to say, primary enforcement by search engines themselves. In other words, private companies such as Google will act as a sort of "court of first instance" in the implementation of the right, filtering the requests that will eventually end up being analyzed by data protection authorities and official tribunals.

The "outsourcing" of law enforcement to private parties is not necessarily a new issue. The legal system itself cannot be reduced to its formal organizations. Law is constantly enforced without force (or state force) by a variety of people, organizations and social movements that play an active role in the formulation, interpretation and implementation of legal rules and principles, sometimes (or most of

144 Google (2016) 'Adapting our approach to the European right to be forgotten'. Geolocation and geoblocking technologies, however, may be easily bypassed by other technologies, such as Virtual Private Networks (VPNs), which hide the effective IP number of the user and provide him/her with a virtual IP number, associated with a specific territorial region that may be freely chosen.

145 CJEU (2017) *Case C-507/17: Google Inc. v Commission nationale de l'informatique et des libertés*. The Advocate General has already delivered his opinion on the case, proposing a sort of European-wide delisting as a solution to the controversy: independently of the specific national version of Google's website used in the search, and with the help of geolocation and geoblocking technologies, the objected results should be made unavailable for anyone making the search in the territory of the EEA. Besides this legal dispute concerning the territorial scope of the right to be forgotten, the CNIL imposed a €50 million fine on Google in January 2019 for irregularities concerning its privacy policy, which was the first fine applied by a European data protection authority based on the new legal framework provided by the GDPR. See: CNIL (2019) *La formation restreinte de la CNIL prononce une sanction de 50 millions d'euros à l'encontre de la société GOOGLE LLC.*

146 Bernal (2014) 'The EU, the US and right to be forgotten', p. 73ff.

the time) even pushing well-established legal boundaries and meanings beyond their accepted official standards.[147]

The day-to-day decisions of big private companies and providers of public utilities usually affect large numbers of people in their respective markets and beyond, people who are generally subsumed into the large and diffuse category of consumers. When consumers have a complaint about a product or service, they usually get back to the provider before considering the eventual recourse to the more expensive and time-consuming formal procedures of the law.

Google and other online platforms, however, are constantly taking vast amounts of automated and semi-automated decisions that have an immediate impact on people and their personal data that go well beyond the boundaries of economic and consumer law, especially with regard to the first index, the content available on the Web that is automatically stored, processed and transmitted worldwide.

As already discussed in Chapter 2, the important and influential role of private intermediaries such as Google in the circulation of data and information through the Internet is widely acknowledged, as well as their strategic position as "bottlenecks" or "points of control" for the regulation of conduct online, a regulation that has a strong impact on human rights such as privacy and freedom of expression.

Given Google's leading position in Europe and the huge number of requests for removal of search results it has been receiving day-by-day since the CJEU decision in *Google Spain*, specific concerns have been raised over the constitutional adequacy of leaving the primary enforcement of such a relevant right in the hands of a private company. Something that could risk turning a basic conflict over human rights into a "customer service" issue.[148]

Although acknowledging its own reluctance to assume such a prominent enforcement role,[149] not least because of the additional costs involved, Google has taken some steps to influence the public debate and to make its decision-making more transparent and predictable. The company has commissioned an independent council of experts to provide it with specific advice on the implementation of the judgment.[150] It has also created a specific section in its "transparency report" that contains statistics on how the requests are being handled, as well as information about the most common grounds for their approval and rejection – information about its own "case law", one might say.[151]

147 Luhmann (2008 [1993]) *Law as a Social System*, p. 274ff.

148 Zittrain (2014) 'Righting the right to be forgotten'.

149 According to Google's own instructions to its users (https://www.google.it/intl/en/policies/faq): "These are difficult judgments and as a private organisation, we may not be in a good position to decide on your case. If you disagree with our decision you can contact your local DPA."

150 Google (2015) *The Advisory Council to Google on the Right to be Forgotten*. The Advisory Council came up with four basic criteria to assess the requests for removal: (i) the data subject's role in public life; (ii) the nature of the information; (iii) the specific source; and (iv) the time elapsed since the first publication (Google (2015) *The Advisory Council to Google on the Right to be Forgotten*, p. 7ff).

151 Google's Transparency Report is available on the website: https://www.google.com/transparencyreport.

The increasing assumption of enforcement responsibilities by Google also has a potential impact on the very issue of territorial and national jurisdiction, an impact that does not seem to have been properly considered yet.

In its preliminary ruling in *Google Spain*, the CJEU took the facts of the case into consideration only in order to provide an adequate interpretation of the DPD. The application of the relevant EU norms, as interpreted by the CJEU, to the facts of the case is always the responsibility of the referring court. An "application" that obviously involves further interpretative steps.

This division of tasks between European and national courts is particularly important to the European multilevel legal system. The very separation of interpretative steps is a way of reconciling unity with diversity, of forcing the courts to engage in an interpretative dialogue in which the unsettling question of final authority may remain strategically hidden. The "primary competence" to interpret European law is assigned to the European courts, while the national courts retain the competence to apply the norms to the facts, an activity that always entails some degree of adaptation or modulation in the re-framing of norms already interpreted in abstract in order to match the concrete facts of the case. This is what provides, for instance, the "margin of maneuver" for Sweden to criminally punish an indiscrete churchgoer who publishes trivial facts about her peers on the Web, as was the case in *Bodil Lindqvist*. The same "margin of maneuver" that was used by a Spanish court in *Google Spain* in order to give more weight to privacy than to freedom of expression when giving its final word about the right to be forgotten of Mr. Gonzáles.

However, if Google increasingly assumes the role of a "court of first instance" for the whole of Europe, this very peculiar potential for national diversification in face of the unifying primacy of EU law will tend to be suppressed or significantly diminished. The need for increased convergence, uniformity and repeatability of a transnational corporate bureaucracy will tend to prevail over the more fragmentary contextual demands of different national legal systems. It is much easier for the company to change its legal and technological "code" for the whole of the EU than to adapt it to different national preferences and "sensitivities" on a country-by-country basis. For better or worse, the right to be forgotten will probably gain in terms of redundancy and lose in terms of variety.

The issue of private enforcement by Google compounds the more general concerns that have been raised over the impact of the right to be forgotten on other fundamental rights such as freedom of expression and access to information. The CJEU has already been criticized for its deficit of reasoning and argumentation, as well as its limited balancing approach,[152] but the technologically enhanced balancing to be automatically or semi-automatically struck by search engines in a multitude of different situations seems even more problematic. Instead of public authorities making use of legally regulated procedures, private companies, with the

152 Kulk and Borgesius (2014) '*Google Spain v. González*'; Kuner (2015) 'The Court of Justice of the EU judgment on data protection and Internet search engines'.

help of their secret and proprietary algorithms, will be deciding, in the first instance, what should be remembered and forgotten online.

Regarding the procedural aspects, the main challenge seems to be how to guarantee some form of due process in the context of private enforcement by search engines. If some balance is to be effectively struck, the freedom of expression of publishers, as well as the right of access to information of the general public of online readers (or searches), should also be taken into consideration. After all, in the context of online search, free speech also implies the right to find and to be found.

It has therefore been suggested that search engines should follow, whenever feasible, a more adversarial procedure, offering the original webpublisher the possibility of commenting on a request before deciding on its merits. More elements would then be gathered in order to help search engines assess whether the contested search results contain personal data that is really "inadequate, irrelevant or no longer relevant, or excessive in relation to the purposes of its original processing".[153]

The so-called "Streisand effect", which characterized the original case, paradoxically making Mr. Gonzáles so "unforgettable", will certainly not follow the multitude of other requests for removal of search results that are currently being, and will continue to be, granted, resulting in more restricted "personal searchability" online that almost nobody will notice.[154] This is especially the case when search engines themselves directly approve the request, so that no public authority gets involved and no official procedure is initiated. Providing publishers, even if only in certain and more relevant circumstances, with a sort of procedural guarantee in the form of a right to be listened to and to take part in the decision might be a way to re-introduce free speech into the balance.

Regarding the more substantial aspects, the distinction between public and private seems to be "re-entering" itself on the side of privacy. A "re-entry" that leads to a further distinction between personal data that is public and personal data that is private. While one may ask for certain aspects of one's private life to be legitimately forgotten, one's public life may, instead, be the legitimate object of automatic remembrance. The CJEU itself has stressed in its ruling that the role played by the data subject in "public life" should be given an appropriate weight on the data protection balance: an exception to the *prima facie* primacy of privacy that

153 Google (2015) *The Advisory Council to Google on the Right to be Forgotten*, p. 15ff; Zittrain (2014) 'Righting the right to be forgotten'. According to WP29 (2014) *Guidelines on the Implementation of the Court of Justice of the European Union Judgment on "Google Spain and Inc v. Agencia Española de Protección de Datos (AEPD) and Mario Costeja Gonzáles" C-131/12*, p. 10, in order to further preserve the privacy of the data subject, the notification of the original webpublisher and its participation in the proceedings would only be justified in particularly difficult and controversial cases.

154 When a privacy request for search removal is granted, Google removes the links to the contested webpages (or URLs) from the list of results shown when a search for the requester's name is made. Moreover, the list of results for any search for a person's name that may fall under the scope of European data protection law automatically shows at the bottom of the page the following message: "Some results may have been removed under data protection law in Europe".

will have to be, and is already being, further elaborated by search engines and national authorities.[155]

Legally enforced forgetting against automatic and widely available remembrance in the first index does not necessarily affect, however, the selectivity and the surveillance potential of the second index. Privacy and data protection may be even more difficult to enforce here, as the power of digital bureaucracies over global data flows seem to be much more secret and opaque.

4.4.2 The second index and the power of digital bureaucracies

In contrast to its decision in *Google Spain*, the main purpose of the CJEU in invalidating the Data Retention Directive in *Digital Rights Ireland*, and especially the Safe Harbour Agreement in *Schrems*, was to enforce the rights to privacy and data protection against the second index, whose global data flows run in a more centralized way through multiple closed intranets, owned by either corporations or governments. Here, personal data is generally collected in the context of some specific transaction conducted with data subjects, who usually give their consent by accepting the inflexible conditions imposed by standard contractual clauses, privacy policies and general terms of use.[156] This personal data is originally collected by private companies – to a great extent, by transnational corporations like Google – and further provided on "bulk demand" to public authorities, especially in the US.

The second index exacerbates the privacy risks posed by "digital bureaucracies". The risks of having both public and private organizations constantly collecting and processing personal data by automatic means. Data that is further used to inform concrete measures and decisions that directly affect the lives of people, their social identity and principally their general prospects of inclusion. Automatic processing also generates automatic discrimination, automated patterns of inclusion and exclusion that are increasingly difficult to understand and to meaningfully regulate and control.[157]

155 According to WP29 (2014) *Guidelines on the Implementation of the Court of Justice of the European Union Judgment on "Google Spain and Inc v. Agencia Española de Protección de Datos (AEPD) and Mario Costeja Gonzáles" C-131/12*, p. 6: "Although all data relating to a person is personal data, not all data about a person is private. There is a basic distinction between a person's private life and their public or professional persona. The availability of information in a search result becomes more acceptable the less it reveals about a person's private life." It is interesting to note that, according to Google's Transparency Report (https://www.google.com/transparencyreport/removals/europeprivacy), the websites most impacted by search removals are those of social media like Facebook, YouTube and Twitter, which generally contain personal data that may be more easily classified as private.

156 On the shortcomings of "user consent" as a legal basis for the processing of personal data: Zanfir (2014) 'Forgetting about consent'; Belli and Venturini (2016) 'Private ordering and the rise of terms of service as cyber-regulation'; Custers (2016) 'Click here to consent forever'.

157 Solove (2001) 'Privacy and power'; Citron (2008) 'Technological due process'; Barocas (2014) 'Data mining and the discourse on discrimination'; Barocas and Selbst (2016) 'Big data's disparate impact'.

These risks are exacerbated because the second index works online. It takes advantage of ubiquitous computing and networking to sift through the digital traces that people leave in cyberspace. Growing access to the Internet generates ever more transaction data that flow through multiple intranets, ending up on the databases of various corporate and governmental bureaucracies: digital archives that constitute important elements of power and wealth.

The main problem here is not exactly (or not only) one of increased exposure, of having one's own private life subjected to constant public scrutiny, of not being "let alone". The second index is not available to the public, who barely knows how it works. It is more like a business secret that, besides being constantly monetized for marketing purposes, is also secretly shared with secret services. With the exception of some leak or other, the rule is secrecy, not publicity. People may have the right to access their personal data, but it is very difficult for them to know where these data are and how they are being used.

Widespread and automatic surveillance (or "dataveillance") in the second index is the job of machines, not people.[158] They are the ones programmed to remember what is relevant and forget what is not, to determine which differences should make a difference. This certainly does not eliminate the risk of unauthorized access to personal data due to cyber-attacks, or indiscrete access by "cyber-bureaucrats" themselves. However, it is not the public gaze that constitutes the main threat, but the secret and opaque ways in which decisions are taken based on these personal data. Decisions that may arbitrarily discriminate and that always have an unevenly distributed (or asymmetric) exclusionary effect.[159]

More than the increased exposure of people and their data, it is the opacity of the second index that is worrisome, as well as this very contrast between transparency and secrecy. The contrast of making private lives ever more transparent to automated bureaucracies that work in the utmost secret, very far from the public. With the help of the second index, people become more exposed to organizations whose decision-making procedures become more opaque to them.

Both the DPD of 1995 and the GDPR of 2016 that has replaced it have tried to address this sort of problem: the constitutional problem which originates from the powerlessness of individuals in relation to "digital bureaucracies" that are constantly processing their data in order to make more and more automated decisions that have an impact on their lives. A problem that has been exacerbated by the rise of the Internet and the consequent spread of the "computational turn" to the whole of society and people's day-to-day lives.

The aim of the European data protection legislation is to regulate and constrain the power of databases by providing a sort of "technological due process". A due

158 Clarke (1988) 'Information technology and dataveillance'; Clarke (1997) 'Introduction to dataveillance and information privacy'; Clarke (2003) 'Dataveillance – 15 years on'.

159 Newman (2014) 'The costs of lost privacy'; Larnier (2011) 'The local-global flip'; Solove (2001) 'Privacy and power'; Citron (2008) 'Technological due process'; Barocas (2014) 'Data mining and the discourse on discrimination'; Barocas and Selbst (2016) 'Big data's disparate impact'.

process that confers on individuals the rights to access their data, take part in their processing and eventually request their rectification or even erasure. The right to ask for human intervention against the automatic decision-making procedures of the machine.[160] Rights that must count for their effectiveness on the institution of independent authorities with a specific mandate to impose and enforce checks and balances on the data and media power of both public and private organizations. And as global data flows are increasingly blind to territorial borders, the transnationality of the problem also requires transnational solutions. Solutions that come in the form of a complex and rather convoluted transnational network of laws and legal provisions that make cross-references to each other in the hope of providing "safe harbors" and privacy shields to the global network of data flows.[161]

In *Digital Rights Ireland*, the CJEU established a clear limit to the mandatory surveillance and data retention practices imposed on the private sector by the EU. In *Schrems*, the court took a step forward and established a limit, even if an indirect one, to the political, economic and media power of transnational corporations and US intelligence agencies. It recognized that the previous data protection arrangement between the EU and the US was not adequate to protect the privacy of European citizens and residents. The limit was established (or re-established) mainly by re-affirming the power of European data protection authorities over transnational (or transatlantic) data flows. A limit whose concrete effectiveness has yet to be proven, since the new Privacy Shield framework is already the object of controversy and will soon be assessed by the CJEU itself.

Besides having to enforce the right to be forgotten in its first index, Google, as well as other transnational corporations of the digital economy, is now compelled to mistrust the safety of any "harbor" or "shield" provided by the EU and the US to the global data flows generated by their respective second indexes. After all, these "harbors" and "shields" seem to be provided mainly for the sake of the stability and predictability of transatlantic trade, rather than for the protection of people and their personal data.

4.4.3 Profiles, exposure and discrimination

One last distinction between the two indexes of Google may be drawn based on the way they allow people to be "profiled". Different forms of profiling in the first

160 Protection against "automated individual decisions" is provided both by Article 15 of the DPD and Articles 21 and 22 of the GDPR.

161 Compared to traditional international law treaties, both the Safe Harbour Agreement and the new Privacy Shield framework are much more informal and flexible. They articulate the joint operation of multiple public authorities in the EU and the US to supervise a mechanism that consists basically of the voluntary self-certification of private companies. Instead of two or more clearly defined state parties, the actors are much more diversified: the European Commission, European Data Protection Authorities, the US Department of Commerce, the US Federal Trade Commission, the US "intelligence community" and, last but not least, big transnational corporations of the digital economy.

and second index raise different, even if interrelated, questions of remembrance, forgetting and surveillance. Schematically, we may say that profiles in the first index are mainly sources of exposure, while profiles in the second index are mainly technologies of discrimination. Exposure and discrimination that, in the same way as the two indexes, work together and are constantly overlapping and reinforcing each other.

The "detailed profiles" that, according to the CJEU in *Google Spain*, characterize the risk posed by the processing of personal data carried out by search engines, are publicly available profiles, profiles created by the first index. They are made up of the condensation of scattered pieces of data on the Web that, when put together, may expose a lot of information about a person. These are individualized profiles, profiles that provide identification, the condensation of information that identifies people and exposes their lives to anyone who simply searches for their name online. A form of mass exposure that may cause shame and embarrassment and may have a chilling effect on opinions, behaviors and dissent more generally.

Profiles in the second index, on the other hand, do not serve primarily to identify and expose someone, but to commodify, discriminate and make predictions. Profiling here means building impersonal models of human behavior, choices, preferences and attributes from the statistical analysis of huge amounts of data – first and foremost, transaction data – and then applying the models to concrete individuals in order to predict and influence their conduct.[162] Individuals are treated as objects not of curiosity, but rather of bureaucratic indifference. They are analyzed in terms of costs and benefits, opportunities and risks by both private and public organizations. These are profiles that categorize and classify, helping "digital bureaucracies" to take automatic or semi-automatic decisions on inclusion and exclusion. In other words, profiles that asymmetrically exclude and discriminate.

The kind of mass surveillance by the masses allowed by the "detailed profiles" of the first index are a constant source of exposure that may cause shame, embarrassment and even discrimination, but the risks are more decentralized and evenly distributed. The exercise of the right to be forgotten against this more diffuse form of surveillance does not necessarily cause personal data to be erased, but only to become more difficult to find. It is a right against the automatic and widespread remembrance made possible by digital media in general and search engines in particular. A right against the sort of mass exposure produced by the technologies of online search. Forgetting here is not a means to be "let alone" by search engines, but to be "let alone" by other people, who are able to easily get an individualized profile about almost anyone by simply searching for them in the first index.

Mass surveillance in the context of the second index, however, is not carried out by the masses, but by formal organizations that collect and process personal data in a more secret and centralized way. It is a bureaucratic and highly automated form of surveillance. Forgetting here means basically erasing personal data from

162 Otterlo (2013) 'A machine learning view on profiling', p. 41ff.

corporate and governmental databases.[163] It is not a protection against increased exposure to the public, but against the secret and exclusionary effect of discriminatory profiles. Moreover, these databases are much more opaque. They may be spread around the world (or the "cloud") and are usually protected by business and national security secrets, which makes forgetting (or erasure) much more difficult. Curbing the indiscrete gaze of the public, therefore, seems to be much easier than countering the discriminatory power of digital bureaucracies.

In order to limit the "environmental harm" of profiling techniques that both expose and discriminate, a specific solution that has been suggested several times consists of giving people a sort of property right over their personal data. Personal data would be legally modeled in terms of intellectual property rights, rights over immaterial things that people may sell, buy, negotiate and bargain over. To a certain extent, this would amount to a legal formalization of the current structures of "digital markets", where people allegedly "pay" with their own data for the "free services" provided online.[164]

This solution might address, in theory, some private law concerns. Given that personal data is widely exploited by economic purposes, treating them as formal property would at least re-establish some balance in the market, empowering consumers and giving them a larger share of the monetary value actually attributed to their data.

The main problem, however, is not one of private law, but one of constitutional law. As already stressed more than once, users cannot be reduced to consumers, just as the Internet cannot be reduced to one huge digital market. As a medium of global communication, its effects go well beyond the economic system. Privacy and data protection are constitutional artefacts invented to empower individuals beyond their role of consumers and to constrain the power of formal organizations beyond their "disturbing" interventions in the market.

The monetization of profiles may increase the opportunities for personal gain, but it does nothing to counter the risks of automated exposure and discrimination exemplified by the two indexes of Google. Risks that the CJEU has tried to address by recognizing a right to be forgotten against search engines and by establishing (or re-establishing) some limits to the transnational (or transatlantic) power of corporate and governmental databases.

The power of mass surveillance provided by digital media and digital bureaucracies, by the first and second indexes, is not exactly a coordinated and unified power that comes from above, from some hierarchical center that is able to watch, read and listen to everything, manipulating the whole of society and the day-to-day lives of people according to some previously established plan or overall goal. As Daniel Solove has already stressed, the main threat does not come from an

163 The GDPR, in Article 17, refers primarily to a "right to erasure", mentioning the denomination "right to be forgotten" only in brackets.

164 On current proposals to treat personal data as private property: Lessig (2006) *Code*, p. 200ff; Larnier (2014) 'Whoever owns our data will determine our fate'. For a critical assessment of these proposals: Litman (2000) 'Information privacy/information property'.

oppressive "big brother" that knows everything with the help of its "little brothers", being able, thus, to exercise overwhelming command and control. In a functionally differentiated society that has no top or center, the technologically enhanced threat to privacy comes when "Kafka goes online". It is not the interest of the media and of corporate and governmental bureaucracies in people and the minutest details of their lives that is threatening, but their complete indifference. The sense of powerlessness and vulnerability that comes when the differences that are most relevant to someone, who can be anyone, make no difference to others, either to their peers or to those with real power to take decisions over their lives.[165]

165 According to Solove (2001) 'Privacy and power', p. 1429: "We are not heading toward a world of Big Brother or one composed of Little Brothers, but toward a more mindless process—of bureaucratic indifference, arbitrary errors, and dehumanization—a world that is beginning to resemble Kafka's vision in *The Trial*". In Foucauldian terms, it is not the hierarchical power of sovereignty, but the normalizing effect of more diffused forms of discipline that is really threatening. See: Foucault (1979) *Microfísica do Poder*.

Conclusion

> A constitution is not a thing in name only, but in fact. It has not an ideal, but a real existence; and wherever it cannot be produced in a visible form, there is none.
>
> (Thomas Paine)[1]

More than two hundred years after Thomas Paine's famous and influential definition of constitution as "a thing antecedent to a government" that constitutes this same government,[2] it is still hard to find a "visible" constitutional form beyond government, that is to say, beyond the traditional nation state.

Paine's insistence on the "visibility" of the constitution was directed against the British government, whose lack of a written constitution, a constitution decided by the people, would be at the root of the tyranny of both its parliament and monarchy. This insistence was also a provocation to conservative thinkers like Edmund Burke, who praised the British "ancient constitution" for its stability and criticized the French Revolution for its brutal break with the past and its naïve proclamation of "abstract principles" such as the "rights of man".[3]

Leaving aside Paine's revolutionary rhetoric, few people would deny that the UK has a constitution even in the absence of a written and unified document. British exceptionalism in constitutional matters is the result of historical evolution, which has provided the country with its own particular institutions for the self-limitation of power, including the relatively recent formal protection of the "rights of men" by means of the participation of the UK in international regimes such as the European system of human rights.

1 Paine (1817 [1792]) *The Rights of Man*, p. 29.

2 In the words of Paine (1817 [1792]) *The Rights of Man*, pp. 29–30: "A constitution is a thing antecedent to a government, and a government is only the creature of a constitution. The constitution of a country is not the act of its government, but of the people constituting its government. It is the body of elements, to which you can refer, and quote article by article; and which contains the principles on which the government shall be established, the manner in which it shall be organised, the powers it shall have, the mode of elections, the duration of Parliaments, or by what other name such bodies may be called; the powers which the executive part of the government shall have; and in fine, everything that relates to the complete organisation of a civil government, and the principles on which it shall act, and by which it shall be bound."

3 Burke (1790) *Reflections on the Revolution in France*, p. 44ff.

As the concrete example of a process of social institutionalization of constitutional norms without a clear-cut constitutional moment or constitutional text, the exceptional case of British constitutionalism might inspire the constitutionalization of other sectors and regimes of world society beyond state politics (or simply, beyond "governments"). This has been suggested by Gunther Teubner, according to whom "civil constitutions" are emerging from the structural couplings of law with other subsystems of world society in an evolutionary process that bears some similarities with the constitutionalization of British politics.[4]

As also indicated by Teubner, companies like Google would be at the center of the new constitutional question of our times, which would concern, first and foremost, the taming of the destructive energies released by the increasing globalization, privatization and digitalization of the world. The expansionist tendencies of Google, together with its "information monopoly", would pose, then, a threat to the constitution of the economy, the constitution of the new media and the constitution of the Internet itself.[5]

Transnational constitutional conflicts over global data flows

Notwithstanding the appeal and the epistemic potential of this heterodox approach, we have followed a more traditional path through this book and have stuck to the sociological definition of constitution as a structural coupling between politics and law.[6] A structural coupling that influences (or "irritates"), as well as is influenced (or "irritated") by, the structural coupling of the legal and political systems with other social systems, especially the economy. Instead of looking for new civil or societal constitutions, which do not seem to be "visible" yet – if not in "name", at least in "fact" – we have focused on the actual conflicts between Google and the EU in order to investigate their transnational constitutional (or transconstitutional) dimension.[7]

4 According to Teubner (2004) 'Societal constitutionalism', pp. 14–15: "As so often, hereto much can be learned from the special case of Britain. Though the prejudice is readily cultivated on the continent that Britain has no constitution at all or is at least constitutionally underdeveloped, nonetheless, in the light of Dicey's analyses, the constitutional qualities of the British polity and the common law have repeatedly been clearly worked out. Its substantive qualities in relation to state organisation and fundamental rights, in particular their protective intensity, can stand any comparison with continental constitutions. The point is social institutionalisation, not the formal existence of a constituent assembly, a constitutional document, norms of explicitly constitutional quality, or a court specialised in constitutional questions. *Mutatis mutandis*, this is also true of the civil constitutions of global society. Actualising the latency of constitutional elements would then also imply normatively reflecting the de facto course of constitutionalisation, and being in a position to influence its direction."

5 Teubner (2013) 'The project of constitutional sociology', p. 44ff.

6 Luhmann (1996) 'La costituzione come acquisizione evolutiva'; Luhmann (2008 [1993]) *Law as a Social System*, p. 381ff.

7 Neves (2013 [2009]) *Transconstitutionalism*.

Systems theory itself has proved to be an adequate theoretical framework for the main analyses of the book. Conceiving of: (i) society as communication; and (ii) modern society as world society, that is to say, a global system (or network) of communication, the theory is well suited to the investigation of the constitutional conflicts that take place in cyberspace, which is nothing more than the technological medium that allows communication and information to flow globally (or transnationally) with increasing independence from physical space and territorial borders.

Taking into consideration some global asymmetries of functional differentiation – in other words, the fact that the economy, science and technology and the mass media operate more easily at the global level than politics an law – the investigation was framed, at a general level, by the question of how different legal and political orders (or segments) of world society are dealing with the ever more accelerated global flows of money, technology and information, flows that have been enhanced and enlarged by the rise and spread of the Internet.

Then we came to the specifics. On the one hand, Google is one of the wealthiest and most powerful transnational corporations of the Internet economy. A company that has been very successful in leveraging its innovative technologies for the sake of constantly turning global flows of data and information into global flows of money, also creating, in the meantime, new problems for the competitive potential of other companies, for the tax bases of governments and for the protection of fundamental rights. On the other hand, the EU is the most advanced institutional experiment to date of expanding not only markets, but also law and politics, as well as the very idea of constitution, beyond the nation state.

The recent conflicts between Google and the EU in the areas of competition, taxation and human rights may be seen, therefore, as a good "proxy" for the more general economic, legal and political (to a certain extent, also constitutional) disputes related to the regulation and control of the Internet.

As the Snowden revelations have shown, these disputes also have a clear geopolitical and geoeconomic relevance. They are influenced by the ability of certain nation states, mainly the US, to tap global networks of communication, the very "materialities of cyberspace", in order to secretly extract data and information and to turn them into opportunities to extend political power and to increase economic gain.

The EU itself seems to keep a somewhat paradoxical relationship with transnational corporations of US origin, especially in the new media sector, where these companies are clearly dominant. At the same time as the process of economic integration and the rules of the single market facilitate the penetration of US companies, their dominance tends to be perceived as a threat to the European "economic constitution", to the public finances of Member States and to the privacy of European citizens.

The three sets of conflicts between Google and the EU are all connected in some way with the disturbing effects of global data flows, that is to say, with the use of digital technologies to accelerate the circulation of wealth and information around the world, something that challenges the traditional regulatory powers of nation states and the effectiveness of their constitutions. Considering that data is now "everywhere", the conflicts are basically related to the competition for data, the taxation of data and the protection from data. The economic and political exploitation of data and information by technological means is, therefore, at the center of the debate.

The transconstitutional protection of privacy

From a constitutional (or transconstitutional) perspective, the main concern related to the conflicts is with the enforcement of fundamental rights against the threats stemming from these global flows of data that transcend territorial borders and national jurisdictions. As shown by the analysis of the case law of the CJEU, these flows create common constitutional problems for more than one legal order that none of them can solve alone.

These constitutional problems are related mainly to the protection of privacy. Contrary to the prospects and interests of the business and intelligence sectors, the rise and spread of the Internet and the consequent acceleration and amplification of global data flows do not entail the end of privacy, but its re-birth. Economic, political and technological changes also cause privacy itself to change, to expand its scope to the protection of personal data against the automatic means of data processing, the increasing capacities of data storage and the ubiquitous possibilities of data collection and exchange. Beyond its liberal role as a negative liberty, privacy has also developed a more positive and active dimension. It has come to be understood as a general guarantee of freedom, equality and dues process online against the power of public and private organizations. Digital bureaucracies that both expose and discriminate, directly affecting the lives of people, while their inner workings remain relatively secret and unknown.

Privacy, just like the other "rights of men", has a constitutional dimension that is common to multiple legal orders. It is recognized as a human right in international law and as a fundamental right in the constitutional law of many nation states, as well as in the supranational legal order of the EU. It is also increasingly used to shape (or to claim the shaping of) the more or less autonomous forms of law-making of Internet companies and the "multistakeholder" organizations of the global regime of Internet governance, be it in the formulation of their privacy policies and general terms of use, be it in the very design of their technologies and technological standards – the so-called *lex digitalis.*

As a right that may be invoked against either the state or "private parties", it has both "vertical" and "horizontal" effects. It is a legal artefact for the protection of people and their personal data that simultaneously puts limits on and provides legitimacy for the exercise of power in any given political order or "community", be it national, supranational, international or even transnational, such as the "global Internet community" – a community that is certainly fictitious, but probably no less real than the "international community of states" or even the "European community" itself, not to mention the various national and subnational "communities" of our contemporary world society.

The protection of privacy in cyberspace, as well as the protection of other human or fundamental rights in general, tends to raise constitutional problems that are potentially global or transnational in nature.[8] This is the case for the implementation of the right to be forgotten, as well as of the imposition of limits on public and private organizations that exploit personal data for political and economic purposes. In other words, this applies to both the Google indexes.

In *Google Spain*, the CJEU recognized a right against search engines that is European-wide. It is based on the rights to privacy and to the protection of personal data provided for in the Charter of Fundamental Rights of the EU. A supranational right that is binding in all the Member States, and not only in Spain.

The ensuing debates about the implementation of the decision, however, have shown that the recognition of a right to be forgotten has consequences that are not restricted to Europe, or to the EU's supranational legal order.

First of all, regarding the issue of territorial jurisdiction, while Google has tried to restrict as much as possible the territorial scope of the right, European data protection authorities have claimed that the right should be implemented globally, that is to say, on all versions of Google's website, so that no one, no matter the territorial location from where the Internet is accessed, is able to search and find the links that are the object of legally enforced forgetting. The right to be forgotten, however, is a European invention. It does not necessarily match international human rights standards, not to mention the multiple national constitutional standards of different nation states outside Europe.

Second, regarding the issue of enforcement, or private enforcement, the EU is already relying on Google and other search engines as the "courts of first instance" to implement the right. This has an impact on the so-called *lex digitalis*. The privacy policies and the general terms of use generally employed by Internet companies around the world to regulate their relationships with their users (or consumers) must now take this new right into consideration. Google itself has implemented changes in its internal mechanisms of corporate governance in order to implement the decision. It commissioned an independent advisory council of experts to formulate the criteria that allegedly orient its internal "case law", whose details are now regularly published in its transparency report, together with other data and statistics about its "rulings" on the so-called "European privacy requests for search removals". Its own technology or "code" also had to be adapted in order to deal with the vast number of these requests, which, when granted, also require further technological implementation that changes the very configuration of the "first index".

8 Neves (2013 [2009]) *Transconstitutionalism*, p. 157ff, speaks of the "pluridimensional transconstitutionalism of human rights", the fact that the violation of human rights tend to raise constitutional problems that are common to more than one legal order and whose solution may require some degree of dialogue and mutual understanding between different courts. In a rather similar vein, Marramao (2008) *La Passione del Presente*, p. 169ff, also stresses the process of "de-territorialization" of law that follows the global recognition of human rights.

Third, regarding the balance to be struck between privacy and freedom of expression, since the very exercise of the right to be forgotten depends on the "role played by the data subject in public life", complex and difficult collisions may be expected to arise in future cases. If the right is to be enforced in the EU only, the transconstitutional solutions to the collisions may come from the already established mechanisms for the judicial dialogue between European and national courts. However, if the courts and data protection authorities in Europe are to insist on the global enforcement of the right, then a much broader transconstitutional dialogue will be required in order to accommodate different conceptions of privacy and freedom of expression beyond Europe – for instance, the European strong data protection framework may be expected to collide with the very permissive US tradition on free speech, not to mention other different national and international interpretations of privacy and freedom of expression.

In relation to the "second index", the CJEU has attempted, first, to impose some limitations to the bulk collection of personal data inside the EU by invalidating the Data Retention Directive in *Digital Rights Ireland*, and, then, to establish (or re-establish) some limits to transnational (or transatlantic) data flows by invalidating the Safe Harbour Agreement in *Schrems*. Two typical exercises of judicial review: one directed against EU legislation, the other against a decision of the European Commission that, in practice, had declared US law to be compatible with European privacy standards.

The second decision is very instructive, even if its practical effects may turn out to be very limited. The Safe Harbour Agreement provided a framework for the self-certification of companies under the oversight of US public authorities. Instead of the adoption of a traditional international treaty clearly defining the legal obligations of the parties, the EU and the US opted for a more informal agreement that established a complex network of mutual legal compromises between different legal orders: (i) companies pledged to observe, in their internal practices and governance structures, privacy standards allegedly similar to those valid in Europe, (ii) US public authorities promised to oversee the promises of these companies, while (iii) the EU Commission, against the advice of the European Parliament and European data protection authorities, declared (or promised) that all these promises ensured an "adequate level of protection" to the privacy of European citizens.

In the end, after the Snowden leaks, it became clear that the main problem was not only the level of protection offered by the companies themselves with regard to the transborder flows of data over their own intranets, but the lack of protection against mass surveillance by US public authorities. And it remains to be seen if the Privacy Shield, with its new round of mutual compromises and its brand-new "Ombudsperson", will offer any additional protection against the US "intelligence community".

What is certain is that the privacy risks posed by the activities of companies like Google to European citizens are global or transnational in nature. They present constitutional (or transconstitutional) problems related to the enforcement of fundamental rights recognized at the supranational level – rights that, according to international standards, are valid "online", as well as "offline" – against global flows of data controlled mainly by transnational corporations and available on "bulk demand" to the intelligence services of multiple nation states, especially the US.

Therefore, the protection of privacy must also be articulated transnationally (or transconstitutionally). That is to say, it must take into consideration the various legal orders involved, which include EU law, the law of EU Member States, US law, international law and even the more or less autonomous forms of law-making of transnational corporations of the digital economy.

Even with all the eventual shortcomings of the initial solutions proposed to address the problem, the EU has, nonetheless, set the stage for a sort of transconstitutional debate. It has recognized a new right – or a new dimension of already existing rights, which is basically the same – against new media companies like Google, a right to reinstate some degree of forgetting in face of the automatic forms of remembrance made possible with the worldwide spread of digital technologies.[9] It has also attempted to curb the power of public and private organizations over global data flows, re-enforcing the role of data protection authorities vis-à-vis "digital bureaucracies" that operate transnationally.

Constitutionalizing markets over politics

These European efforts to extend the protection of privacy in cyberspace are a sign that constitutionalism itself may be expanded at the level of world society even without the emergence of constitutions beyond the nation state. However, the EU represents a more ambitious project of supranational integration that might (or should) eventually count on a real and effective constitution at the supranational level, even if it is a "plural" and "multilevel" one.

If the human rights conflicts involving Google illustrate the potential role of the EU in the expansion of constitutionalism beyond the state, the competition and fiscal conflicts show, instead, some of its limits. Here we turn again to the often-criticized democratic deficit of the EU, which is itself a deficit of politics, or democratic and redistributive politics.

Google's leading position as both the worldwide most popular search engine and the platform most used for mobile navigation gives the company significant control over global flows of data and information. Whether or not this may be characterized as a monopoly, Google's dominance poses serious problems in terms of the concentration of markets, as well as the concentration of the media. It raises not only antitrust concerns, but concerns over media pluralism online and the very conditions for the exercise of the fundamental rights to freedom of expression and access to information, not to mention the rights to privacy and data protection.

Notwithstanding all the exaggerated media rhetoric over the recent antitrust investigations and proceedings carried out by the European Commission against

9 This right has been ascertained based on the assessment of the economic reality of the operations of Google in Europe, an assessment that might eventually prove to be useful also for tax purposes.

Google, the legal cases themselves must be constructed based on the more restricted and very specific mechanisms of competition law. They do not (and probably cannot) address the more general problems of freedom to communicate and to exchange information on the Internet, which may be negatively affected by Google's secret algorithm, but only the more limited aspects of freedom to shop online and to eventually download more apps. Inflated expectations are probably to be met with great frustration.

After all, the European "economic constitution" – that is to say, the four fundamental freedoms of movement and the basic rules and principles on competition and state aid contained in the founding treaties, and further developed in secondary legislation and the case law of the European courts, that work as supranational constraints on national state politics – is tailored to protect markets and consumers, and not democratic institutions and fundamental rights, on which it may only have an indirect effect.

This corpus of supranational economic law that may potentially reduce the market power of Google in Europe is paradoxically the same that allows the company to generate huge profits in the continent with minimal tax burdens. Google's very mobile income is able to move freely in the single market in search of the most favorable tax rules. An income that depends on the integration of activities carried out in multiple nation states, but which, in practice, ends up being taxed in none of them.

While "fearful" companies and dissatisfied consumers may count on the European institutions and the European founding treaties for economic law enforcement against Google, nation states and taxpayers are still searching in vain for supranational action in the field of corporate taxation that would effectively prevent transnational corporations like Google from avoiding taxes in the continent. An indication that the digital single market seems to get along well with the digital avoidance of taxes.[10]

The different ways of dealing with the competition and fiscal conflicts involving Google may be described as a consequence of the limitations and structural imbalances of the European constitutional project itself. Notwithstanding some positive developments in terms of the enforcement of privacy and data protection online, when it comes to cyberspace, the EU's "plural" and "multilevel" constitutional system also favors the supranational integration of markets in relation to that of politics.

10 It is probably not by chance that the most relevant actions related to tax avoidance are currently being taken by the commissioner for competition, who has recently "condemned" some Member States for recovering "illegal state aid" granted to transnational corporations in the form of "tax rulings" that, in practice, officially approved the tax avoidance strategies of these companies. For instance, Ireland has been recently "sanctioned" to recover thirteen billion euros of "illegal state aid" granted to Apple. See: European Commission (2016) *State aid: Ireland gave illegal tax benefits to Apple worth up to €13 billion*. To the European Commission, however, it seems that the problem is not tax avoidance itself, but the disruption of market competition when the possibility of avoiding taxes is selectively granted to a few companies only.

From the perspective of systems theory, the structural coupling between law and politics at the supranational level works, basically, to limit the range of action of Member States in the regulation of the single market without providing the EU institutions with the legitimacy and adequate powers to compensate this loss of public regulatory capacity. While freedom of contract, property rights and competition acquire a sort of constitutional status due to the primacy of EU economic law over national law, the historically very important issue of taxation is only addressed at the supranational level when it comes to removing the obstacles to economic integration. To a certain extent, the constitutionalization of markets outpaces the constitutionalization of politics, as the unfolding of the competition and fiscal conflicts involving Google seems to corroborate.

If the constitution is a form of two sides, a paradoxical form that serves to hide (or unfold) the very unity of the difference between the legal and political systems, the conflicts between Google and the EU may also indicate that, while the legal side of constitutionalism has been expanding beyond its traditional national settings, its political side is still evolving at a slower pace. In other words, that the discourses and practices related to the global (or transconstitutional) protection of rights have not been followed by the institutionalization of more inclusive organizations and procedures for collective decision-making.

At the level of the EU, this corresponds to the fact that the single market, as well as its "digital counterpart", has a much stronger structural coupling with EU law than with EU politics, so that it is easier to enforce private competition for data than to tax the wealth extracted from global data flows.[11] In the conflicts with Google, it is possible to see some of the same systemic asymmetries and structural imbalances of functional differentiation reproduced in the EU, asymmetries and imbalances that the normative demands of constitutionalism (or transconstitutionalism) are supposed to counter.[12]

Human contingency and data determinism

As a global network for the worldwide circulation of communication and information, the Internet intensifies old problems and conflicts at the same time as it gives rise to new ones. The concentration of markets is now pursued by means of the concentration of data, as well as the challenges to the taxation of an ever more

11 Neves (2015) 'Comparing transconstitutionalism in an asymmetric world society', p. 7, refers to this general problem as a sort of asymmetry between the forms of law: "The legal forms of contract and property affirm themselves expansively against the legal forms of environment and inclusion. In the context of new developments in world society, the functionally determined forms of economic law are increasingly stronger than the territorially conditioned forms of political law in the constitutional state".

12 In the words of Neves (2016) 'Paradoxes of transconstitutionalism in Latin America', e-book 82%: "Transconstitutionalism takes the form of a basic normative counterpoint to both the expansionary primacy of the cognitive structures of world society (linked to the economy, technology and science) and the semantics of the control of information (and knowledge) by the mass media".

globalized economy now extend to the taxation of its ever more accelerated global data flows. Moreover, the concern over the power of databases and the risks posed by the automatic processing of personal data become even more relevant now that data, or "big data", seem to be "everywhere".

To a certain extent, the main problem with databases and the automatic processing of personal data is not what they show about people, but rather what they hide. Not what they record, but what they cannot access. Not what they remember, but what they forget. In other words, their selectivity is just as threatening, or even more threatening, than their massive capacity to record and process data.[13]

This forgotten side is the "real side" of people beyond all profiles, that which they really are and that no machine can guess, because it is uncertain and undetermined. The consciousness is also a "black box". Even in the context of "big data" and mass surveillance, the consciousness remains a mystery. For an effective protection of privacy and personal data, it is the mystery of the consciousness that must be remembered, that should not be forgotten.[14]

The success of Google seems to come mainly from the recognition of this mystery, from the way the company capitalizes the very contingency of its users in the form of the "virtual contingency" that is constantly being fed back into its machines. It is a pardox, therefore, that Google itself, together with its two indexes, ends up banalizing and somehow hiding this same mystery. Google does that by creating both (i) profiles that expose only limited (and at times inconvenient) data fragments of people to their peers, and (ii) profiles that help other organizations to constantly classify, categorize and discriminate them. As a result, the uniqueness and unpredictability of the user is turned into the fragmented and routinized calculability of the profile.

It seems reasonable, then, to insist, as the EU is currently trying to, on a sort of "data ecology" that legally protects forgetting as a dimension of freedom.[15] Freedom against mass surveillance by digital bureaucracies, as well as mass surveillance by the masses themselves. That is why forgetting has become an element of privacy and data protection. A form of protecting and reinforcing the indeterminacy and contingency of people against the behaviorism and determinism of data and global data flows.

13 According to Solove (2001) 'Privacy and power', p. 1425: "The privacy problem stems paradoxically from the pervasiveness of this data—the fact that it encompasses much of our lives—as well as from its limitations— how it fails to capture us, how it distorts who we are".

14 In the words of Esposito (2013) 'Digital prophecies and Web intelligence', p. 138: "We should not keep a secret, but preserve a mystery: the mystery of the black box of the individual psyche".

15 Mayer-Schönberger (2007) 'Useful void'; Rodotà (2014) *Il Mondo nella Rete*, e-book 37%ff; Rodotà (2012) *Il Diritto di Avere Diritti*, p. 404ff; Rouvroy (2007) 'Réinventer l'art d'oublier et de se faire oublier dans la société de l'information?'.

Bibliography

Articles, books and conferences

Abbate, Janet (1999) *Inventing the Internet*, Cambridge (MA): MIT Press.

Agamben, Giorgio (2003) *Stato di Eccezione*, Torino: Bollati Borighieri.

Albers, Marion (2014) 'Realizing the complexity of data protection', in Serge Gutwirth, Ronald Leenes and Paul De Hert (eds) *Reloading Data Protection: Multidisciplinary Insights and Contemporary Challenges*, Heidelberg: Springer.

Alexy, Robert (2003) 'Constitutional rights, balancing and rationality', *Ration Juris* 16(2): 139–151.

Almunia, Joaquín (2014) 'We discipline Google', *Franfurter Allgemeine*, 13 May 2014, <http://www.faz.net/aktuell/feuilleton/debatten/the-digital-debate/joaquin-almunia-we-discipline-google-12937515.html>.

Alston, Philip (ed) (2005) *Non-State Actors and Human Rights*, Oxford: Oxford University Press.

Alves Jr, Sergio (2013) 'Internet governance in the age of surveillance', *Berkeley Technology Law Journal*, 21 October 2013, <http://btlj.org/?p=3066>.

Alves Jr, Sergio (2014) 'The Internet Balkanization fragmentation', DiploFoundation, 2 October 2014, <http://www.diplomacy.edu/blog/internet-balkanization-fragmentation>.

Anderson, Chris (2008) 'The end of theory: the data deluge makes the scientific method obsolete', *Wired*, 23 June 2008, <http://archive.wired.com/science/discoveries/magazine/16-07/pb_theory>.

Anderson, Nate (2010) 'Google demands neutrality (just don't apply it to them)', *Ars Technica*, 27 April 2010, <http://arstechnica.com/tech-policy/2010/04/google-demands-neutrality-just-dont-apply-it-to-them>.

Anderson, Nate (2010) 'Search neutrality? How Google became a neutrality target', *Ars Technica*, 30 April 2010, <http://arstechnica.com/tech-policy/2010/04/search-neutrality-google-becomes-neutraliy>.

Arendt, Hannah (1998 [1958]) *The Human Condition*, Chicago: The University of Chicago Press.

Argenton, Cédric and Jens Prüfer (2012) 'Search engine competition with network externalities', *Journal of Competition Law & Economics* 8(1): 73–105.

Arrighi, Giovanni (1994) *The Long Twentieth Century: Money, Power, and the Origins of Our Times*, London: Verso.

Arrighi, Giovanni and Beverly G. Silver eds (1999) *Chaos and Governance in the Modern World System*, Minneapolis: University of Minnesota Press.

Arrow, Kenneth (1996) 'The economics of information', *Empirica* 23: 119–128.

Askitas, Nikolaos (2015) 'Google search activity data and breaking trends', *IZA World of Labour*, November 2015.

Assange, Julian (2014) *When Google Met WikiLeaks*, New York: OR Books.

Assmann, Aleida (2008) 'Canon and archive', in Astrid Erll and Ansgar Nünnin (eds) *Cultural Memory Studies: An International and Interdisciplinary Handbook*, Berlin: Walter de Gruyter.

Assmann, Jan (2008) 'Communicative and cultural memory', in Astrid Erll and Ansgar Nünnin (eds) *Cultural Memory Studies: An International and Interdisciplinary Handbook*, Berlin: Walter de Gruyter.

Aujean, Michel (2010) 'Tax policy in the EU: between harmonisation and coordination?', *Transfer: European Review of Labour and Research* 16(1): 11–22.

Ausloos, Jef (2012) 'The "right to be forgotten" – worth remembering?', *Computer Law & Security Review* 28(2): 143–152.

Backer, Larry Catá (2006) 'The autonomous global corporation: on the role of organizational law beyond asset partitioning and legal personality', *Tulsa Law Review* 41(3): 541–572.

Backer, Larry Catá (2012) 'Transnational corporate constitutionalism: the emergence of a constitutional order for economic enterprises', *EUI Working Papers*, <http://ssrn.com/abstract=2038081>.

Bain, Malcom (2012) 'Google Chrome and Android: legal aspects of open source software', in Aurelio Lopez-Tarruella (ed) *Google and the Law: Empirical Approaches to Legal Aspects of Knowledge-Economy Business Models*, The Hague: T.M.C. Asser Press.

Bakan, Joel (2004) *The Corporation: The Pathological Pursuit of Profit and Power*, New York: Free Press.

Baker, Stewart (2010) 'The privacy problem: what's wrong with privacy?', in Berin Szoka and Adam Marcus (eds) *The Next Digital Decade: Essays on the Future of the Internet*, Washington: TechFreedom.

Balkin, Jack M. (2004) 'Digital speech and democratic culture: a theory of freedom of expression for the information society', *New York University Law Review* 79(1): 1–55.

Ballon, Pieter and Eric Van Heesvelde (2011) 'ICT platforms and regulatory concerns in Europe', *Telecommunications Policy* 35(8): 702–714.

Bamford, James (1982) *The Puzzle Palace: A Report on America's Most Secret Agency*, Boston: Houghton-Mifflin.

Bamford, James (2002) *Body of Secrets: Anatomy of the Ultra-Secret National Security Agency*, New York: Anchor Books.

Bamford, James (2008) *The Shadow Factory: the Ultra-Secret NSA from 9/11 to the Eavesdropping on America*, New York: Doubleday.

Barbrook, Richard and Andy Cameron (1996) 'The Californian ideology', *Science as Culture* 6(1): 44–72.

Barlow, John (1992) 'Decrypting the Puzzle Palace', *Communications of the ACM* 35(7): 25–31.

Barlow, John (1996) 'A declaration of the independence of cyberspace', <https://www.eff.org/cyberspace-independence>.

Barocas, Solon (2014) 'Data mining and the discourse on discrimination', Conference on Knowledge Discovery and Data Mining (KDD), Proceedings of the Data Ethics Workshop, 24–27 August 2014, New York City.

Barocas, Solon and Andrew D. Selbst (2016) 'Big data's disparate impact', *California Law Review* 104: 671–732.

Bateson, Gregory (1972) *Steps to an Ecology of Mind*, London: Jason Aronson Inc.

Bechmann, Anja (2013) 'Internet profiling: the economy of data intraoperability on Facebook and Google', *MedieKultur* 29(55): 72–91.

Becker, Konrad (2009) 'The power of classification: culture, context, command, control, communications, computing', in Konrad Becker and Felix Stalder (eds) *Deep Search: The Politics of Search Beyond Google*, Innsbruck: Studien Verlag.

Becker, Konrad and Felix Stalder (eds) (2009) *Deep Search: The Politics of Search Beyond Google*, Innsbruck: Studien Verlag.

Belli, Luca and Jamila Venturini (2016) 'Private ordering and the rise of terms of service as cyber-regulation', *Internet Policy Review* 5(4): 1–17.

Benkler, Yochai (2006) *The Wealth of Networks: How Social Production Transforms Markets and Freedom*, New Haven: Yale University Press.

Benvenisti, Eyal (2008) 'Reclaiming democracy: the strategic uses of foreign and international law by national courts', *American Journal of International Law* 102: 241–274.

Bernal, Paul (2014) 'The EU, the US and right to be forgotten', in Serge Gutwirth, Ronald Leenes and Paul De Hert (eds) *Reloading Data Protection: Multidisciplinary Insights and Contemporary Challenges*, Heidelberg: Springer.

Bernardi, Luigi (2015) 'Internet and taxation in the European Union: a primer', *Munich Personal RePEc Archive*, Paper No. 65638, 17 July 2015, <https://mpra.ub.uni-muenchen.de/65638>.

Blau, John (2014) 'NSA surveillance sparks talk of national Internets', *IEEE Spectrum* 51(2): 14–16.

Borden, Charles E. and Claire Rajan (2013) 'Transnational human rights litigation after *Kiobel*', *The Business and Human Rights Review*, Spring2013, Issue 2: 30–32.

Borges, Jorge Luís (1962 [1942]) 'Funes the memorious', in *Labyrinths*, New Directions.

Borges, Jorge Luís 1983) *La Memoria de Shakespeare*, Madrid: Alianza.

Böröcz, József and Mahua Sarkar (2005) 'What is the EU?', *International Sociology* 20(2): 153–173.

Börzel, Tanja A. (2010) 'European governance: governing with or without the state?', in Petra Dobner and Martin Loughlin (eds) *The Twilight of Constitutionalism?*, Oxford: Oxford University Press.

Boyle, James (1997) 'Foucault in cyberspace: surveillance, sovereignty, and hardwired censors', *University of Cincinnati Law Review* 66(1): 177–205.

Brin, Sergay and Larry Page (1998) 'The anatomy of a large-scale hypertextual Web search engine', *Computer Networks and ISDN Systems* 30(1): 107–117.

Brown, George Spencer (1972) *Laws of Form*, New York: The Julian Press.

Brunkhorst, Hauke (2010) 'Constitutionalism and democracy in the world society', in Petra Dobner and Martin Loughlin (eds) *The Twilight of Constitutionalism?*, Oxford: Oxford University Press.

Brunkhorst, Hauke (2014) 'The beheading of the legislator: the European crisis – paradoxes of constitutionalizing democratic capitalism', *Direito.UnB* 1(1): 89–112.

Brunton, Finn and Helen Nissenbaum (2013) 'Political and ethical perspectives on data obfuscation', in Mireille Hildebrandt and Katja de Vries (eds) *Privacy, Due Process and the Computational Turn: The Philosophy of Law Meets the Philosophy of Technology*, New York: Routledge.

Búrca, Gráinne and Neil Walker (2003) 'Law and transnational civil society: upsetting the agenda?', *European Law Journal* 9(4): 387–400.

Burke, Edmund (1790) *Reflections on the Revolution in France, and on the Proceedings in Certain Societies in London Relative to that Event*, London: J. Dodsley.

Burrell, Jenna (2016) 'How the machine "thinks": understanding opacity in machine learning algorithms', *Big Data & Society* 3(1): 1–12.

Calliess, Gralf-Peter (2011) 'Transnational corporations revisited', *Indiana Journal of Global Legal Studies* 18(2): 601–615.

Calliess, Gralf-Peter and Peer Zumbansen (2010) *Rough Consensus and Running Code: A Theory of Transnational Private Law*, Oxford: Hart Publishing.

Calvino, Italo (1988) *Lezioni Americane: Sei Proposte per il Prossimo Millennio*, Milano: Garzanti.

Calvino, Italo (1988) *Six Memos for the Next Millennium*, Cambridge (MA): Harvard University Press.

Cassese, Sabino (1986) 'The rise and decline of the notion of state', *International Political Science Review* 7(2): 120–130.

Cassese, Sabino (2002) *La Crisi dello Stato*, Roma: Laterza.

Cassese, Sabino (2006) 'Administrative law without the state? The challenge of global regulation', *International Law and Politics* 37(4): 663–694.

Cassese, Sabino (2006) *Oltre lo Stato*, Roma: Laterza.

Cassese, Sabino (2009) *I Tribunali di Babele: I Giudici alla Ricerca di un Nuovo Ordine Globale*, Roma: Donzelli.

Cassese, Sabino *et a.* (eds) (2008) *Global Administrative Law: Cases, Materials, Issues*, Istituto di Ricerche sulla Pubblica Amministrazione (IRPA) and Institute for International Law and Justice (IILJ), <http://www.iilj.org/gal/documents/GALCasebook2008.pdf>.

Castells, Manuell (2010) *End of Millennium*, Oxford and Cambridge (MA): Wiley-Blackwell.

Castells, Manuell (2010) *The Rise of the Network Society*, Oxford and Cambridge (MA): Wiley-Blackwell.

Christensen, John (2011) 'The looting continues: tax havens and corruption', *Critical Perspectives on International Business* 7(2): 177–196.

Christensen, John and Richard Murphy (2004) 'The social irresponsibility of corporate tax avoidance: taking CSR to the bottom line', *Development* 47(3): 37–44.

Citron, Danielle Keats (2008) 'Technological due process', *Washington University Law Review* 85(6): 1249–1313.

Clapham, Andrew (2006) *Human Rights Obligations of Non-State Actors*, Oxford: Oxford University Press.

Clarke, Roger (1988) 'Information technology and dataveillance', *Communications of the ACM* 31(5) 498–512.

Clarke, Roger (1997) 'Introduction to dataveillance and information privacy', 15 August 2017, <http://www.rogerclarke.com/DV/Intro.html>.

Clarke, Roger (2003) 'Dataveillance – 15 years on', 31 March 2003, <http://www.rogerclarke.com/DV/DVNZ03.html>.

Cohen, Jean L. (2008) 'A global state of emergency or the further constitutionalization of international law: a pluralist approach', *Constellations* 15(4): 456–484.

Cohen, Jean L. (2010) 'Constitutionalism beyond the state: myth or necessity?', *RECON Online*, Working Paper 2010/16, <http://www.reconproject.eu/main.php/RECON_wp_1016.pdf?fileitem=50511999>.

Cohen, Julie E. (2013) 'What privacy is for', *Harvard Law Review* 126(7): 1904–1933.

Corkery, Jim, Jay Forder, Dan Svantesson and Enrico Mercuri (2015) 'Taxes, the Internet and the digital economy', *Revenue Law Journal* 23(1): Article 7.

Corsi, Giancarlo (2000) 'Protest and decision-making in a society of blame', *Democracy & Nature* 6(3): 361–374.

Corsi, Giancarlo (2002) 'Sociologia da constituição', *Revista Jurídica UNIGRAN* 4(2): 97–115.

Corsi, Giancarlo (2007) 'La finzione dello Stato. La nascita del medium politico (secoli XVI–XVIII)', in Alberto Cevolini (ed), *Potere e Modernità. Stato, Diritto, Costituzione*, Milano: Franco Angeli.

Corsi, Giancarlo (2016) 'On paradoxes in constitutions', in Alberto Febbrajo and Giancarlo Corsi (eds) *Sociology of Constitutions: A Paradoxical Perspective*, New York: Routledge.

Costa, Pietro (2004) 'Immagini della sovranità fra medioevo ed età moderna: la metafora della "verticalità"', *Scienza & Politica* 16(31): 9–19.

Crane, Daniel A. (2012) 'Search neutrality as an antitrust principle', *George Mason Law Review* 19(5): 1199–1209.

Crane, Daniel A (2014) 'After search neutrality: drawing a line between promotion and demotion', *I/S: A Journal of Law and Policy for the Information Society* 9(3): 397–406.

Custers, Bart (2016) 'Click here to consent forever: expiry dates for informed consent', *Big Data & Society* 3(1): 1–6.

Darby III, Joseph B. and Kelsey Lemaster (2007) 'Double Irish more than doubles the tax savings: hybrid structure reduces Irish, U.S. and worldwide taxation', *Practical US/International Tax Strategies* 11(9): 2–16.

Darnton, Robert (2009) 'Google & the future of books', *The New York Review of Books*, 12 February 2009, <http://www.nybooks.com/articles/archives/2009/feb/12/google-the-future-of-books>.

Darnton, Robert (2009) 'The library in the information age: 6000 years of script', in Konrad Becker and Felix Stalder (eds) *Deep Search: The Politics of Search Beyond Google*, Innsbruck: Studien Verlag.

Davenport, Thomas H. and D. J. Patil (2012) 'Data scientist: the sexiest job of the 21st century', *Harvard Business Review*, October 2012, <https://hbr.org/2012/10/data-scientist-the-sexiest-job-of-the-21st-century>.

De Busser, Els (2014) 'Privatization of information and the data protection reform', in Serge Gutwirth, Ronald Leenes and Paul De Hert (eds) *Reloading Data Protection: Multidisciplinary Insights and Contemporary Challenges*, Heidelberg: Springer.

De Filippi, Primavera (2013) 'Taxing the cloud: introducing a new taxation system on data collection?', *Internet Policy Review* 2(2): 1–7.

DeNardis, Laura (2010) 'The emerging field of Internet governance', *Yale Information Society Project Working Paper Series*, <https://papers.ssrn.com/sol3/papers.cfm?abstract_id=1678343>.

DeNardis, Laura (2014) *The Global War for Internet Governance*, New Haven: Yale University Press.

Diez, Fernando (2012) 'Google, in the aftermath of Microsoft and Intel: the right approach to antitrust enforcement in innovative High Tech Platform Markets?', <https://papers.ssrn.com/sol3/papers.cfm?abstract_id=2082882>.

Doane, Deborah (2005) 'The myth of CSR: the problem with assuming that companies can do well while also doing good is that markets really don't work that way', *Stanford Social Innovation Review*, Fall 2005: 23–29, <http://www.ssireview.org/articles/entry/the_myth_of_csr>.

Dobner, Petra and Martin Loughlin (eds) (2010) *The Twilight of Constitutionalism?*, Oxford: Oxford University Press. Döpfner, Mathias (2014) 'Why we fear Google – an open letter to Eric Schmidt', *Franfurter Allgemeine*, 17 April 2014, <https://archive.is/LTL6l>.

Downes, Larry (2010) 'A market approach to privacy policy', in Berin Szoka and Adam Marcus (eds) *The Next Digital Decade: Essays on the Future of the Internet*, Washington: TechFreedom.

Dunning, John H. (2001) 'The key literature on IB activities', in Alan M. Rugman and Thomas L. Brewer (eds) *The Oxford Handbook of International Business*, Oxford: Oxford University Press.

Eco, Umberto (1975) *Tratatto di Semiotica Generale*, Milano: Bompiani.

Eco, Umberto (1988) 'An *ars oblivionalis*? Forget it!', *Modern Language Association* 103(3): 254–261.

Eco, Umberto (2009) *Vertigine della Lista*, Milano: Bompiani.

Eden, Lorraine (2001) 'Taxes, transfer pricing, and the multinational enterprise', in Alan M. Rugman and Thomas L. Brewer (eds), *The Oxford Handbook of International Business*, Oxford: Oxford University Press.

Eidenmüller, Horst (2011) 'The transnational law market, regulatory competition, and transnational corporations', *Indiana Journal of Global Legal Studies* 18(2): 707–749.

Erixon, Fredrik (2015) 'The Google case and the promotion of the European digital economy', *ECIPE – European Center for International Political Economy*, Bulletin No. 1/2015, <http://www.ecipe.org/publications/the-google-case-promotion-of-europes-digital-economy>.

Esposito, Elena (2001) *La Memoria Sociale: Mezzi per Comunicare e Modi per Dimenticare*, Roma: Laterza.

Esposito, Elena (2004) 'The arts of contingency', *Critical Enquiry* 31(1): 7–25.

Esposito, Elena (2008) 'Social forgetting: a systems-theory approach', in Astrid Erll and Ansgar Nünnin (eds) *Cultural Memory Studies: An International and Interdisciplinary Handbook*, Berlin: Walter de Gruyter.

Esposito, Elena (2011) 'A time of divination and a time of risk: social preconditions for prophecy and prediction', *International Consortium for Research in the Humanities – Selected Lectures*, 30 November 2011, <http://ikgf.fau.de/content/articles/Elena_Esposito_-_Time_of_Divination.pdf>.

Esposito, Elena (2013) 'Digital prophecies and Web intelligence', in Mireille Hildebrandt and Katja de Vries (eds) *Privacy, Due Process and the Computational Turn: The Philosophy of Law Meets the Philosophy of Technology*, New York: Routledge.

Esposito, Elena (2013) 'The structures of uncertainty: performativity and unpredictability in economic operations', *Economy and Society* 42(1): 102–129.

Esposito, Elena (2014) 'Virtual contingency: digital techniques of remembering and forgetting', *ICI Lecture Series – Constituting Wholes II*, 27 January 2014, <https://legacy.ici-berlin.org/event/579>.

Esposito, Elena (2017) 'Algorithmic memory and the right to be forgotten on the Web', *Big Data & Society* 4(1): 1–11.

Esposito, Elena (2017) 'An ecology of differences. Communication, the Web and the question of borders', in Erich Hörl and James Burton, *General Ecology. The New Ecological Paradigm*, London and New York: Bloomsbury.

Esposito, Elena (2017) 'Artificial communication? The production of contingency by algorithms', *Zeitschrift für Soziologie* 46(4): 249–265.

Esposito, Elena (2017) 'Organizing without understanding: lists in ancient and in digital cultures', *Lili – Zeitschrift fur Literaturwissenschaft und Linguistik*, August 2017.

Evans, David S. (2008) 'Antitrust issues raised by the emerging global Internet economy', *Northwestern University Law Review* 102(4): 1987–2008.

Fassbender, Bardo (2007) '"We the peoples of the United Nations": constituent power and constituent form in international law', in Martin Loughlin and Neil Walker (eds) *The Paradox of Constitutionalism: Constituent Power and Constitutional Form*, Oxford: Oxford University Press.

Fassbender, Bardo (2009) *The United Nations Charter as the Constitution of the International Community*, Boston: Martinus Nijhoff Publishers.

Featherstone, Mike (2009) 'Ubiquitous media: an introduction', *Theory, Culture & Society* 26(2–3): 1–22.

Febbrajo, Alberto and Giancarlo Corsi (eds) (2016) *Sociology of Constitutions: A Paradoxical Perspective*, London and New York, Routledge.

Fioravanti, Maurizio (1999) *Costituzione*, Bologna: Il Mulino.

Fiormonte, Domenico, Teresa Numerico and Francesca Tomasi (2015) *The Digital Humanist: A Critical Inquiry*, New York: Punctum Books.

Fischer-Lescano, Andreas and Gunther Teubner (2004) 'Regime-collisions: the vain search for legal unity in the fragmentation of global law', *Michigan Journal of International Law* 25(4): 999–1046.

Fortunato, Santo, Alessandro Flammini, Filippo Menczer and Alessandro Vespignani (2006) 'The egalitarian effect of search engines', <https://arxiv.org/pdf/cs/0511005.pdf>.

Foucault, Michel (1979) *Microfísica do Poder*, Rio de Janeiro: Graal.

Froomkin (2003) 'HABERMAS@DISCOURSE.NET: toward a critical theory of cyberspace', *Harvard Law Review* 116(3): 749–873.

Ganghof, Steffen and Philipp Genschel (2008) 'Taxation and democracy in the EU', *Journal of European Public Policy* 15(1): 58–77.

Garcia, Flora J. (2005) 'Bodil Lindqvist: a Swedish churchgoer's violation of the European Union's Data Protection Directive should be a warning to U.S. legislators', *Fordham Intellectual Property, Media and Entertainment Law Journal* 15(4): 1204–1243.

Geist, Michael (2003) 'Cyberlaw 2.0', *Boston College Law Review* 44(2): 323–358.

Genschel, Philipp, Achim Kemmerling and Eric Seils (2011) 'Accelerating downhill: how the EU shapes corporate tax competition in the single market', *Journal of Common Market Studies* 49(3): 585–606.

Genschel, Philipp and Markus Jachtenfuchs (2011) 'How the European Union constrains the state: multilevel governance of taxation', *European Journal of Political Research* 50 (3): 293–314.

Gillespie, Tarleton (2010) 'The politics of "platforms"', *New Media & Society* 12(3): 347–364.

Ginzburg, Carlo (2010) *A História na Era Google*, Fronteiras do Pensamento, 29 November 2010, <https://www.youtube.com/watch?v=CqxP9taRUvA>.

Goldman, Eric (2006) 'Search engine bias and the demise of search engine utopianism', *Yale Journal of Law and Technology* 8(1): 111–123.

Goldman, Eric (2011) 'Revisiting search engine bias', *William Mitchell Law Review* 38(1): 96–110.

Goldsmith, Jack and Tim Wu (2006) *Who Controls the Internet? Illusions of a Borderless World*, Oxford: Oxford University Press.

Gordon, Scott (2002) *Controlling the State: Constitutionalism from Ancient Athens to Today*, Cambridge (MA): Harvard University Press.

Graef, Inge (2015) 'Stretching EU competition law tools for search engines and social networks', *Internet Policy Review* 4(3): 1–10.

Granka, Laura A. (2010) 'The politics of search: a decade retrospective', *The Information Society* 26(5): 364–374.

Greene, Jay (2011) 'Why Microsoft is taking on Google in Europe', *CNET*, 31 March 2011, <http://www.cnet.com/news/why-microsoft-is-taking-on-google-in-europe>.

Greenwald, Glenn (2014) *No Place to Hide: Edward Snowden, the NSA, and the U.S. Surveillance State*, New York: Metropolitan.

Greer, Steven (2000) *The Margin of Appreciation: Interpretation and Discretion under the European Convention on Human Rights*, Human Rights Files No. 17, Council of Europe Publishing, <http://www.echr.coe.int/LibraryDocs/DG2/HRFILES/DG2-EN-HRFILES-17(2000).pdf>.

Grimm, Dieter (1995) 'Does Europe need a constitution?', *European Law Journal* 1(3): 282–302.

Grimm, Dieter (2010) 'The achievement of constitutionalism and its prospects in a changed world', in Petra Dobner and Martin Loughlin (eds) *The Twilight of Constitutionalism?*, Oxford: Oxford University Press.

Grimmelmann, James (2007) 'Don't censor search', *The Yale Law Journal Pocket Part* 117: 48–52, <http://www.yalelawjournal.org/forum/dont-censor-search>.

Grimmelmann, James (2007) 'The structure of search engine law', *Iowa Law Review* 93(1): 1–63.

Grimmelmann, James (2009) 'The Google dilemma', *New York Law School Law Review* 53(4): 939–950.

Grimmelmann, James (2010) 'Some skepticism about search neutrality', in Berin Szoka and Adam Marcus (eds) *The Next Digital Decade: Essays on the Future of the Internet*, Washington: TechFreedom.

Grimmelmann, James (2014) 'Speech engines', *Minnesota Law Review* 98(3): 868–952.

Grimwood, Daniel (2013) 'Human rights in a post-*Kiobel* landscape', *The Business and Human Rights Review* 3: 33.

Gumbrecht, Hans Ulrich (2003) 'Why intermediality – if at all?', *Intermédialités* 2: 173–178.

Gumbrecht, Hans Ulrich (2014) *Our Broad Present: Time and Contemporary Culture*, New York: Columbia University Press.

Gumbrecht, Hans Ulrich and K. Ludwig Pffeifer (eds) (1994) *Materialities of Communication*, Stanford: Stanford University Press.

Gutwirth, Serge, Ronald Leenes and Paul De Hert (eds) (2014) *Reloading Data Protection: Multidisciplinary Insights and Contemporary Challenges*, Heidelberg: Springer.

Habermas, Jürgen (1991 [1962]) *The Structural Transformation of the Public Sphere: An Inquiry into a Category of Bourgeois Society*, Cambridge (MA): MIT Press.

Habermas, Jürgen (1995) 'Remarks on Dieter Grimm's "Does Europe need a constitution?"', *European Law Journal* 1(3): 303–307.

Habermas, Jürgen (1996 [1992]) *Between Facts and Norms: Contributions to a Discourse Theory of Law and Democracy*, Cambridge (MA): The MIT Press.

Habermas, Jürgen (2001 [1998]) *The Postnational Constellation: Political Essays*, Cambridge (MA): MIT Press.

Habermas, Jürgen (2002 [1996]) *The Inclusion of the Other: Studies in Political Theory*, Cambridge: Polity Press.

Habermas, Jürgen (2006 [2004]) *The Divided West*, Malden: Polity.

Habermas, Jürgen (2006 [2001]) *Time of Transitions*, Cambridge: Polity Press.

Habermas, Jürgen (2008) 'The constitutionalization of international law and the legitimation problems of a constitution for world society', *Constellations* 15(4): 444–455.

Habermas, Jürgen (2009) *Europe: The Faltering Project*, Cambridge: Polity Press.

Habermas, Jürgen (2012) *The Crisis of the European Union: A Response*, Cambridge: Polity Press.

Habermas, Jürgen (2015) *The Lure of Technocracy*, Cambridge: Polity Press.

Hafner, Katie and Matthew Lyon (1998) *Where Wizards Stay Up Late: The Origins of the Internet*, New York: Simon & Schuster.

Heidegger, Martin (1977) *The Question Concerning Technology and Other Essays*, New York: Grand Publishing.

Heider, Fritz (2017 [1926]) *Chose et médium*, Paris: Librarie Philosophique J. Vrin.

Hildebrandt, Mireille (2013) 'Profile transparency by design? Re-enabling double contingency', in Mireille Hildebrandt and Katja de Vries (eds) *Privacy, Due Process and the Computational Turn: The Philosophy of Law Meets the Philosophy of Technology*, New York: Routledge.

Hildebrandt, Mireille and Katja de Vries (eds) (2013) *Privacy, Due Process and the Computational Turn: The Philosophy of Law Meets the Philosophy of Technology*, New York: Routledge.

Hindman, Matthew, Kostas Tsioutsiouliklis and Judy A. Johnson (2003) '"Googlearchy": how a few heavily-linked sites dominate politics on the Web ', <http://citeseerx.ist.psu.edu/viewdoc/download?doi=10.1.1.160.8347&rep=rep1&type=pdf>.

Hobbes, Thomas (1651) *Leviathan, or the Matter, Form, & Power of a Common-wealth Ecclesiasticall and Civill*, London: Andrew Crooke.

Hoboken, Joris van (2009) 'Search engine law and freedom of expression: a European perspective', in Konrad Becker and Felix Stalder (eds) *Deep Search: The Politics of Search Beyond Google*, Innsbruck: Studien Verlag.

Holmes, Pablo (2011) 'The rhetoric of "legal fragmentation" and its discontents: evolutionary dilemmas in the constitutional semantics of global law', *Utrecht Law Review* 7 (2): 113–140.

Holmes, Stephen (1988) 'Precommitment and the paradox of democracy', in Jon Elster and Rune Slagstad (ed) *Constitutionalism and Democracy*, Cambridge: Cambridge University Press.

Holmes, Stephen and Cass R. Sustein (2000) *The Cost of Rights: Why Liberty Depends on Taxes*, New York: W. W. Norton and Company.

Hong, Qing and Michael Smart (2010) 'In praise of tax havens: international tax planning and foreign direct investment', *European Economic Review* 54: 82–95.

Howard, Philip N. (2004) 'Embedded media: who we know, what we know, and society online', in Philip N. Howard and Steve Jones (eds) *Society Online: The Internet in Context*, Thousand Oaks: SAGE Publications.

Hymer, Stephen (1970) 'The efficiency (contradictions) of multinational corporations', *The American Economic Review* 60(2): 441–448.

Ietto-Gillies, Grazia (2012) *Transnational Corporations and International Production: Concepts, Theories and Effects*, Cheltenham: Edward Elgar.

Interdisciplinary Internet Institute (2015) '*Taxing Internet use: the failed Hungarian proposal*', Interview with Balázs Gulyás, 2 November 2015, <http://www.theiii.org/index.php/1824/taxing-internet-use-the-failed-hungarian-proposal-interview-with-balazs-gulyas>.

Introna, Lucas D. and Helen Nissenbaum (2000) 'Shaping the Web: why the politics of search engines matters', *The Information Society* 16(3): 169–185.

Ippolita (2014) 'The dark side of Google: pre-afterword – social media times', in René König and Miriam Rasch (eds) *Society of the Query Reader: Reflections on Web Search*, Amsterdam: Institute of Network Cultures.

Johnson, David R. and David Post (1996) 'Law and borders: the rise of law in cyberspace', *Stanford Law Review* 48(5): 1367–1402.

Juncker, Jean-Claude (2014) *A New Start for Europe: My Agenda for Jobs, Growth, Fairness and Democratic Change*, Political Guidelines for the Next European Commission, <https://ec.europa.eu/commission/publications/president-junckers-political-guidelines_en>.

Kallinikos, Jannis (2009) 'On the computational rendition of reality: artefacts and human agency', *Organization* 16(2): 183–202.

Kallinikos, Jannis (2009) 'The making of ephemeria: on the shortening life spans of information', *The International Journal of Interdisciplinary Social Sciences* 4(3): 227–236.

Kallinikos, Jannis (2013) 'The allure of big data', *Mercury Magazine* 2(3): 40–43.

Kallinikos, Jannis, Aleksi Aaltonen and Attila Marton (2010) 'A theory of digital objects', *First Monday* 15(6–7), <http://journals.uic.edu/ojs/index.php/fm/article/view/3033/2564>.

Karavas, Vaios (2009) 'The force of code: law's transformation under information-technological conditions', *German Law Journal* 10(4): 463–481.

Karavas, Vaios and Gunther Teubner (2005) 'www.CompanyNameSucks.com: the horizontal effect of fundamental rights on "private parties" within autonomous Internet law', *Constellations* 12(2): 262–282.

Katz, Andrew (2012) 'Google, APIs, and the law: use, reuse and lock-in', in Aurelio Lopez-Tarruella (ed) *Google and the Law: Empirical Approaches to Legal Aspects of Knowledge-Economy Business Models*, The Hague: T.M.C. Asser Press.

Kello, Lucas (2017) *The Virtual Weapon and International Order*, New Haven: Yale University Press.

Kennedy, David (2008) 'The mystery of global governance', *Ohio Northern University Law Review* 34: 827–860.

Kerr, Ian (2013) 'Prediction, pre-emption, presumption: the path of law after the computational turn', in Mireille Hildebrandt and Katja de Vries (eds) *Privacy, Due Process and the Computational Turn: The Philosophy of Law Meets the Philosophy of Technology*, New York: Routledge.

Kingsbury, Benedict, Nico Krisch and Richard B. Stewart (2005) 'The emergence of global administrative law', *Law and Contemporary Problems* 68: 15–61.

Kittler, Friedrich (1996) 'The history of communication media', *CTHEORY*, <http://www.ctheory.net/articles.aspx?id=45>.

Kittler, Friedrich (1999 [1986]) *Gramophone, Film, Typewriter*, Stanford: Stanford University Press.

Kittler, Friedrich (2013) *The Truth of the Technological World*, Stanford: Stanford University Press.

Kittler, Friedrich (2014 [1986]) 'No such agency', *Theory, Culture & Society*, <http://www.theoryculturesociety.org/kittler-on-the-nsa>.

Kjaer, Paul (2011) 'Law and order within and beyond national configurations', in Paul F Kjaer, Gunther Teubner and Alberto Febbrajo (eds) *The Financial Crisis in Constitutional Perspective: The Dark Side of Functional Differentiation*, Oxford: Hart Publishing.

Kjaer, Paul, Gunther Teubner and Alberto Febbrajo (eds) (2011) *The Financial Crisis in Constitutional Perspective: The Dark Side of Functional Differentiation*, Oxford: Hart Publishing.

Klein, Naomi (2000) *No Logo: Taking Aim at the Brand Bullies*, New York: Picador.

Kleinbard, Edward D. (2011) 'Stateless income', *Florida Tax Review* 11(9): 699–773.

Kleinbard, Edward D (2011) 'The lessons of stateless income', *Tax Law Review* 65(1): 99–171.

Kobrin, Stephen J. (2001) 'Sovereignty@Bay: globalization, multinational enterprise, and the international political system', in Alan M. Rugman and Thomas L. Brewer (eds), *The Oxford Handbook of International Business*, Oxford: Oxford University Press.

Kobrin, Stephen J (2004) 'Safe harbours are hard to find: the trans-Atlantic data privacy dispute, territorial jurisdiction and global governance', *Review of International Studies* 30(1): 111–131.

König, René and Miriam Rasch (eds) (2014) *Society of the Query Reader: Reflections on Web Search*, Amsterdam: Institute of Network Cultures.

Koops, Bert-Jaap (2011) 'Forgetting footprints, shunning shadows: a critical analysis of the "right to be forgotten in big data practice"', *Scripted* 8(3): 229–256.

Koops, Bert-Jaap (2013) 'On decision transparency, or how to enhance data protection after the computational turn', in Mireille Hildebrandt and Katja de Vries (eds) *Privacy, Due Process and the Computational Turn: The Philosophy of Law Meets the Philosophy of Technology*, New York: Routledge.

Koselleck, Reinhart (1998 [1959]) *Critique and Crisis: Enlightenment and the Pathogenesis of Modern Society*, Cambridge (MA): MIT Press.

Koselleck, Reinhart (2004 [1979]) *Futures Past: On the Semantics of Historical Time*, New York: Columbia University Press.

Koskenniemi, Martti (2004) 'International law and hegemony: a reconfiguration', *Cambridge Review of International Affairs* 17(2): 197–218.

Koskenniemi, Martti (2005) *Global Legal Pluralism: Multiple Regimes and Multiple Modes of Thought*, <http://www.helsinki.fi/eci/Publications/Koskenniemi/MKPluralism-Harvard-05d%5B1%5D.pdf>.

Koskenniemi, Martti (2007) 'Constitutionalism as mindset: reflections on Kantian themes about international law and globalization', *Theoretical Inquiries in Law* 8(1): 9–36.

Koskenniemi, Martti (2011) 'Empire and international law: the real Spanish contribution', *University of Toronto Law Review* 61(1): 1–36.

Krämer, Jan, Lukas Wiewiorra and Christof Winhardt (2013) 'Net neutrality: a progress report', *Telecommunications Policy* 37(9): 794–813.

Krisch, Nico (2005) 'International law in times of hegemony: unequal power and the shaping of the international legal order', *The European Journal of International Law* 16(5): 369–408.

Krugman, Paul R., Maurice Obstfeld and Marc J. Melitz (2012) *International Economics: Theory & Policy*, Boston: Addison-Wesley.

Kulk, Stefan and Frederik Borgesius (2014) '*Google Spain v. González*: did the court forget about freedom of expression?', *European Journal of Risk Regulation* 5(3): 389–398, <https://ssrn.com/abstract=2491486>.

Kumm, Mattias (2010) 'The best of times and the worst of times: between constitutional triumphalism and nostalgia', in Petra Dobner and Martin Loughlin (eds) *The Twilight of Constitutionalism?*, Oxford: Oxford University Press.

Kuner, Christopher (2011) 'Regulation of transborder data flows under data protection and privacy law: past, present and future', OECD Digital Economy Papers, N. 187, Paris: OECD Publishing.

Kuner, Christopher (2015) 'The Court of Justice of the EU judgment on data protection and Internet search engines', *LSE Law, Society and Economy Working Papers*, 3/2015.

Kuner, Christopher, Fred H. Cate, Christopher Millard, and Dan JerkerB. Svantesson (2012) 'The challenge of "big data" for data protection", *International Data Privacy Law* 2(2): 47–49.

Kurbalija, Jovan (2014) *An Introduction to Internet Governance*, Geneva: DIPLO Foundation.

Ladeur, Karl-Heinz (1997) 'Towards a theory of supranationality – the viability of the network concept', *European Law Journal* 3(1): 33–54.

Larnier, Jaron (2011) 'The local-global flip, or, "The Larnier Effect"', *Edge*, 29 August 2011, <https://www.edge.org/conversation/jaron_lanier-the-local-global-flip-or-the-lanier-effect>.

Larnier, Jaron (2014) 'Whoever owns our data will determine our fate', *Franfurter Allgemeine*, 24 April 2014, <http://www.faz.net/aktuell/feuilleton/debatten/the-digital-debate/almighty-google-whoever-owns-our-data-will-determine-our-fate-12908348.html>.

Leiner, Barry M.*et al* (2009) 'A brief history of the Internet', *ACM SIGCOMM Computer Communication Review* 39(5): 22–31.

Lessig, Lawrence (2006) *Code – Version 2.0*, New York: Basic Books.

Levy, Steven (2011) *In the Plex: How Google Thinks, Works, and Shapes Our Lives*, New York: Simon & Schuster.

Lewandowski, Dirk (2014) 'Why we need an independent index of the Web', in René König and Miriam Rasch (eds) *Society of the Query Reader: Reflections on Web Search*, Amsterdam: Institute of Network Cultures.

Lima, Pascal de (2014) 'Google ou la route de la servitude', *Le Monde*, 3 April 2014, <http://www.lemonde.fr/economie/article/2014/04/03/google-ou-la-route-de-la-servitude_4395186_3234.html>.

Litman, Jessica (2000) 'Information privacy/information property', *Stanford Law Review* 52: 1283–1313.

Loon, Sophie van (2012) 'The power of Google: first mover advantage or abuse of a dominant position?', in Aurelio Lopez-Tarruella (ed) *Google and the Law: Empirical Approaches to Legal Aspects of Knowledge-Economy Business Models*, The Hague: T.M.C. Asser Press.

Lopez-Tarruella, Aurelio (ed) (2012) *Google and the Law: Empirical Approaches to Legal Aspects of Knowledge-Economy Business Models*, The Hague: T.M.C. Asser Press.

Loughlin, Martin (2010) 'What is constitutionalization?', in Petra Dobner and Martin Loughlin (eds) *The Twilight of Constitutionalism?*, Oxford: Oxford University Press.

Loughlin, Martin and Neil Walker (eds) (2007) *The Paradox of Constitutionalism: Constituent Power and Constitutional Form*, Oxford: Oxford University Press.

Luhmann, Niklas (1982) *The Differentiation of Society*, New York: Columbia University Press.

Luhmann, Niklas (1990 [1981]) *Political Theory in the Welfare State*, Berlin: Walter de Gruyter.

Luhmann, Niklas (1993) 'The code of moral', *Cardozo Law Review* 14: 995–1009.

Luhmann, Niklas (1995) 'Legal argumentation: an analysis of its form', *The Modern Law Review* 58(3): 285–298.

Luhmann, Niklas (1995 [1984]) *Social Systems*, Stanford: Stanford University Press.

Luhmann, Niklas (1995) 'Why does society describe itself as postmodern?', *Cultural Critique* 30(1): 171–186.

Luhmann, Niklas (1996) 'La costituzione come acquisizione evolutiva', in Gustavo Zagrebelsky, Pier Paolo Portinaro and Jörg Luther (eds) *Il Futuro della Costituzione*, Torino: Einaudi.

Luhmann, Niklas (1997) 'Capitalisme et utopie', *Archives de Philosophie du Droit* 41: 483–492.

Luhmann, Niklas (1997) 'Globalization or world society: how to conceive of modern society', *International Review of Sociology* 7(1): 67–79.

Luhmann, Niklas (2000 [1996]) *The Reality of the Mass Media*, Stanford: Stanford University Press.

Luhmann, Niklas (2002 [1965]) *I Diritti Fondamentali come Istituzione*, Bari: Dedalo.

Luhmann, Niklas (2002) *Theories of Distinction: Redescribing the Distinctions of Modernity*, Stanford: Stanford University Press.

Luhmann, Niklas (2005 [1991]) *Risk: A Sociological Theory*, New York: Routledge.

Luhmann, Niklas (2008 [1993]) *Law as a Social System*, Oxford: Oxford University Press.

Luhmann, Niklas (2012 [1997]) *Theory of Society*, Vol. 1, Stanford: Stanford University Press.

Luhmann, Niklas (2013 [1997]) *Theory of Society*, Vol. 2, Stanford: Stanford University Press.

Luhmann, Niklas (2018 [2000]) *Organization and Decision*, Cambridge: Cambridge University Press.

Lynskey, Orla (2015) 'Control over personal data in a digital age: *Google Spain v AEPD and Mario Costeja Gonzalez*', *The Modern Law Review* 75(3): 522–548.

MacKinnon, Rebecca (2012) *Consent of the Networked: The Worldwide Struggle for Internet Freedom*, New York: Basic Books.

MacKinnon, Rebecca (2014) 'Playing favorites', *Guernica*, 3 February 2014, <https://www.guernicamag.com/features/playing-favorites>.

Maduro, Miguel Poiares (1998) *We the Court: The European Court of Justice and the European Economic Constitution*, Oxford: Hart Publishing.

Maduro, Miguel Poiares (2005) 'The importance of being called a constitution: constitutional authority and the authority of constitutionalism', *International Journal of Constitutional Law* 3(2–3): 332–356.

Magnani, Lorenzo (2013) 'Abducting personal data, destroying privacy: diagnosing profiles through artefactual mediators', in Mireille Hildebrandt and Katja de Vries (eds) *Privacy, Due Process and the Computational Turn: The Philosophy of Law Meets the Philosophy of Technology*, New York: Routledge.

Manne, Geoffrey A. (2010) 'The problem of search engines as essential facilities: an economic & legal assessment', in Berin Szoka and Adam Marcus (eds) *The Next Digital Decade: Essays on the Future of the Internet*, Washington: TechFreedom.

Manne, Geoffrey A. and Joshua D. Wright (2011) 'Google and the limits of antitrust: the case against the case against Google', *Harvard Journal of Law and Public Policy* 34(1): 171–244.

Manne, Geoffrey A. and Joshua D. Wright (2012) 'If search neutrality is the answer, what is the question?', *Columbia Business Law Review* 2012(1): 151–239.

Marramao, Giacomo (2000) *Dopo il Leviatano: Individuo e Comunità*, Torino: Bollati Boringhieri.

Marramao, Giacomo (2008) *La Passione del Presente*, Torino: Bollati Boringhieri.

Marramao, Giacomo (2009) *Passaggio a Occidente: Filosofia e Globalizzazione*, Torino: Bollati Boringhieri.

Marramao, Giacomo (2011) *Contro il Potere: Filosofia e Scrittura*, Milano: Bompiani.

Marton, Attila (2011) '*Forgotten as data – remembered through information. Social memory institutions in the digital age: the case of the European initiative*', PhD Dissertation, London School of Economics and Political Science.

Marton, Attila (2011) 'Social memory and the digital domain: the canonization of digital cultural artefacts', 27th European Group for Organizational Studies Colloquium (EGO), 6–9 July 2011, Gothenburg – Sweden.

Marton, Attila, Michel Avital and Tina Bleging Jensen (2013) 'Reframing open big data', *European Conference on Information Systems – ECIS*, Paper 169.

Mayer-Schönberger, Viktor (2007) 'Useful void: the art of forgetting in the age of ubiquitous computing', John F. Kennedy School of Government, *Faculty Working Paper Series*, RWP7–22.

McLuhan, Marshall (1964) *Understanding Media: The Extensions of Man*, New York: Sphere Books.

Miconi, Andrea (2014) 'Dialectic of Google', in René König and Miriam Rasch (eds) *Society of the Query Reader: Reflections on Web Search*, Amsterdam: Institute of Network Cultures.

Morozov, Evgeny (2011) *The Net Delusion: The Dark Side of Internet Freedom*, New York: Public Affairs.

Muchlinski, Peter (2001) 'Human rights and multinationals: is there a problem?', *International Affairs* 77(1): 31–47.

Mueller, Milton L. (2002) *Ruling the Root: Internet Governance and the Taming of Cyberspace*, Cambridge (MA): MIT Press.

Mueller, Milton L (2010) *Networks and States: The Global Politics of Internet Governance*, Cambridge (MA): MIT Press.

Mueller, Milton L (2017) *Will the Internet Fragment? Sovereignty, Globalization, and Cyberspace*, Cambridge: Polity Press.

Muth, Karl T. (2009) 'Googlestroika: privatizing privacy', *Duquesne Law Review* 47(2): 337–353.

Neves, Marcelo (2007) 'The symbolic force of human rights', *Philosophy & Social Criticism*, 33(4): 411–444.

Neves, Marcelo (2013 [2009]) *Transconstitutionalism*, Oxford: Hart Publishing.

Neves, Marcelo (2015) 'Comparing transconstitutionalism in an asymmetric world society: conceptual background and self-critical remarks', *Adam Smith Research Foundation – Working Paper Series*, University of Glasgow.

Neves, Marcelo (2016) 'Paradoxes of transconstitutionalism in Latin America', in Alberto Febbrajo and Giancarlo Corsi (eds) *Sociology of Constitutions: A Paradoxical Perspective*, New York: Routledge.

Newman, Nathan (2014) 'The costs of lost privacy: consumer harm and rising economic inequality in the age of Google', *William Mitchell Law Review* 40(2): 849–889.

Nissenbaum, Helen (2004) 'Privacy as contextual integrity', *Washington Law Review* 79: 101–139.

Nissenbaum, Helen (2010) *Privacy in Context: Technology, Policy, and the Integrity of Social Life*, Stanford: Stanford University Press.

Nissenbaum, Helen (2011) 'A contextual approach to privacy online', *Daedalus* 140(4): 32–48.

Odlyzko, Andrew (2009) 'Network neutrality, search neutrality, and the never-ending conflict between efficiency and fairness in markets', *Review of Network Economics* 8(1): 40–60.

Offe, Claus (2015) *Europe Entrapped*, Cambridge: Polity Press.

O'Reilly, Tim (2007) 'What is Web 2.0: design patterns and business models for the next generation of software', *Communications & Strategies* 65(1): 17–37.

Otterlo, Martijn van (2013) 'A machine learning view on profiling', in Mireille Hildebrandt and Katja de Vries (eds) *Privacy, Due Process and the Computational Turn: The Philosophy of Law Meets the Philosophy of Technology*, New York: Routledge.

Paine, Thomas (1817 [1792]) *The Rights of Man; Being an Answer to Mr. Burke's Attack on the French Revolution*, Los Angeles: University of California.

Paixão, Cristiano and Renato Bigliazzi (2008) *História Constitucional Inglesa e Norte-Americana: Do Surgimento à Estabilização da Forma Constitucional*, Brasília: Editora da UnB.

Palmisano, Giuseppe (2004) 'Spunti internazionalistici di riflessione sul trattato "costituzionale" e sulla natura dell'Unione Europea', *Costituzionalismo.it* 3 <http://www.costituzionalismo.it/articoli/166>.

Palmisano, Giuseppe (2010) 'Dal diritto internazionale al diritto cosmopolitico? Riflessioni a margine de la democrazia nell'età della globalizzazione', *Jura Gentium* 7(1): 114–131.

Pariser, Eli (2011) *The Filter Bubble: What the Internet is Hiding from You*, London: Penguin Books.

Pasquale, Frank (2008) 'Internet nondiscrimination principles: commercial ethics for carriers and search engines', *The University of Chicago Legal Forum*, <https://papers.ssrn.com/sol3/papers.cfm?abstract_id=1134159>.

Pasquale, Frank (2010) 'Dominant search engines: an essential cultural & political facility', in Berin Szoka and Adam Marcus (eds) *The Next Digital Decade: Essays on the Future of the Internet*, Washington: TechFreedom.

Pasquale, Frank (2010) 'Trusting (and verifying) online intermediaries' policing', in Berin Szoka and Adam Marcus (eds) *The Next Digital Decade: Essays on the Future of the Internet*, Washington: TechFreedom.

Pasquale, Frank (2013) 'Privacy, antitrust, and power', *George Mason Law Review* 20(4): 1009–1024.

Pasquale, Frank and Oren Bracha (2008) 'Federal search commission – access, fairness, and accountability in the law of search', *Cornell Law Review* 93(6): 1149–1210.

Pentland, Alex (2012) 'Reinventing society in the wake of big data', *Edge*, 30 August 2012, <https://www.edge.org/conversation/alex_sandy_pentland-reinventing-society-in-the-wake-of-big-data>.

Pernice, Ingolf (2001) 'Multilevel constitutionalism in the European Union', *Walter Hallstein-Institut*, Paper 5/02, <http://www.whi-berlin.de/documents/whi-paper0502.pdf>.

Pernice, Ingolf (2009) 'The Treaty of Lisbon: multilevel constitutionalism in action', *The Columbia Journal of European Law* 15(3): 349–407.

Petersmann, Ernst-Ulrich (2000) 'The WTO Constitution and human rights', *Journal of International Economic Law* 3: 19–25.

Petersmann, Ernst-Ulrich (2006) 'Human rights, constitutionalism and the World Trade Organization: challenges for World Trade Organization jurisprudence and civil society', *Leiden Journal of International Law* 19: 663–667.

Polanyi, Karl (1944) *The Great Transformation: The Political and Economic Origins of Our Time*, Boston: Beacon Press.

Pollock, Rufus (2010) 'Is Google the next Microsoft: competition, welfare and regulation in online search', *Review of Network Economics* 9(4): 1–29.

Preuss, Ulrich K. (2010) 'Disconnecting constitutions from statehood: is global constitutionalism a viable concept?', in Petra Dobner and Martin Loughlin (eds) *The Twilight of Constitutionalism?*, Oxford: Oxford University Press.

Ratner, Steven R. (2001) 'Corporations and human rights: a theory of legal responsibility', *The Yale Law Journal* 111: 443–545.

Reidenberg, Joel (1997) 'Lex informatica: the formulation of information policy rules through technology', *Texas Law Review* 76(3): 553–593.

Reidenberg, Joel (2002) 'Yahoo and democracy on the Internet', *Jurimetrics* 42: 261–280.

Reidenberg, Joel (2005) 'Technology and Internet jurisdiction', *University of Pennsylvania Law Review* 153(6): 1951–1974.

Renda, Andrea (2015) 'Antitrust on the "G string": What's behind the Commission's investigations of Google and Gazprom?', *CEPS Commentary*, 15 June 2015.

Renda, Andrea (2015) 'Antitrust, regulation and the neutrality trap: a plea for a smart, evidence-based internet policy', *CEPS Special Report*, N. 104, April 2015.

Renda, Andrea (2015) 'Searching for harm or harming search? A look at the European Commission's antitrust investigation against Google', *CEPS Special Report*, N. 118, September 2015.

Rieder, Bernhard (2009) 'Democratizing search? From critique to society-oriented design', in Konrad Becker and Felix Stalder (eds) *Deep Search: The Politics of Search Beyond Google*, Innsbruck: Studien Verlag.

Riekmann, Sonja P. (2010) 'Constitutionalism and representation: European parliamentarism in the Treaty of Lisbon', in Petra Dobner and Martin Loughlin (eds) *The Twilight of Constitutionalism?*, Oxford: Oxford University Press.

Rodotà, Stefano (2005) *Intervista su Privacy e Libertà*, Roma: Laterza.

Rodotà, Stefano (2012) *Il Diritto di Avere Diritti*, Roma: Laterza.

Rodotà, Stefano (2014) *Il Mondo nella Rete: Quali i Diritti, Quali i Vincoli*, Roma: Laterza.

Rogers, Richard (2009) 'The Googlization question: towards the inculpable engine?', in Konrad Becker and Felix Stalder (eds) *Deep Search: The Politics of Search Beyond Google*, Innsbruck: Studien Verlag.

Röhle, Theo (2009) 'Dissecting the gatekeepers: relational perspectives on the power of search engines', in Konrad Becker and Felix Stalder (eds) *Deep Search: The Politics of Search Beyond Google*, Innsbruck: Studien Verlag.

Rosas, Allan and Lorna Armati (2012) *EU Constitutional Law: An Introduction*, Oxford: Hart Publishing.

Rosen, Jeffrey (2010) 'The Web means the end of forgetting', *New York Times*, 21 July 2010, <http://www.nytimes.com/2010/07/25/magazine/25privacy-t2.html?pagewanted=all>.

Rosen, Jeffrey (2012) 'The deciders: the future of privacy and free speech in the age of Facebook and Google', *Fordham Law Review* 80(4): 1525–1538.

Rosen, Jeffrey (2012) 'The right to be forgotten', *Stanford Law Review Online* 64 (Symposium Issue): 88–92.

Rosenfeld, Michel (2008) 'Rethinking constitutional ordering in an era of legal and ideological pluralism', *Cardozo Legal Studies Research*, Paper N. 242

Rouvroy, Antoinette (2007) 'Réinventer l'art d'oublier et de se faire oublier dans la société de l'information?', *Colloque asphalès sur la protection de l'individu numérisé*, Paris: CNRS.

Rouvroy, Antoinette (2013) 'The end(s) of critique: data behaviourism versus due process', in Mireille Hildebrandt and Katja de Vries (eds) *Privacy, Due Process and the Computational Turn: The Philosophy of Law Meets the Philosophy of Technology*, New York: Routledge.

Ruggie, John (2007) 'Business and human rights: the evolving international agenda', *Corporate Social Responsibility Initiative*, Working Paper N. 31, Cambridge (MA): John F. Kennedy School of Government, Harvard University.

Ruggie, John (2014) 'Regulating multinationals: the UN Guiding Principles, civil society, and international legalization', in César Rodriguez-Garavito (ed), *Business and Human Rights: Beyond the End of the Beginning*, <http://papers.ssrn.com/sol3/papers.cfm?abstract_id=2474236>.

Russell, Andrew L. (2006) 'Rough consensus and running code and the Internet-OSI standards war', *IEEE Annals of the History of Computing* 28(3): 48–61.

Sajó, András (1999 [1995]) *Limiting Government: An Introduction to Constitutionalism*, Budapest: Central European University Press.

Sajó, András (2005) 'Constitution without the constitutional moment: a view from the new Member States', *International Journal of Constitutional Law* 3(2–3): 243–261.

Sajó, András and Renáta Uitz (eds) (2005) *The Constitution in Private Relations: Expanding Constitutionalism*, Utrecht: Eleven International.

Sassen, Saskia (2004) 'Sited materialities with global span', in Philip N. Howard and Steve Jones (eds) *Society Online: The Internet in Context*, Thousand Oaks: SAGE Publications.

Scharpf, Fritz W. (2010) 'Legitimacy in the multi-level European polity', in Petra Dobner and Martin Loughlin (eds) *The Twilight of Constitutionalism?*, Oxford: Oxford University Press.

Schmidt, Eric (2014) 'A chance for growth', *Franfurter Allgemeine*, 9 April 2014, <http://www.faz.net/aktuell/feuilleton/debatten/eric-schmidt-about-the-good-things-google-does-a-chance-for-growth-12887909.html>.

Schmitt, Carl (1985 [1922]) *Political Theology: Four Chapters on the Concept of Sovereignty*, Cambridge (MA): The MIT Press.

Schumpeter, Joseph A. (1991) *The Economics and Sociology of Capitalism*, Princeton: Princeton University Press.

Schutter, Olivier De (2005) 'The accountability of multinationals for human rights violation in European law', in Philip Alston (ed) *Non-State Actors and Human Rights*, Oxford: Oxford University Press.

Sciulli, David (2001) *Corporate Power in Civil Society: An Application of Societal Constitutionalism*, New York: New York University Press.

Scott, Craig and Robert Wai (2004) 'Transnational governance of corporate conduct through the migration of human rights norms: the potential contribution of transnational private litigation', in Christian Joerges et al (eds) *Transnational Governance and Constitutionalism*, Oxford: Hart Publishing.

Shannon, Claude and Warren Weaver (1964) *The Mathematical Theory of Communication*, Urbana: The University of Illinois Press.

Simon, Herbert A. (1991) 'Organizations and markets', *Journal of Economic Perspectives* 5 (2): 25–44.

Simser, Jeffrey (2008) 'Tax evasion and avoidance typologies', *Journal of Money Laundering Control* 11(2): 123–134.

Singer, Hal (2012) 'Who competes with Google Search? Just Amazon, Apple and Facebook', *Forbes*, 18 September 2012, <http://www.forbes.com/sites/halsinger/2012/09/18/who-competes-with-google-in-search-just-amazon-apple-and-facebook/ - 3c3aacf77459>.

Slaughter, Anne-Marie (2004) 'Disaggregated sovereignty: towards the public accountability of global government networks', *Government and Opposition* 39(2): 159–190.

Sluis, Katrina (2010) 'Algorithmic memory? Machinic vision and database culture', in Aris Mousoutzanis and Daniel Riha (eds) *New Media and the Politics of Online Communities*, Oxford: Inter-Disciplinary Press.

Solove, Daniel J. (2001) 'Privacy and power: computer databases and metaphors for information privacy', *Stanford Law Review* 53(6): 1393–1462.

Solove, Daniel J. (2006) 'A taxonomy of privacy', *University of Pennsylvania Law Review* 154(3): 477–560.

Solove, Daniel J. (2008) 'The end of privacy?', *Scientific American* 299(3): 100–106.

Solum, Lawrence B. and Minn Chung (2004) 'The Layers Principle: Internet architecture and the law', *Notre Dame Law Review* 79(3): 815–948.

Stalder, Felix and Christine Mayer (2009) 'The second index: search engines, personalization and surveillance', in Konrad Becker and Felix Stalder (eds) *Deep Search: The Politics of Search Beyond Google*, Innsbruck: Studien Verlag.

Streeck, Wolfgan (2011) 'The crises of democratic capitalism', *New Left Review* 71: 5–29.

Streeck, Wolfgan (2013) 'The politics of public debt: neoliberalism, capitalist development and the restructuring of the state', *German Economic Review* 15(1): 143–165.

Stute, David J. (2015) 'Privacy almighty? The CJEU's judgment in *Google Spain SL v. AEPD*', *Michigan Journal of International Law* 36: 649–680.

Sustein, Cass R. (2007) *Republic.com 2.0*, Princeton: Princeton University Press.

Svantesson, Dan Jerker B. (2014) 'The extraterritoriality of EU data privacy law – its theoretical justification and its practical effects on U.S. businesses', *Stanford Journal of International Law* 54: 53–102.

Sweeney, Latanya (2013) 'Discrimination in online ad delivery', *Communications of the ACM* 56(5): 44–54.

Szoka, Berin and Adam Marcus (eds) (2010) *The Next Digital Decade: Essays on the Future of the Internet*, Washington: TechFreedom.

Tamò, Aurelia and Damien George (2014) 'Oblivion, erasure and forgetting in the digital age', *Journal of Intellectual Property, Information Technology and Electronic Commerce Law* 5(2): 71–87.

Tene, Omar and Jules Polonetsky (2012) 'Privacy in the age of big data: a time for big decisions', *Stanford Law Review Online* 64(Symposium Issue): 63–69.

Teubner, Gunther (1993) *Law as an Autopoietic System*, Oxford: Blackwell.

Teubner, Gunther (1997) 'Global bukowina: legal pluralism in the world society', in Gunther Teubner (ed) *Global Law Without a State*, Aldershot: Dartmouth Gower.

Teubner, Gunther (2002) 'Breaking frames: economic globalization and the emergence of *lex mercatoria*', *European Journal of Social Theory* 5(2): 199–217.

Teubner, Gunther (2004) 'Societal constitutionalism: alternatives to state-centred constitutional theory', in Christian Joerges, Inger-Johane Sand and Gunther Teubner (eds) *Transnational Governance and Constitutionalism*, Oxford: Hart Publishing, <http://www.jura.uni-frankfurt.de/42852793/societal_constitutionalism.pdf>.

Teubner, Gunther (2006) 'Coincidentia oppositorum: hybrid networks beyond contract and organization', in Robert Gordon and Mort Horwitz (eds), *Festschrift in Honour of Lawrence Friedman*, Stanford: Stanford University Press, <http://ssrn.com/abstract=876939>.

Teubner, Gunther (2006) 'The anonymous matrix: human rights violations by "private" transnational actors', *Modern Law Review* 69: 327–346.

Teubner, Gunther (2009) 'The corporate codes of multinationals: company constitutions beyond corporate governance and co-determination', in Rainer Nickel (ed) *Conflict of Laws and Laws of Conflict in Europe and Beyond: Patterns of Supranational and Transnational Juridification*, Oxford: Hart Publishing.

Teubner, Gunther (2010) 'Fragmented foundations: societal constitutionalism beyond the nation state', in Petra Dobner and Martin Loughlin (eds) *The Twilight of Constitutionalism?*, Oxford: Oxford University Press.

Teubner, Gunther (2011) 'A constitutional moment? The logics of "hitting the bottom"', in Paul Kjaer, Gunther Teubner and Alberto Febbrajo (eds) *The Financial Crisis in Constitutional Perspective: The Dark Side of Functional Differentiation*, Oxford: Hart Publishing.

Teubner, Gunther (2011) 'Self-constitutionalizing TNCs? On the linkage of "private" and "public" corporate codes of conduct', *Indiana Journal of Global Legal Studies* 18(2): 17–38.

Teubner, Gunther (2012) *Constitutional Fragments: Societal Constitutionalism and Globalization*, Oxford: Oxford University Press.

Teubner, Gunther (2013) 'The project of constitutional sociology: irritating nation state constitutionalism', *Transnational Legal Theory* 4(1): 44–58.

Thornhill, Chris (2010) 'Niklas Luhmann and the sociology of the constitution', *Journal of Classical Sociology* 10(4): 315–337.

Thornhill, Chris (2011) *A Sociology of Constitutions: Constitutions and State Legitimacy in Historical-Sociological Perspective*, Cambridge: Cambridge University Press.

Thornhill, Chris (2011) 'The future of the state', in Paul F Kjaer, Gunther Teubner and Alberto Febbrajo (eds) *The Financial Crisis in Constitutional Perspective: The Dark Side of Functional Differentiation*, Oxford: Hart Publishing.

Tribe, Lawrence (1991) 'The constitution in cyberspace: law and liberty beyond the electronic frontier', Electronic Privacy Information Center, <https://epic.org/free_speech/tribe.html>.

Trovato, Massimiliano (2014) 'La tassazione dell'economia digitale: una soluzione in cerca di un problema?', *IBL Special Report*, 18 October 2014.

Tushnet, Mark (2009) 'The inevitable globalization of constitutional law', *Virginia Journal of International Law* 50(1): 985–1006.

Vaidhyanathan, Siva (2011) *The Googlization of Everything (and Why We Should Worry)*, Berkeley and Los Angeles: University of California Press.

Vanderstraeten, Raf (2002) 'Parsons, Luhmann and the Theorem of Double Contingency', *Journal of Classical Sociology* 2(1): 77–92.

Varoufakis, Yanis (2013) *The Global Minotaur: America, Europe and the Future of the Global Economy*, London: Zed Books.

Verschraegen, Gert (2002) 'Human rights and modern society: a sociological analysis from the perspective of systems theory', *Journal of Law and Society* 9(2): 258–281.

Vestager, Margrethe (2015) 'Competition policy in the EU: outlook and recent developments in antitrust', European Commission, Speech of Commissioner Margrethe Vestager at the Peterson Institute for International Economics, 16 April 2015, <https://ec.europa.eu/commission/2014-2019/vestager/announcements/competition-policy-eu-outlook-and-recent-developments-antitrust_en>.

Vise, David A. and Mark Malseed (2008) *The Google Story*, New York: Delta.

Vries, Katja de (2013) 'Privacy, due process and the computational turn: A parable and a first analysis', in Mireille Hildebrandt and Katja de Vries (eds) *Privacy, Due Process and the Computational Turn: The Philosophy of Law Meets the Philosophy of Technology*, New York: Routledge.

Wai, Robert (2003) 'Countering, branding, dealing: using economic and social rights in and around the international trade regime', *European Journal of International Law* 14 (1): 35–84.

Wai, Robert (2005) 'Transnational private law and private ordering in a contested global society', *Harvard International Law Journal* 46(2): 471–486.

Walker, Neil (2002) 'The idea of constitutional pluralism', *The Modern Law Review* 65(3): 317–359.

Walker, Neil (2007) 'Post-constituent constitutionalism? The case of the European Union', in Martin Loughlin and Neil Walker (eds) *The Paradox of Constitutionalism: Constituent Power and Constitutional Form*, Oxford: Oxford University Press.

Walker, Neil (2008) 'Taking constitutionalism beyond the state', *Political Studies* 56(3): 519–543.

Walker, Neil (2009) 'Multilevel constitutionalism: looking beyond the German debate', *LSE 'Europe in Question' Discussion Paper Series*, Paper 08/2009, <http://papers.ssrn.com/sol3/papers.cfm?abstract_id=1550912>.

Walker, Neil (2010) 'Beyond the holistic constitution?', in Petra Dobner and Martin Loughlin (eds) *The Twilight of Constitutionalism?*, Oxford: Oxford University Press.

Warren, Samuel D. and Louis D. Brandeis (1890) 'The right to privacy', *Harvard Law Review* 4(5): 193–220.

Wasserfallen, Fabio (2014) 'Political and economic integration in the EU: the case of failed tax harmonization', *Journal of Common Market Studies* 52(2): 420–435.

Weber, Max (1978 [1922]) *Economy and Society: An Outline of Interpretative Sociology*, Los Angeles: University of California Press.

Westney, D. Eleanor and Srilata Zaheer (2001) 'The multinational enterprise as an organization', in Alan M. Rugman and Thomas L. Brewer (eds), *The Oxford Handbook of International Business*, Oxford: Oxford University Press.

Westwood, Sean (2010) 'How to measure public opinion in the networked age: working in a Googleocracy or a Googlearchy?', in Jacques Berleur, Magda David Hercheui and Lorenz M. Hilty (eds) *What Kind of Information Society? Governance, Virtuality, Surveillance, Sustainability, Resilience*, Heidelberg: Springer, IFIP Advances in Information and Communication Technology, <https://link.springer.com/chapter/10.1007/978-3-642-15479-9_14>.

Whitman, James Q. (2004) 'The two Western cultures of privacy: dignity versus liberty', *Yale Law Journal* 113(6): 1151–1222.

Wilkins, Mira (2001) 'The history of multinational enterprise', in Alan M. Rugman and Thomas L. Brewer (eds), *The Oxford Handbook of International Business*, Oxford: Oxford University Press.

Winthrop-Young, Geoffrey (2000) 'Silicon sociology, or, two kings on Hegel's throne? Kittler, Luhmann, and the posthuman merger of German Media Theory', *The Yale Journal of Criticism* 13(2): 391–420.

Zagrebelsky, Gustavo, Pier Paolo Portinaro and Jörg Luther (eds) (1996) *Il Futuro della Costituzione*, Torino: Einaudi.

Zanfir, Gabriela (2014) 'Forgetting about consent. Why the focus should be on "suitable safeguards" in data protection law', in Serge Gutwirth, Ronald Leenes and Paul De Hert (eds) *Reloading Data Protection: Multidisciplinary Insights and Contemporary Challenges*, Heidelberg: Springer.

Zierold, Martin (2008) 'Memory and media cultures', in Astrid Erll and Ansgar Nünnin (eds) *Cultural Memory Studies: An International and Interdisciplinary Handbook*, Berlin: Walter de Gruyter.

Zimmer, Miachael (2007) 'The panoptic gaze of Web 2.0: how Web 2.0 platforms act as infrastructure of dataveillance', *Social Software and Web 2.0: Critical Perspectives and Challenges for Research and Business*, <http://michaelzimmer.org/files/Zimmer Aa lborg talk.pdf>.

Zimmer, Miachael (2010) 'Privacy protection in the next digital decade: "trading up" or "race to the bottom"?', in Berin Szoka and Adam Marcus (eds) *The Next Digital Decade: Essays on the Future of the Internet*, Washington: TechFreedom.

Zittrain, Jonathan (2008) *The Future of the Internet – and How to Stop It*, New Haven and London: Yale University Press.

Zittrain, Jonathan (2014) 'Righting the right to be forgotten', 14 July 2014, <http://blogs.harvard.edu/futureoftheinternet/2014/07/14/righting-the-right-to-be-forgotten>.

Zuboff, Shoshana (2014) 'Dark Google', *Franfurter Allgemeine*, 30 April 2014, <http://www.faz.net/aktuell/feuilleton/debatten/the-digital-debate/shoshanna-zuboff-dark-google-12916679.html>.

Zucman, Gabriel (2013) *La richesse cachée des nations: enquête sur les paradis fiscaux*, Paris: Seuil.

Zucman, Gabriel (2014) 'Taxing across borders: tracking personal wealth and corporate profits', *Journal of Economic Perspectives* 28(4): 121–148.

Zumbansen (2010) 'Neither "public" nor "private", "national" nor "international": transnational corporate governance from a legal pluralistic perspective', *CLPE Research Paper Series*, 6(5), <http://www.comparativeresearch.net>.

Documents, reports and press releases

Autorità Garante della Concorrenza e del Mercato (2010) '*Antitrust accetta impegni di Google e chiede al parlamento di adeguare le norme sul diritto d'autore*', *Comunicato Stampa*, 17 January 2010, <http://www.agcm.it/stampa/comunicati/5194-a420-as787-antitrust-accetta-impegni-di-google-e-chiede-al-parlamento-di-adeguare-le-norme-sul-diritto-dautore.html>.

Autorité de la Concurrence (2010) '*L'autorité de la concurrence estime que Google est en position dominante sur le marché de la publicité liée aux moteurs de recherche*', *Communiqués*, 14 December 2010, <http://www.autoritedelaconcurrence.fr/user/standard.php?id_rub=367&id_article=1513>.

Business & Human Rights Resource Center (2014) '*Information technology: the power and responsibility of business*', <https://business-humanrights.org/sites/default/files/media/documents/information-technology-briefing-feb-2014.pdf>.

CNIL – Commission Nationale de l'Informatique et des Libertés (2015) '*CNIL orders Google to apply delisting on all domain names of the search engine*', 12 June 2015, <http://www.cnil.fr/english/news-and-events/news/article/cnil-orders-google-to-apply-delisting-on-all-domain-names-of-the-search-engine>.

CNIL – Commission Nationale de l'Informatique et des Libertés (2019) 'La formation restreinte de la CNIL prononce une sanction de 50 millions d'euros à l'encontre de la société GOOGLE LLC', 21 January 2019, <https://www.cnil.fr/fr/la-formation-restreinte-de-la-cnil-prononce-une-sanction-de-50-millions-deuros-lencontre-de-la>.

Collin, Pierre et Nicolas Colin (2013) *Mission d'expertise sur la fiscalité de l'économie numérique*, Rapport au Ministre de l'économie et des finances, au Ministre du redressement productif, au Ministre délégué chargé du budget et à la Ministre déléguée chargée des petites et moyennes entreprises, de l'innovation et de l'économie numérique, January 2013, <https://www.economie.gouv.fr/files/rapport-fiscalite-du-numerique_2013.pdf>.

Congressional Research Service (2016) *The Internet Tax Freedom Act: In Brief*, CRS Report, 13 April 2016, <https://fas.org/sgp/crs/misc/R43772.pdf>.

Council of Europe (2011) *Recommendation CM/Rec(2011)7 of the Committee of Ministers to Member States on a New Notion of Media*, Adopted by the Committee of Ministers on 21 September 2011 at the 1121st meeting of the Ministers' Deputies.

EDPS – European Data Protection Supervisor (2016) *Opinion on the EU-U.S. Privacy Shield Draft Adequacy Decision*, Opinion 4/2016, 30 May 2016.

European Commission (2002) *VAT: Commission welcomes Council adoption of rules for application of VAT to electronically delivered services*, Press Release: IP/02/673, Brussels: 7 May 2002.

European Commission (2008) *Mergers: Commission clears proposed acquisition of DoubleClick by Google*, Press Release: IP/08/426, Brussels: 11 March 2008.

European Commission (2009) *Taxation and good governance: the European Commission proposes actions to improve transparency, exchange of information and fair tax competition*, Press Release: IP/09/650, Brussels: 28 April 2009.

European Commission (2010) *Antitrust: Commission probes allegations of antitrust violations by Google*, Press Release: IP/10/1624, Brussels: 30 November 2010.

European Commission (2011) *European corporate tax base: making business easier and cheaper*, Press Release: IP/11/319, Brussels: 16 March 2011.

European Commission (2012) *Clamping down on tax evasion and avoidance: Commission presents the way forward*, Press Release: IP/12/1325, Brussels: 6 December 2012.

European Commission (2012) *Commission proposes a comprehensive reform of data protection rules to increase users' control of their data and to cut costs for businesses*, Press Release: IP/12/46, Brussels: 25 January 2012.

European Commission (2012) *Europe 2020: Europe's Growth Strategy*, The European Union Explained, Luxembourg: Publications Office of the European Union.

European Commission (2012) *Mergers: Commission approves acquisition of Motorola Mobility by Google*, Press Release: IP/12/129, Brussels: 13 February 2012.

European Commission (2012) *Statement of VP Almunia on the Google antitrust investigation*, SPEECH/12/372, Brussels: 21 May 2012.

European Commission (2012) *Stimulating growth and employment: an action plan for doubling the volume of e-commerce in Europe by 2015*, Press Release: IP/12/10, Brussels: 11 January 2012.

European Commission (2013) *Rebuilding Trust in EU-US Data Flows*, Communication from the Commission to the European Parliament and the Council, COM(2013) 846 final, Brussels: 27 November 2013.

European Commission (2014) *Antitrust: Commission obtains from Google comparable display of specialised search rivals*, Press Release: IP/14/115, Brussels: 5 February 2014.

European Commission (2014) *Digital Agenda for Europe*, The European Union Explained, Luxembourg: Publications Office of the European Union.

European Commission (2014) *Inspiring trust: stronger data protection rules to boost the Digital Single Market*, SPEECH/14/2504, Brussels: 9 December 2014.

European Commission (2014) *Questions & Answers: VAT changes from 2015*, MEMO/14/448, Brussels: 1 July 2014.

European Commission (2014) *Report of the Commission Expert Group on Taxation of the Digital Economy*, <https://ec.europa.eu/taxation_customs/sites/taxation/files/resources/documents/taxation/gen_info/good_governance_matters/digital/report_digital_economy.pdf>.

European Commission (2014) *Statement on the Google investigation*, Vice President of the European Commission responsible for Competition Policy Joaquín Almunia, SPEECH/14/93, Brussels: 5 February 2014.

European Commission (2014) *Taxation: countdown to simpler and fairer VAT system*, Press Release: IP/14/758, Brussels: 1 July 2014.

European Commission (2015) *A Digital Single Market Strategy for Europe – Analysis and Evidence*, Commission Staff Working Document, COM(2015) 192 final, Brussels: 6 May 2015.

European Commission (2015) *Antitrust: Commission sends Statement of Objections to Google on comparison shopping service; opens separate formal investigation on Android*, Press Release: IP/15/4780, Brussels: 15 April 2015.

European Commission (2015) *Combatting corporate tax avoidance: Commission presents Tax Transparency Package*, Press Release: IP/15/4610, Brussels: 18 March 2015.

European Commission (2015) *Commission presents Action Plan for Fair and Efficient Corporate Taxation in the EU*, Press Release: IP/15/5188, Brussels: 17 June 2015.

European Commission (2015) *First Vice-President Timmermans and Commissioner Jourová's press conference on Safe Harbour following the Court ruling in case C-362/14 (Schrems)*, STATEMENT 15/5782, Strasbourg: 6 October 2015.

European Commission (2015) *Taxation*, The European Union Explained, Luxembourg: Publications Office of the European Union.

European Commission (2016) *Antitrust: Commission sends Statement of Objections to Google on Android operating system and applications*, Press Release: IP/16/1492, Brussels: 20 April 2016.

European Commission (2016) *Antitrust: Commission takes further steps in investigations alleging Google's comparison shopping and advertising-related practices breach EU rules*, Press Release: IP/16/2532, Brussels: 14 July 2016.

European Commission (2016) *European Commission proposes public tax transparency rules for multinationals*, Press Release: IP/16/1349, Brussels: 12 April 2016.

European Commission (2016) *Fair taxation: Commission presents new measures against corporate tax avoidance*, Press Release: IP/16/159, Brussels: 28 January 2016.

European Commission (2016) *Proposal for a Directive of the European Parliament and of the Council on copyright in the Digital Single Market*, COM(2016) 593 final, Brussels: 14 September 2016.

European Commission (2016) *State aid: Ireland gave illegal tax benefits to Apple worth up to €13 billion*, Press Release, IP/16/2923, Brussels: 30 August 2016.

European Commission (2016) *VAT Action Plan: Commission presents measures to modernise VAT in the EU*, Press Release, IP/16/1022, Brussels: 7 April 2016.

European Commission (2017) *Antitrust: Commission fines Google €2.42 billion for abusing dominance as search engine by giving illegal advantage to own comparison shopping service*, Press Release: IP/17/1784, Brussels: 27 June 2017.

European Commission (2017) *Commission Decision of 27.6.2017 relating to proceedings under Article 102 of the Treaty on the Functioning of the European Union and Article 54 of the Agreement on the European Economic Area (AT.39740 – Google Search (Shopping))*, C(2017) 4444final, Brussels: 27 June 2017, <http://ec.europa.eu/competition/antitrust/cases/dec_docs/39740/39740_14996_3.pdf>.

European Commission (2017) *Commission proposes high level of privacy rules for all electronic communications and updates data protection rules for EU institutions*, Press Release: IP/17/16, Brussels: 10 January 2017.

European Commission (2018) *A multi-dimensional approach to disinformation: report of the independent High Level Group on fake news and online disinformation*, <https://ec.europa.eu/digital-single-market/en/news/final-report-high-level-expert-group-fake-news-and-online-disinformation>.

European Commission (2018) *Antitrust: Commission fines Google €4.34 billion for illegal practices regarding Android mobile devices to strengthen dominance of Google's search engine*, Press Release: IP/18/4581, Brussels: 18 July 2018.

European Commission (2018) *Digital taxation: Commission proposes new measures to ensure that all companies pay fair tax in the EU*, Press Release: IP/18/2041, Brussels: 21 March 2018.

European Commission (2018) *Questions and Answers on a Fair and Efficient Tax System in the EU for the Digital Single Market*, MEMO/18/2141, Brussels: 21 March 2018.

European Commission (2019) *Antitrust: Commission fines Google €1.49 billion for abusive practices in online advertising*, Press Release: IP/19/1770, Brussels: 20 March 2019.

European Parliament (2000) *Report on the draft Commission decision on the adequacy of the protection afforded by the 'Safe Harbor Privacy Principles' and related frequently asked questions issued by the United States Department of Commerce*, FINAL A5–0177/2000, 22 June 2000, <http://ec.europa.eu/justice/policies/privacy/docs/adequacy/0117-02_en.pdf>.

European Parliament (2001) *Report on the existence of a global system for the interception of private and commercial communications (ECHELON interception system)*, FINAL A5–0264/2001 PAR1, 11 July 2001, <http://www.europarl.europa.eu/sides/getDoc.do?pubRef=-//EP//NONSGML+REPORT+A5-2001-0264+0+DOC+PDF+V0//EN>.

European Parliament (2013) *Corporate tax avoidance by multinational firms*, Library Briefing, 23 September 2013, <http://www.europarl.europa.eu/RegData/bibliotheque/briefing/2013/130574/LDM_BRI(2013)130574_REV1_EN.pdf>.

European Parliament (2014) *EU and US competition policies: similar objectives, different approaches*, European Parliamentary Research Service, Briefing, 27 March 2014, <http://www.europarl.europa.eu/RegData/bibliotheque/briefing/2014/140779/LDM_BRI(2014)140779_REV1_EN.pdf>.

European Parliament (2014) *Inquiry on electronic mass surveillance of EU citizens*, Protecting Fundamental Rights in a Digital Age: Proceedings, Outcome and Background Documents 2013–2214, <http://www.europarl.europa.eu/document/activities/cont/201410/20141016ATT91322/20141016ATT91322EN.pdf>.

European Parliament (2014) *Resolution on supporting consumer rights in the Digital Single Market*, Document: B8–0286/2014, Procedure: 2014/2973(RSP), 27 November 2014, <http://www.europarl.europa.eu/sides/getDoc.do?pubRef=-//EP//TEXT+MOTION+B8-2014-0286+0+DOC+XML+V0//EN>.

European Parliament (2015) *Google antitrust proceedings: digital business and competition*, European Parliamentary Research Service, Briefing, 14 July 2015, <http://www.europarl.europa.eu/thinktank/en/document.html?reference=EPRS_BRI(2015)565870>.

European Parliament (2015) *Taxation and good governance: issues and challenges*, European Parliamentary Research Service, February 2015, <http://www.europarl.europa.eu/RegData/etudes/IDAN/2015/549001/EPRS_IDA(2015)549001_EN.pdf>.

European Parliament (2016) *Resolution on transatlantic data flows*, Document: RC-B8–0623/2016, Procedure: 2016/2727(RSP), 24 May 2016, <http://www.europarl.europa.eu/sides/getDoc.do?pubRef=-//EP//TEXT+MOTION+P8-RC-2016-0623+0+DOC+XML+V0//EN>.

European Parliament (2017) *Resolution on the adequacy of the protection afforded by the EU-US Privacy Shield*, Document: B8–0235/2017, Procedure: 2016/3018(RSP), 29 March 2017, <http://www.europarl.europa.eu/sides/getDoc.do?pubRef=-//EP//TEXT+TA+P8-TA-2017-0131+0+DOC+XML+V0//EN>.

FRA – European Union Agency for Fundamental Rights and Council of Europe (2014) *Handbook on European Data Protection Law*, Luxembourg: Publications Office of the European Union, <http://fra.europa.eu/en/publication/2014/handbook-european-data-protection-law>.

FCC – Federal Communications Commission (2015) *FCC adopts strong, sustainable rules to protect the open Internet*, Press Release, 26 February 2015, <https://apps.fcc.gov/edocs_public/attachmatch/DOC-332260A1.pdf>.

FTC – Federal Trade Commission (2013) *Google agrees to change its business practices to resolve FTC competition concerns in the markets for devices like smart phones, games and tablets, and in online search*, Press Release, 3 January 2013, <https://www.ftc.gov/news-events/press-releases/2013/01/google-agrees-change-its-business-practices-resolve-ftc>.

Global Network Initiative (2016) *Public Report on the 2015/2016 Independent Company Assessments*, <http://globalnetworkinitiative.org/sites/default/files/Public-Report-2015-16-Independent-Company-Assessments.pdf>.

Google (2010) *Search Engine Optimization Starter Guide*, <https://static.googleusercontent.com/media/www.google.com/en//webmasters/docs/search-engine-optimization-starter-guide.pdf >.

Google (2015) *The Advisory Council to Google on the Right to be Forgotten*, 6 February 2015, <https://buermeyer.de/wp/wp-content/uploads/2012/02/Report-of-the-Advisory-Committee-to-Google-on-the-Right-to-be-Forgotten.pdf>.

Human Rights Watch (2014) *With Liberty to Monitor All: How Large-Scale US Surveillance is Harming Journalism, Law and American Democracy*, <https://www.hrw.org/report/2014/07/28/liberty-monitor-all/how-large-scale-us-surveillance-harming-journalism-law-and>.

ILO – International Labour Organization (2017) *Tripartite Declaration of Principles Concerning Multinational Enterprises and Social Policy*, <http://www.ilo.org/wcmsp5/groups/public/—ed_emp/—emp_ent/—multi/documents/publication/wcms_094386.pdf>.

ISO – International Standardization Organization (2010) *ISO 26000 – Guidance on Social Responsibility*, <https://www.iso.org/obp/ui/ - iso:std:iso:26000:ed-1:v1:en>.

OECD – Organization for Economic Cooperation and Development (1998) *Electronic Commerce: Taxation Framework Conditions*, <https://www.oecd.org/ctp/consumption/1923256.pdf>.

OECD – Organization for Economic Cooperation and Development (1998) *Harmful Tax Competition: An Emerging Global Issue*, <http://www.oecd-ilibrary.org/taxation/harmful-tax-competition_9789264162945-en>.

OECD – Organization for Economic Cooperation and Development (2011) *OECD Guidelines for Multinational Enterprises*, Paris: OECD Publishing, <http://dx.doi.org/10.1787/9789264115415-en>.

OECD – Organization for Economic Cooperation and Development (2013) *Action Plan on Base Erosion and Profit Shifting*, Paris: OECD Publishing, <http://dx.doi.org/10.1787/9789264202719-en>.

OECD – Organization for Economic Cooperation and Development (2013) *Addressing Base Erosion and Profit Shifting*, Paris: OECD Publishing, <http://dx.doi.org/10.1787/9789264192744-en>.

OECD – Organization for Economic Cooperation and Development (2013) *The OECD Privacy Framework*, Paris: OECD Publishing, <http://www.oecd.org/sti/ieconomy/oecd_privacy_framework.pdf>.

OECD –- Organization for Economic Cooperation and Development (2014) *Model Tax Convention on Income and on Capital: Consolidated Version 2014*, Paris: OECD Publishing, <http://dx.doi.org/10.1787/mtc_cond-2014-en>.

OECD – Organization for Economic Cooperation and Development (2015) *Addressing the Tax Challenges of the Digital Economy*, Action 1–2015 Final Report, OECD/G20 Base Erosion and Profit Shifting Project, Paris: OECD Publishing, <http://dx.doi.org/10.1787/9789264218789-en>.

OECD – Organization for Economic Cooperation and Development (2015) *Countering Harmful Tax Practices More Effectively, Taking into Account Transparency and Substance*, Action 5–2015 Final Report, OECD/G20 Base Erosion and Profit Shifting Project, Paris: OECD Publishing, <http://dx.doi.org/10.1787/9789264241190-en>.

OECD – Organization for Economic Cooperation and Development (2015) *G20/OECD Principles of Corporate Governance*, Paris: OECD Publishing, <http://dx.doi.org/10.1787/9789264236882-en>.

OECD – Organization for Economic Cooperation and Development (2015) *OECD Guidelines on Corporate Governance of State-Owned Enterprises*, Paris: OECD Publishing, <http://dx.doi.org/10.1787/9789264244160-en>.

OECD –- Organization for Economic Cooperation and Development (2016) *Multilateral Convention to Implement Tax Treaty Related Measures to Prevent Base Erosion and Profit Shifting*, Paris: OECD Publishing, <http://www.oecd.org/ctp/transfer-pricing/transfer-pricing-guidelines.htm https://www.oecd.org/tax/multilateral-convention-to-implement-tax-treaty-related-measures-to-prevent-beps.htm>.

OECD – Organization for Economic Cooperation and Development (2017) *Model Tax Convention on Income and on Capital: Consolidated Version 2017*, Paris; OECD Publishing, <https://dx.doi.org/10.1787/mtc_cond-2017-en>.

OECD – Organization for Economic Cooperation and Development (2017) *Transfer Pricing Guidelines for Multinational Enterprises and Tax Administrations*, Paris: OECD Publishing, <http://www.oecd.org/ctp/transfer-pricing/transfer-pricing-guidelines.htm>.

OECD – Organization for Economic Cooperation and Development (2018) *OECD/G20 Inclusive Framework on BEPS – Progress Report July 2017–June 2018*, Paris: OECD Publishing, <https://www.oecd.org/tax/beps/inclusive-framework-on-beps-progress-report-june-2017-july-2018.htm>.

OECD – Organization for Economic Cooperation and Development (2018) *Tax Challenges Arising from Digitalisation – Interim Report 2018: Inclusive Framework on BEPS*, OECD/G20 Base Erosion and Profit Shifting Project, Paris: OECD Publishing, <https://www.oecd.org/ctp/tax-challenges-arising-from-digitalisation-interim-report-9789264293083-en.htm>.

Reuters (2013) *It's not just Google ...*, Special Report, 23 July 2013, <http://graphics.thomsonreuters.com/13/07/BIGTECH-TAXES.pdf>.

Tax Justice Network (2015) *Ten Reasons to Defend the Corporation Tax*, <http://www.taxjustice.net/wp-content/uploads/2013/04/Ten_Reasons_Full_Report.pdf>.

The Economist (2010) *Data, Data Everywhere: A Special Report on Managing Information*, 27 February 2010, <https://www.emc.com/collateral/analyst-reports/ar-the-economist-data-data-everywhere.pdf>.

The Privacy Surgeon (2014) *A Crisis of Accountability: A Global Analysis of the Impact of the Snowden Revelations*, <http://www.privacysurgeon.org/blog/resources/a-crisis-of-accountability-report>.

UN – United Nations (2011) *Guiding Principles on Business and Human Rights*, <http://www.ohchr.org/Documents/Publications/GuidingPrinciplesBusinessHR_EN.pdf>.

UN – United Nations (2011) *Model Double Taxation Convention between Developed and Developing Countries*, <http://www.un.org/esa/ffd/documents/UN_Model_2011_Update.pdf>.

UN – United Nations (2014) *Guide to Corporate Sustainability: Shaping a Sustainable Future*, <https://www.unglobalcompact.org/docs/publications/UN_Global_Compact_Guide_to_Corporate_Sustainability.pdf>.

UN – United Nations (2014) *The Mapping of International Internet Public Policy Issues*, <http://unctad.org/meetings/en/SessionalDocuments/CSTD_2014_Mapping_Internet_en.pdf>.

UN – United Nations (2017) *Model Double Taxation Convention between Developed and Developing Countries*, <https://www.un.org/esa/ffd/wp-content/uploads/2018/05/MDT_2017.pdf>.

UNCCPR – United Nations Human Rights Committee (2011) *General comment No. 34 – Article 19: freedoms of opinion and expression*, CCPR/C/GC/34, 12 September 2011.

UNCCPR – United Nations Human Rights Committee (2014) *Concluding observations on the fourth periodic report of the United States of America*, CCPR/C/USA/CO/4, 23 April 2014.

UNCTAD – United Nations Conference on Trade and Development (2017) *World Investment Report 2017: Investment and the Digital Economy*, <http://unctad.org/en/PublicationsLibrary/wir2017_en.pdf>.

UNGA – United Nations General Assembly (1990) *Guidelines for the Regulation of Computerized Personal Data Files*, A-RES-45–95, 14 December 1990.

UNGA – United Nations General Assembly (2011) *Report of the Special Rapporteur on the promotion and protection of the right to freedom of opinion and expression*, A/66/290, 10 August 2011.

UNGA – United Nations General Assembly (2013) *Resolution on the right to privacy in the digital age*, A/RES/68/167, 18 December 2013.

UNGA – United Nations General Assembly (2014) *Report of the Special Rapporteur on the promotion and protection of human rights and fundamental freedoms while countering terrorism*, A/69/397, 23 September 2014.

UNHRC – United Nations Human Rights Council (2012) *Resolution on the promotion, protection and enjoyment of human rights on the Internet*, A/HRC/RES/20/8, 16 July 2012.

UNHRC – United Nations Human Rights Council (2014) *Report on the right to privacy in the digital age*, A/HCR/27/37, 30 June 2014.

World Economic Forum (2011) *Personal Data: The Emergence of a New Asset Class*, <http://www3.weforum.org/docs/WEF_ITTC_PersonalDataNewAsset_Report_2011.pdf>.

WP29 – Article 29 Data Protection Working Party (2000) *Opinion 4/2000 on the level of protection provided by the "Safe Harbor Principles"*, WP 32, 16 May 2000.

WP29 – Article 29 Data Protection Working Party (2008) *Opinion 1/2008 on data protection issues related to search engines*, WP 148, 4 April 2008. WP29 – Article 29 Data Protection Working Party (2014) *Guidelines on the implementation of the Court of Justice of the European Union judgment on "Google Spain and Inc v. Agencia Española de Protección de Datos (AEPD) and Mario Costeja Gonzáles" C-131/12*, WP 225, 26 November 2014.

WP29 – Article 29 Data Protection Working Party (2016) *Opinion 01/2016 on the EU–U. S. Privacy Shield draft adequacy decision*, WP 238, 13 April 2016.

WTO – World Trade Organization (1998) *Declaration on Global Electronic Commerce*, WT/MIN(98)/DEC/2, 25 May 1998.

WTO – World Trade Organization (2017) *Work Programme on Electronic Commerce*, WT/MIN(17)/65, 18 December 2017.

News, blogs and posts

Ars Technica (2008) '*Court rejects appeal over student-teacher drunk MySpace pics*', 5 December 2008, <https://arstechnica.com/tech-policy/2008/12/court-rejects-appeal-over-student-teacher-drunk-myspace-pics>.

Ars Technica (2014) '*Google changes stance on Net neutrality four years after Verizon deal*', 9 September 2014, <https://arstechnica.com/tech-policy/2014/09/four-years-after-deal-with-verizon-google-changes-mind-on-net-neutrality>.

Ars Technica (2015) '*Google ramps up EU lobbying as antitrust charges proceed*', 17 December 2015, <https://arstechnica.com/tech-policy/2015/12/google-ramps-up-eu-lobbying-as-antitrust-charges-proceed>.

Bloomberg (2010) '*Google 2.4% rate shows how $60 billion is lost to tax loopholes*', 21 October 2010, <http://www.bloomberg.com/news/articles/2010-10-21/google-2-4-rate-shows-how-60-billion-u-s-revenue-lost-to-tax-loopholes>.

Bloomberg (2012) '*Google revenues sheltered in no-tax Bermuda soar to $10 billion*', 10 December 2012, <http://www.bloomberg.com/news/articles/2012-12-10/google-revenues-sheltered-in-no-tax-bermuda-soar-to-10-billion>.

Bloomberg (2019) '*Google cuts taxes by shifting billions to Bermuda—again*', 3 January 2019, <https://news.bloombergtax.com/daily-tax-report-international/google-cuts-taxes-by-shifting-billions-to-bermudaagain>.

Business Insider (2014) '*Spain just passed an insane law taxing Google for linking to news*', 28 July 2014, <http://www.businessinsider.com/spain-google-tax-2014-7>.

Corriere della Sera (2014) '*L'iter (finito) della Web Tax*', 21 November 2014, <http://www.corriere.it/tecnologia/economia-digitale/14_novembre_21/iter-finito-web-tax-86a9267a-7187-11e4-b9c7-dbbe3ea603eb.shtml>.

Corriere della Sera (2016) '*Google e il fisco italiano: verso una richiesta da 227 milioni di euro*', 28 January 2016, <http://www.corriere.it/economia/16_gennaio_28/google-fisco-italiano-richiesta-150-milioni-euro-aeda11ae-c587-11e5-b3b7-699cc16119c2.shtml?refresh_ce-cp>.

Derecho a Leer (2014), *The unforgettable history of the seizure to the defaulter Mario Costeja Gonzáles that happened in 1998*, 30 May 2014, <http://derechoaleer.org/en/blog/2014/05/the-unforgettable-story-of-the-seizure-to-the-defaulter-mario-costeja-gonzalez-that-happened-in-1998.html>.

Deutsche Welle (2018) '*Austria to implement digital tax for tech giants*', 29 December 2018, <https://www.dw.com/en/austria-to-implement-digital-tax-for-tech-giants/a-46894297>.

El Pais (2016) '*Hacienda busca en Google Spain y Google Ireland indicios de fraude fiscal*', 30 June 2016, <https://economia.elpais.com/economia/2016/06/30/actualidad/1467280502_356974.html>.

EurActiv (2014) '*France, Germany back MEPs against Google*', 28 November 2014, <http://www.euractiv.com/section/digital/news/france-germany-back-meps-against-google>.

EurActiv (2014) '*Google, Apple and Amazon under fire in OECD war on tax evasion*', 18 September 2014, <http://www.euractiv.com/sections/innovation-enterprise/google-apple-and-amazon-under-fire-oecd-war-tax-evasion-308548>.

EurActiv (2018) '*Google appeals record EU fine over Android*', 10 October 2018, <https://www.euractiv.com/section/digital/news/google-appeals-record-eu-fine-over-android>.

Financial Times (2013) '*Brussels furious over claims UK and US spied on Almunia*', 20 December 2013, <https://www.ft.com/content/7d853cec-699e-11e3-aba3-00144feabdc0>.

Forbes (2014) '*Ireland declares "double Irish" tax scheme dead*', 15 October 2014, <http://www.forbes.com/sites/kellyphillipserb/2014/10/15/ireland-declares-double-irish-tax-scheme-dead>.

Google (2007) '*Google begins move to universal search*', 16 May 2007, <http://googlepress.blogspot.hu/2007/05/google-begins-move-to-universal-search_16.html>.

Google (2015) '*Implementing a European, not global, right to be forgotten*', 30 July 2015, <http://googlepolicyeurope.blogspot.hu/2015/07/implementing-european-not-global-right.html>.

Google (2015) '*Improving quality isn't anti-competitive*', 27 August 2015, <http://googlepolicyeurope.blogspot.hu/2015/08/improving-quality-isnt-anti-competitive.html>.

Google (2016) '*Adapting our approach to the European right to be forgotten*', 4 March 2016, <https://googlepolicyeurope.blogspot.hu/2016/03/adapting-our-approach-to-european-right.html>.

Google (2016) '*Android's model of open innovation*', 20 April 2016, <https://www.blog.google/topics/google-europe/androids-model-of-open-innovation>.

Guardian (2010) '*Privacy no longer a social norm, says Facebook founder*', 11 January 2010, <https://www.theguardian.com/technology/2010/jan/11/facebook-privacy>.

Guardian (2014) '*Dane investigating EU tax deals says Luxleaks trail will lead to fair pay*', 19 December 2014, <http://www.theguardian.com/world/2014/dec/19/vestager-tax-inquiry-luxleaks-juncker-eu-pay>.

Guardian (2014) '*Google to sell Motorola Mobility to Lenovo in $2.9bn deal*', 30 January 2014, <https://www.theguardian.com/technology/2014/jan/29/google-motorola-lenovo-sale>.

Guardian (2014) 'Obama's speech on N.S.A. phone surveillan, 1 April 2014, <https://www.theguardian.com/world/2014/apr/01/nsa-surveillance-loophole-americans-data>.

Guardian (2015) '*Revealed: how Google enlisted members of US Congress it bankrolled to fight $6bn EU antitrust case*', 17 December 2015, <https://www.theguardian.com/world/2015/dec/17/google-lobbyists-congress-antitrust-brussels-eu>.

Guardian (2016) '*France to seek €1.6bn in back taxes from Google, says official*', 24 February 2016, <https://www.theguardian.com/technology/2016/feb/24/france-google-tax-avoidance-back-taxes>.

Guardian (2016) '*Google agrees to pay British authorities £130m in back taxes*', 23 January 2016, <https://www.theguardian.com/technology/2016/jan/22/google-agrees-to-pay-hmrc-130m-in-back-taxes>.

Guardian (2016) '*Quietly, symbolically, US control of the Internet was just ended*', 14 March 2016, <https://www.theguardian.com/technology/2016/mar/14/icann-internet-control-domain-names-iana>.

Guardian (2017) '*Google ad controversy: what the row is all about*', 17 March 2017, <https://www.theguardian.com/technology/2017/mar/17/youtube-and-google-search-for-answers>.

Guardian (2017) '*Google appeals against EU's €2.4bn fine over search engine results*', 11 September 2017, <https://www.theguardian.com/technology/2017/sep/11/google-appeals-eu-fine-search-engine-results-shopping-service>.

Guardian (2018) '*Revealed: 50 million Facebook profiles harvested for Cambridge Analytica in major data breach*', 17 March 2018, <https://www.theguardian.com/news/2018/mar/17/cambridge-analytica-facebook-influence-us-election>.

JOTA (2014) '*STF vai julgar direito ao esquecimento em repercussão geral*', 9 December 2014, <https://jota.info/justica/stf-vai-julgar-direito-ao-esquecimento-em-repercussao-geral-09122014>.

La Tribune (2013) '*Pourquoi Quaero n'a pas créé le "Google européen"*', 29 March 2013, <http://www.latribune.fr/technos-medias/internet/20130328trib000756586/pourquoi-quaero-n-a-pas-cree-le-google-europeen-.html>.

Le Figaro (2018) '*Taxe GAFA: la France imposera les géants du numérique à partir du 1er janvier 2019*', 12 December 2018, <http://www.lefigaro.fr/conjoncture/2018/12/17/20002-20181217ARTFIG00166-la-france-taxera-les-geants-du-numerique-a-partir-du-1er-janvier-2019.php>.

Le Monde (2016) '*Une vaste perquisition menée dans les locaux de Google à Paris*', 24 May 2016, <http://www.lemonde.fr/economie/article/2016/05/24/une-vaste-perquisiton-menee-dans-les-locaux-de-google-a-paris_4925428_3234.html>.

Microsoft (2011) '*Adding our voice to concerns about search in Europe*', Microsoft Corporate Blogs, 30 March 2011, <http://blogs.microsoft.com/on-the-issues/2011/03/30/adding-our-voice-to-concerns-about-search-in-europe>.

Msoftnews (2013) '*German parliament passes "Google tax" law, forcing royalty payments for news snippets*', 1 March 2013, <http://msoftnews.com/google/german-parliament-passes-google-tax-law-forcing-royalty-payments-for-news-snippets>.

New York Times (2006) '*Europeans weigh plan on Google challenge*', 17 January 2006, <http://www.nytimes.com/2006/01/17/business/worldbusiness/17iht-quaero.html?pagewanted=all&_r=0>.

New York Times (2013) '*N.S.A. spied on allies, aid groups and businesses*', 20 December 2013, <http://www.nytimes.com/2013/12/21/world/nsa-dragnet-included-allies-aid-groups-and-business-elite.html>.

New York Times (2014) '*Ireland to phase out 'double Irish' tax break used by tech giants*, 14 October 2014, <http://www.nytimes.com/2014/10/15/business/international/ireland-to-phase-out-tax-advantage-used-by-technology-firms.html>.

New York Times (2014) '*Obama's speech on N.S.A. phone surveillance*', 17 June 2014, <https://www.nytimes.com/2014/01/18/us/politics/obamas-speech-on-nsa-phone-surveillance.html>.

New York Times (2015) '*European publishers play lobbying role against Google*', 28 August 2015, <https://www.nytimes.com/2015/08/29/technology/european-publishers-play-lobbying-role-against-google.html>.

New York Times (2015) '*"Right to be forgotten" online could spread*', 5 August 2015, <https://www.nytimes.com/2015/08/06/technology/personaltech/right-to-be-forgotten-online-is-poised-to-spread.html>.

New York Times (2017) '*F.C.C. repeals Net neutrality rules*', 14 December 2017, <https://www.nytimes.com/2017/12/14/technology/net-neutrality-repeal-vote.html>.

Repubblica (2016) '*Google, fisco italiano all'attacco: "Paghi 300 milioni"*', 18 January 2016, <http://www.repubblica.it/economia/2016/01/28/news/google_e_fisco_italiano-132192016>.

Rude Baguette (2013) '*Quaero: sorry no results found*', 2 April 2013, <https://www.rudebaguette.com/2013/04/02/quaero-sorry-no-results-found>.

Rue89 (2015) '*Après les Gafa, les nouveaux maîtres du monde sont les Natu*', 2 August 2015, <http://tempsreel.nouvelobs.com/rue89/20150802.RUE3739/apres-les-gafa-les-nouveaux-maitres-du-monde-sont-les-natu.html>.

Search Engine Land (2007) '*Google launches "universal search" & blended results*', 16 May 2007, <http://searchengineland.com/google-20-google-universal-search-11232>.

Search Engine Land (2007)' *Search 3.0: the blended & vertical search revolution*', 27 November 2007, <http://searchengineland.com/search-30-the-blended-vertical-search-revolution-12775>.

Search Engine Land (2012) '*Google wins major antitrust victory in Brazil*', 10 September 2012, <http://searchengineland.com/google-wins-major-antitrust-victory-in-brazil-does-it-foreshadow-broader-eu-us-wins-132729>.

Telegraph (2012) '*Google's tax avoidance is called "capitalism", says Chairman Eric Schmidt*', 12 December 2012, <http://www.telegraph.co.uk/technology/google/9739039/Googles-tax-avoidance-is-called-capitalism-says-chairman-Eric-Schmidt.html>.

The Economist (1999) '*The end of privacy*', 29 April 1999, <http://www.economist.com/node/202103>.

The Economist (2006) '*Attack of the Eurogoogle*', 9 March 2006, <http://www.economist.com/node/5571496>.

The Economist (2007) '*Who's afraid of Google?*', 30 August 2007, <http://www.economist.com/node/9725272>.

The Economist (2012) '*An ever-deeper democratic deficit*', 26 May 2012, <http://www.economist.com/node/21555927>.

The Economist (2014) '*Hungary's Internet tax: a bit of protest*', 30 October 2014, <http://www.economist.com/blogs/easternapproaches/2014/10/hungarys-internet-tax>.

The Economist (2017) '*YouTube highlights problems with digital advertising*', 30 March 2017, <https://www.economist.com/news/business/21719840-big-brands-protest-about-ads-next-offensive-content-youtube-highlights-problems-digital>.

Telegraph (2012) '*Google's tax avoidance is called "capitalism", says Chairman Eric Schmidt*', 12 December 2012, <http://www.telegraph.co.uk/technology/google/9739039/Googles-tax-avoidance-is-called-capitalism-says-chairman-Eric-Schmidt.html>.

The *Wall Street Journal* (2012) '*So, what's your algorithm?*', 4 January 2012, <https://www.wsj.com/articles/SB10001424052970203462304577138961342097348>.

Wall Street Journal (2013) '*Transcript: Obama's remarks on NSA controversy*', 7 June 2013, <https://blogs.wsj.com/washwire/2013/06/07/transcript-what-obama-said-on-nsa-controversy>.

Wall Street Journal (2014) '*U.K. details "Google tax" plans*', 10 December 2014, <https://www.wsj.com/articles/u-k-details-google-tax-plans-1418239699>.

Wall Street Journal (2015) '*Google's "Don't be evil" becomes Alphabet's "Do the right thing"*', 2 October 2015, <https://blogs.wsj.com/digits/2015/10/02/as-google-becomes-alphabet-dont-be-evil-vanishes/>.

Wall Street Journal (2016) '*Indonesia's "right to be forgotten" raises press freedom issues*', 31 October 2016, <https://www.wsj.com/articles/indonesias-right-to-be-forgotten-raises-press-freedom-issues-1477908348>.

Wired (2016) '*The Internet finally belongs to everyone*', 3 October 2016, <https://www.wired.com/2016/10/internet-finally-belongs-everyone>.

Websites

Alphabet: https://abc.xyz

Alphabet / 'Investor Relations': https://abc.xyz/investor

Business & Human Rights Resource Centre: http://business-humanrights.org

European Commission / 'Competition': http://ec.europa.eu/competition

European Commission / 'State Aid': http://ec.europa.eu/competition/state_aid/register/

Eurostat: http://ec.europa.eu/eurostat

FairSearch: http://fairsearch.org

Global Network Initiative: https://globalnetworkinitiative.org

Google / 'About': https://www.google.com/about

Google / 'AdSense Help': https://support.google.com/adsense/answer/1322028?hl=en&ref_topic=1727162&rd=1

Google / 'AdWords Help': https://support.google.com/adwords/topic/3121938?hl=en&ref_topic=3119101,3181080,3126923

Google / 'Fiber': https://fiber.google.com/about

Google / 'Google Play Help': https://support.google.com/googleplay/answer/2850368?hl=en

Google / 'Google Shopping': https://www.google.com/shopping

Google / 'Google Trends': https://www.google.com/trends

Google / 'How Search Works': http://www.google.com/insidesearch/howsearchworks/?rd=1

Google / 'Privacy & Terms': https://www.google.it/intl/en/policies/faq

Google / 'Privacy Policy': https://www.google.com/policies/privacy

Google / 'Products': http://www.google.com/about/company/products

Google / 'Transparency Report': https://www.google.com/transparencyreport/?hl=en-US

ICANN / 'Stewardship and Accountability': https://www.icann.org/stewardship-accountability

ICOMP: http://i-comp.org

Quaero: http://www.quaero.org

Ranking Digital Rights: https://rankingdigitalrights.org

Search Neutrality: http://www.searchneutrality.org/about

Snowden Archive: https://snowdenarchive.cjfe.org

StatCounter: http://gs.statcounter.com

Statista: http://www.statista.com

International treaties and legislation

Brasil (2014) *Lei Federal n. 12.965, de 16 de Abril de 2014, que estabelce princípios, garantias, direitos e deveres para o uso da Internet no Brasil*, Diário Oficial da União, 24 April 2014 ("Brazilian Internet Civil Act").

Council of Europe (1950) *European Convention on Human Rights*, originally signed in Rome on 4 November 1950, Consolidated Version, <http://www.echr.coe.int/Documents/Convention_ENG.pdf>.

Council of Europe (1981) *Convention for the Protection of Individuals with Regard to Automatic Processing of Personal Data*, originally signed in Strasbourg on 28 January 1981, <http://www.coe.int/en/web/conventions/full-list/-/conventions/treaty/108>.

EEA – European Economic Area (1992) *Agreement on the European Economic Area*, originally signed in Porto on 2 May 1992, Official Journal of the European Communities, L 1/3, 3 January 1994.

EU – European Union (1957) *Treaty on the Functioning of the European Union*, originally signed in Rome on 25 March 1957, Consolidated Version, Official Journal of the European Union, C 83/47, 30 March 2010.

EU – European Union (1992) *Treaty on European Union*, originally signed in Maastricht on 7 February 1992, Consolidated Version, Official Journal of the European Union, C 83/13, 30 March 2010.

EU – European Union (1995) *Directive 95/46/EC of the European Parliament and of the Council of 24 October 1995 on the protection of individuals with regard to the processing of personal data and on the free movement of such data*, Official Journal of the European Communities, L 281/31, 23 November 1995 ("Data Protection Directive").

EU – European Union (1997) *Council Resolution of 1 December 1997 on a Code of Conduct for Business Taxation*, Official Journal of the European Communities, C 2/1, 6 January1998.

EU – European Union (2000) *Charter of Fundamental Rights of the European Union*, originally proclaimed on 7 December 2000, Official Journal of the European Communities, C 364/1, 18 December 2000.

EU – European Union (2000) *Commission Decision 2000/520/EC of 26 July 2000 pursuant to Directive 95/46/EC of the European Parliament and of the Council on the adequacy of the protection provided by the safe harbour privacy principles and related frequently asked questions issued by the US Department of Commerce*, Official Journal of the European Communities, L 215/7, 25 August 2000 ("Safe Harbour Agreement").

EU – European Union (2000) *Directive 2000/31/EC of the European Parliament and of the Council of 8 June 2000 on certain legal aspects of information society services, in particular electronic commerce, in the Internal Market*, Official Journal of the European Communities, L 178/1, 17 July 2000 ("Directive on Electronic Commerce").

EU – European Union (2001) *Council Regulation (EC) No 2157/2001 of 8 October 2001 on the Statute for a European company (SE)*, Official Journal of the European Communities, L 294/1, 10 November 2001.

EU – European Union (2002) *Directive 2002/21/EC of the European Parliament and of the Council of 7 March 2002 on a common regulatory framework for electronic communications networks and services (Framework Directive)*, Official Journal of the European Communities, L 108/33, 24 April 2002.

EU – European Union (2002) *Directive 2002/58/EC of the European Parliament and of the Council of 12 July 2002 concerning the processing of personal data and the protection of privacy in the electronic communications sector*, Official Journal of the European Communities, L 201/37, 31 July 2002 ("Directive on Privacy and Electronic Communications / ePrivacy Directive").

EU – European Union (2004) *Commission Regulation (EC) No 773/2004/EC of 7 April 2004 relating to the conduct of proceedings by the Commission pursuant to Articles 81 and 82 of the EC Treaty*, Official Journal of the European Union, L 123/18, 27 April 2004.

EU – European Union (2006) *Council Directive 2006/112/EC of 28 November 2006 on the common system of value added tax*, Official Journal of the European Union, L 347/1, 11 December 2006.

EU – European Union (2006) *Directive 2006/24/EC of the European Parliament and of the Council of 15 March 2006 on the retention of data generated or processed in connection with the provision of publicly available electronic communications services or of public communications networks and amending Directive 2002/58/EC*, Official Journal of the European Communities, L 105/54, 13 April 2006 ("Data Retention Directive").

EU – European Union (2007) *Treaty of Lisbon amending the Treaty on European Union and the Treaty Establishing the European Community*, originally signed in Lisbon on 13 December 2007, Official Journal of the European Union, C 306/1, 17 December 2007.

EU – European Union (2011) *Council Implementing Regulation (EU) No 282/2011 of 15 March 2011 laying down implementing measures for Directive 2006/112/EC on the common system of value added tax*, Official Journal of the European Union, L 77/1, 23 March 2011.

EU – European Union (2015) *Directive (EU) 2015/1535 of the European Parliament and the Council of 9 September 2015 laying down a procedure for the provision of information in the field of technical regulations and of rules on Information Society services (codification)*, Official Journal of the European Union, L 241/1, 17 September 2015.

EU – European Union (2015) *Regulation (EU) 2015/2120 of the European Parliament and of the Council of 25 November 2015 laying down measures concerning open internet access and amending Directive 2002/22/EC on universal service and users' rights relating to electronic communications networks and services and Regulation (EU) No 531/2012 on public mobile communications networks within the Union*, Official Journal of the European Union, L 310/1, 26 November 2015.

EU – European Union (2016) *Commission Implementing Decision (EU) 2016/1250 of 12 July 2016 pursuant to Directive 95/46/EC of the European Parliament and of the Council on the adequacy of the protection provided by the EU-U.S. Privacy Shield*, Official Journal of the European Union, L 207/1, 1 August 2016 ("EU-US Privacy Shield").

EU – European Union (2016) *Council Directive (EU) 2016/881 of 25 May 2016 amending Directive 2011/16/EU as regards mandatory automatic exchange of information in the field of taxation*, Official Journal of the European Union, L 146/8, 3 June 2016.

EU – European Union (2016) *Council Directive (EU) 2016/1164 of 12 July 2016 laying down rules against tax avoidance practices that directly affect the functioning of the internal market*, Official Journal of the European Union, L 193/1, 19 July 2016.

EU – European Union (2016) *Directive (EU) 2016/680 of the European Parliament and of the Council of 27 April 2016 on the protection of natural persons with regard to the processing of personal data by competent authorities for the purposes of the prevention, investigation, detection or prosecution of criminal offences or the execution of criminal penalties, and on the free movement of such data, and repealing Council Framework Decision 2008/977/JHA*, Official Journal of the European Union, L 119/89, 4 May 2016.

EU – European Union (2016) *Regulation (EU) 2016/679 of the European Parliament and of the Council of 27 April 2016 on the protection of natural persons with regard to the processing of personal data and on the free movement of such data, and repealing Directive 95/46/EC*, Official Journal of the European Union, L 119/1, 4 May 2016 ("General Data Protection Regulation").

EU – European Union (2017) *Council Directive (EU) 2017/952 of 29 May 2017 amending Directive (EU) 2016/1164 as regards hybrid mismatches with third countries*, Official Journal of the European Union, L 144/1, 7 July 2017.

EU – European Union (2018) *Council Directive (EU) 2018/822 of 25 May 2018 amending Directive 2011/16/EU as regards mandatory automatic exchange of information in the field of taxation in relation to reportable cross-border arrangements*, Official Journal of the European Union, L 139/1, 5 June 2018.

EU – European Union (2018) Regulation (EU)2018/1725*of the European Parliament and of the Council of 23 October 2018 on the protection of natural persons with regard to the processing of personal data by the Union institutions, bodies, offices and agencies and on the free movement of such data, and repealing Regulation (EC) No 45/2001 and Decision No 1247/2002/EC*, Official Journal of the European Union, L 295/39, 21 November 2018.

EU – European Union and US – United States (2010) *Agreement between the European Union and the United States of America on the processing and transfer of Financial Messaging Data from the European Union to the United States for the purposes of the Terrorist Finance Tracking Program*, approved by Council Decision 2010/412/EU of 13 July 2010, Official Journal of the European Union, L 195/3, 27 September 2010.

EU – European Union and US – United States (2012) *Agreement between the United States of America and the European Union on the use and transfer of passenger name records to the United States Department of Homeland Security*, approved by Council Decision 2012/472/EU of 26 April 2012, Official Journal of the European Union, L 215/4, 11 August 2012.

EU – European Union and US – United States (2016) *Agreement Between the United States of America and the European Union on the Protection of personal information Relating to the Prevention, Investigation, Detection and Prosecution of Criminal Offences*, approved by Council Decision (EU) 2016/2220 of 2 December 2016, Official Journal of the European Union, L 336/1, 10 December 2016 ("Umbrella Agreement").

UN – United Nations (1966) *International Covenant on Civil and Political Rights*, originally adopted by the United Nations General Assembly with Resolution 2200A (XXI) on 16 December 1966, <https://treaties.un.org/doc/publication/unts/volume 999/volume-999-i-14668-english.pdf >.

US – United States (1787) *The Constitution of the United States*, adopted on 17 September 1787, Consolidated Version, <https://www.senate.gov/civics/constitution_item/constitution.htm>.

Judicial and administrative proceedings

Audiencia Nacional del Reino de España (2014) *Procedimiento Ordinario 725/2010: Google Spain SL, Google Inc. v Agencia Española de Protección de Datos, Mario Costeja González*, Sentencia Final: 29 December 2014.

CJEU – Court of Justice of the European Union (2003) *Case C-101/01: Criminal Proceedings against Bodil Lindqvist*, Final Judgment: 6 November 2003.

CJEU – Court of Justice of the European Union (2015) *Case C-362/14: Maximillian Schrems v Data Protection Commissioner*.

CJEU – Court of Justice of the European Union (2014) *Joined Cases C-293/12 and C-594/12: Digital Rights Ireland and Seitlinger and Others*, Final Judgment: 8 April 2014.

CJEU – Court of Justice of the European Union (2014) *Case C-131/12: Google Spain SL, Google Inc. v Agencia Española de Protección de Datos, Mario Costeja González*, Final Judgment: 13 May 2014.

CJEU – Court of Justice of the European Union (2015), *Case C-230/14: Weltimmo s. r. o. v Nemzeti Adatvédelmi és Információszabadság Hatóság*, Final Judgment: 1 October 2015.

CJEU –- Court of Justice of the European Union (2015) *Case C-362/14: Maximillian Schrems v Data Protection Commissioner*, Final Judgment: 6 October 2015.

CJEU – Court of Justice of the European Union (2016) *Case T-738/16: La Quadrature du Net and Others v Commission*, Application: 25 October 2016.

CJEU – Court of Justice of the European Union (2016) *Joined Cases C-203/15 and C-698/15: Tele2 Sverige and Secretary of State for the Home Department v Post- och telestyrelsen and Others*, Final Judgment: 21 December 2016.

CJEU – Court of Justice of the European Union (2017) *Case C-507/17: Google Inc. v Commission nationale de l'informatique et des libertés*, Reference for a Preliminary Ruling: 21 August 2017.

CJEU – Court of Justice of the European Union (2017) *Case T-670/16: Digital Rights Ireland v Commission*, Order of the Court: 22 November 2017.

CJEU – Court of Justice of the European Union (2018) *Case C-498/16: Maximilian Schrems x Facebook Ireland Limited*, Final Judgment: 25 January 2018.

CJEU – Court of Justice of the European Union (2018) *Case C-311/18: Data Protection Commissioner v Facebook Ireland Limited, Maximillian Schrems*, Reference for a Preliminary Ruling: 9 May 2018.

European Commission (2008) *Case Number M.4731: Google / DoubleClick*, Merger, Final Decision: 11 March 2008.

European Commission (2010) *Case Number 39740: Google Search (Shopping)*, Antitrust, Opening of Proceedings: 30 November 2010.

European Commission (2012) *Case Number M.6381: Google / Motorola Mobility*, Merger, Final Decision: 13 February 2012.

European Commission (2015) *Case Number 40099: Google Android*, Antitrust, Opening of Proceedings: 15 April 2015.

European Commission (2016) *Case Number 40411: Google Search (AdSense)*, Antitrust, Opening of Proceedings: 14 July 2016.

Index

For Product Safety Concerns and Information please contact our EU representative GPSR@taylorandfrancis.com
Taylor & Francis Verlag GmbH, Kaufingerstraße 24, 80331 München, Germany

www.ingramcontent.com/pod-product-compliance
Lightning Source LLC
LaVergne TN
LVHW011128300926
849160LV00008B/563
* 9 7 8 1 0 3 2 2 4 1 0 9 8 *